# Contents

# Foreword

There are two key challenges identified in my State of London report. These are that 'London's prosperity should develop to the maximum' and that 'every citizen of London shares in it'.

More than a third of Londoners are from ethnic minorities and more than a quarter are not white. I am committed to celebrating and developing that diversity to promote London as a great social and cultural, as well as economic, world city.

This report is uplifting, in that it provides evidence of how well some ethnic minorities are doing in London and how they contribute to the cultural diversity that makes London what it is. But there is still a long way to go before we will be able to say, with any real conviction, that all London's citizens share equally in London's prosperity. This report also adds weighty evidence to the fact that many ethnic minorities are suffering the results of discrimination and lack of opportunity in London.

I know that the information contained in this report, on issues such as demographic change, housing, health and employment will be used in the development of strategies to combat discrimination and to offer opportunities to all London's citizens.

Information is vital: I urge you to read it and to use it.

**Ken Livingstone**
Mayor of London

# Chapter 1
# **Introduction**

# Introduction

London is a city of great ethnic diversity. More than one in three of London's residents come from an ethnic minority group.

This report explores in detail the differences between ethnic groups in London at the end of the twentieth century, in relation to a range of topics affecting everyday lives, such as families, health, housing, employment and travel. It also examines the diversity of the population and patterns of migration. This is mainly done through an examination of data provided in the 1991 Census. The report also looks to the future, to the likely changes in London's population, and the information to be gathered in the 2001 Census.

In 1991, for the first time in a British Census, individuals were asked a question on their ethnic group. The London Research Centre (LRC, now part of the Greater London Authority, GLA), on behalf of London's local authorities, commissioned a wide range of tables for London and for individual boroughs from the Office of Population, Censuses and Surveys (now part of the Office for National Statistics, ONS). These large and complex LRC Commissioned tables are not available for other parts of the country and many include ethnic groups as one of the variables. The analysis in this report gives an indication of the range of analyses possible, and explores the Census data in more detail than ever before, although it does not claim to have conveyed every possible aspect. Because of the large amount of detail, much of the analysis is restricted to a London-wide level, but some borough distinctions are included.

The following chapters contain information on the demography of London. There is data and analysis on the diversity of London's population, even within ethnic groups. This covers the differing age structures of the various ethnic groups, and the household and family groupings in which people of different ethnic groups live. Also, there is data on the migration of different ethnic groups within London, to and from the rest of Great Britain and from overseas. Later chapters look at issues related to a number of every day topics. These include:

- Housing – tenure, access to amenities, overcrowding and dwelling type.

- Health – the number of people with a limiting long-term illness by age and gender.

- Employment – full and part-time working, unemployment, students, retired and other economically inactive people, qualifications, occupation, industry, social class and travel.

# Chapter 2
# **Demography**

# Demography

## Introduction

London is one of the most cosmopolitan cities in the world. The Census is one of the main tools which allows us to quantify that diversity. The Census gives us an unprecedented amount of demographic data for different communities, including details of size, distribution, composition and age and gender structures of the different populations. This chapter summarises much of the demographic data available, concentrating on data which are new from commissioned tables.

The first section draws upon data which have been obtained from the questions asking about ethnic group and country of birth. From the answers to both of these questions together, we can obtain an enormous amount of detailed information about the ethnic complexities of different communities in London. The data also highlight the dangers of loose language and assumptions often made by those discussing race/ethnicity issues. For example, the assumptions that all Irish are white or that people from Caribbean islands are black, or that Indians are a homogeneous ethnic group. In fact if there is one main point that can be made from the analysis of this data, it is that many of the ten ethnic groups in the Census for which tables

are published, are not ethnic groups at all in the sense that they do not contain people who share a similar cultural identity. The second section of analysis in this chapter focuses on a gender and age analysis of different communities, which has particular implications for the size of these communities in the future.

Throughout this section there is a distinction made between black/Black and white/White. The capitalised forms refer to the Census categories, whereas the lower case versions relate to the general description of a person's colour. The difference can be illustrated well using the example of Arab people. The majority of Arabs are reported to regard themselves as white in colour, but some, knowing that in Britain the White category has implications of European whiteness, categorised themselves as 'Other' in order to record their Arab origins, even though they would still consider themselves to be white (Al Rasheed, 1996).

## Data sources and ethnic group and country of birth issues

LRC Commissioned tables give us a wealth of new information about the diversity of London's population. The main variables included within the

**Table 2.1 Size of country of birth groups not included in standard Census tables**

| Country of birth | Size of community | Main boroughs of residence |
|---|---|---|
| Brazil | 4,630 | Westminster (635), Kensington & Chelsea (588) |
| Colombia | 3,991 | Kensington & Chelsea (454), Lambeth (444) |
| Iraq | 8,353 | Ealing (1,339), Westminster (831) |
| Jordan | 909 | Westminster (158), Kensington & Chelsea (129) |
| Lebanon | 6,444 | Westminster (1,230) Kensington & Chelsea (1,206) |
| Saudi Arabia | 1,200 | Westminster (212) |
| Syria | 1,505 | Westminster (247), Ealing (186), Kensington & Chelsea (169) |
| Taiwan | 743 | Barnet (93), Westminster (74) |
| Thailand | 3,117 | Kensington & Chelsea (370), Westminster (249) |

*Source: 1991 Census, LRC Commissioned Table LRCT14*

tables are the full breakdown of 120 countries/regions of birth, the full 35 code ethnic group classification before re-coding, the ten-fold ethnic group classification after re-coding, gender and figures for five-year age groups. Each of the tables contains a combination of some of these variables.

Of the 120 countries or regions included in the commissioned data, nine are for countries not included in the standard Census output. The communities include two from South America, five from the Middle East and two from the Far East. The size of those communities in London is shown in Table 2.1. A table showing figures for all boroughs is included in Appendix 1.

Almost all of these groups are concentrated in Central London, in Westminster and in Kensington and Chelsea. Exceptions are the Iraq-born population in Ealing, the Taiwan-born population in Barnet, and the Colombia-born population in Lambeth.

The new commissioned tables allow us to break down regions and examine the ethnic diversity between countries within the same region. Figures for the Old Commonwealth countries of Australia, Canada and New Zealand highlight some of these differences. By far the majority of migrants born in all of these countries were White, yet Canada-born people were more likely to be Indian than people from the other two countries, whereas a number of New Zealand-born people recorded themselves as Black Other or Other – which could include Maoris.

For European Community-born people, again by far the majority (97 per cent) recorded themselves as White. Newham was striking in that less than 90 per cent of its European Community-born population was White. In Newham, those who were not Whites included Black and Asian people from France and people from the Other group who were born in Italy (which might include for example Sardinians or Sicilians who did not consider themselves to be White).

**Table 2.2  Ethnic group by percentage born inside and outside the UK, living in London**

| Ethnic group | % born in UK | % born outside UK |
|---|---|---|
| White | 87.2 | 12.8 |
| Black Caribbean | 53.2 | 46.8 |
| Black African | 35.7 | 64.3 |
| Black Other | 84.1 | 15.9 |
| Indian | 36.4 | 63.6 |
| Pakistani | 45.1 | 54.9 |
| Bangladeshi | 35.0 | 65.0 |
| Chinese | 25.5 | 74.5 |
| Other Asian | 20.7 | 79.3 |
| Other | 53.3 | 46.7 |
| Total percentage | 100.0 | 100.0 |
| Total number | 5,200,000 | 1,500,000 |

*Source: 1991 Census, LRC Commissioned Table LRCT14*

Large differences can be seen in the ethnicity of people from Africa. These differences vary by region, with West Africa-born people being mostly Black, and East Africa-born people including high proportions of Indians. High proportions of people born in Southern Africa are White and many of those from North Africa are Arab.

**Born inside/outside the UK by ethnic group**
Of the 6.7 million people resident in London recorded in the 1991 Census, three quarters (78 per cent) were born in the UK, and one quarter were born outside the UK (see Table 2.2). Of those born in the UK, by far the majority, 5,002,000 were born in England, 113,000 were born in Scotland, 71,000 in Wales, and 42,000 in Northern Ireland.

Of those born in the UK living in London, 89 per cent were White, and 11 per cent from ethnic minority groups. Of those born outside the UK, nearly half (47 per cent) were White.

In the following section each of the main ten ethnic groups for which data are available is analysed, and the composition of each group is described.

## White

The majority (87 per cent) of the White group were born in the UK. Within the UK, 95 per cent were born in England (4,428,463), two per cent in Scotland (110,622), one per cent in Wales (68,661) and less than one per cent in Northern Ireland (41,485). Among the people who said they were born in the UK 251 did not state a particular country.

The country from which most people born abroad came was the Republic of Ireland (210,223 people). A further 180 said they were born in Ireland but did not state which part.

**Table 2.3 Selected countries/regions of birth of White people living in London who were born outside the UK**

| Country/region of birth | Number of White people |
|---|---|
| Irish Republic | 210,223 |
| European Community | 133,147 |
| New Commonwealth | 103,196 |
| *including:* | |
| *Cyprus* | *48,897* |
| *New Commonwealth Asia* | *25,253* |
| *New Commonwealth Africa* | *12,947* |
| *New Commonwealth Caribbean* | *5,293* |
| Other Europe (mostly Scandinavia and Eastern Europe) | 55,174 |
| Old Commonwealth | 51,493 |
| Non New Commonwealth Asia | 33,064 |
| *including:* | |
| *Middle East* | *27,516* |
| USA | 29,793 |
| Non New Commonwealth Africa | 28,023 |
| Turkey | 18,304 |
| Central and South America | 13,109 |
| Total White people born outside UK | 684,098 |

*Source: 1991 Census, LRC Commissioned Table LRCT14*

Around a third of White people born outside the UK were born in the Irish Republic. Almost another third was composed of people born in Europe. Around 100,000 people were from Asia, Africa and the Caribbean combined – both New Commonwealth and other countries, and around 50,000 each from Cyprus and the Old Commonwealth countries of Australia, Canada and New Zealand combined.

The Census ethnic group categories use a mixture of colour, culture and geography to identify different groups. The data are repeatedly put to use to identify disadvantage, and therefore the figures are often used to compare the White group with the non-White ethnic minority group categories. This can often conceal the fact that there are a number of people from minority groups, who given this choice of categories, record themselves as White. The above figures state that of those born outside the UK, nearly half (47 per cent) were White. White people were born in every country/region named in the Census, down to the smallest recorded number of 38 White people born in The Gambia who were living in London in 1991.

Racial discrimination can often be based on a person's colour. It is not possible to know how many people within the White category may be the subject of discrimination, but it is certain that a proportion would identify themselves as being from ethnic minority communities eg, Cypriot or Turkish. If all White people who were born outside the UK were identified as ethnic minorities, there would be a further ten per cent of the population recorded as ethnic minorities added to the 20 per cent identified in the nine non-White categories.

The figures in Table 2.4 show the varying proportions of White people born outside the UK in each borough. Nearly a third of Kensington and Chelsea's White population was born abroad. White people in this borough come from a large variety of countries including the USA, Middle Eastern countries, Irish Republic, Central and South America, Australia,

**Table 2.4  Percentage of the White population born outside the UK living in London, by borough**

| Borough | Total borough population | Whites born outside UK | % of Whites born outside UK |
|---|---|---|---|
| Kensington & Chelsea | 138,394 | 42,362 | 31 |
| Westminster | 174,814 | 44,193 | 25 |
| Camden | 170,444 | 35,275 | 21 |
| Hammersmith & Fulham | 148,502 | 28,290 | 19 |
| Haringey | 202,204 | 33,440 | 17 |
| City of London | 4,142 | 659 | 16 |
| Islington | 164,686 | 2,526 | 15 |
| Brent | 243,025 | 37,345 | 15 |
| Barnet | 293,564 | 41,287 | 14 |
| Ealing | 275,257 | 34,842 | 13 |
| Hackney | 181,248 | 22,785 | 13 |
| Lambeth | 244,834 | 29,189 | 12 |
| Wandsworth | 252,425 | 30,031 | 12 |
| Richmond upon Thames | 160,732 | 18,528 | 12 |
| Enfield | 257,417 | 28,842 | 11 |
| Merton | 168,470 | 16,320 | 10 |
| Southwark | 218,541 | 20,082 | 9 |
| Harrow | 200,100 | 18,230 | 9 |
| Hounslow | 204,397 | 17,299 | 8 |
| Kingston upon Thames | 132,996 | 10,897 | 8 |
| Lewisham | 230,983 | 16,554 | 7 |
| Croydon | 313,510 | 20,210 | 6 |
| Hillingdon | 231,602 | 14,318 | 6 |
| Waltham Forest | 212,033 | 12,756 | 6 |
| Redbridge | 226,218 | 13,111 | 6 |
| Tower Hamlets | 161,064 | 9,215 | 6 |
| Sutton | 168,880 | 9,104 | 5 |
| Greenwich | 207,650 | 11,134 | 5 |
| Bromley | 290,609 | 15,442 | 5 |
| Newham | 212,170 | 8,540 | 4 |
| Bexley | 215,615 | 7,039 | 3 |
| Barking & Dagenham | 143,681 | 4,410 | 3 |
| Havering | 229,492 | 6,843 | 3 |
| Inner London | 2,504,451 | 346,141 | 14 |
| Outer London | 4,175,248 | 337,957 | 8 |
| Greater London | 6,679,699 | 684,098 | 10 |

*Source: 1991 Census, LRC Commissioned Table LRCT14*

Canada and New Zealand. If all these people were considered to be from ethnic minority groups, the total ethnic minority population of Kensington and Chelsea would be 47 per cent of the total population.

The Irish community is the largest migrant community living in London. There were more than a quarter of a million people living in London in 1991 who were born in Ireland (including people of all ethnic groups), with over two hundred thousand people (214,033) born in the Irish Republic, 42,243 in Northern Ireland, and 194 who just wrote Ireland. Because Irish was not included in the ethnic group question as a category in its own right, we do not have a count of the whole Irish community as we cannot tell how many Irish people there were born outside of Ireland, including the many who were born in England. Almost all people (over 98 per cent) born in Ireland recorded themselves as White, but a number wrote in Irish in the any other ethnic group box, and were recoded by ONS back into the White category. A processing fault prevented an accurate count of those people, but ONS has since estimated that some 11,000 people wrote in Irish, around 10,000 of whom lived in London. An additional 20,000 people in London were estimated to have ticked the White box and written in Irish, and these people would have remained in the White group. Of those writing in Irish in London, 60 per cent were born in Ireland and 40 per cent born elsewhere. If this relationship held for the whole Irish community, and those born in Ireland constituted 60 per cent of the whole community, it would number 427,450 people in London – much more than the Indian group at 347,091 which was the largest complete ethnic minority group identified by the Census.

Another large group in London who were contained mostly within the White group were those people born in Europe. In all there were 193,053 people born in European countries (excluding the UK and the Irish Republic), of whom 98 per cent were White. This included 133,147 White people born in European Community countries, and 55,174 White people born

in other European countries. The size of the migrant communities from each of the European countries is shown in Table 2.5.

The largest communities of 19,000 people or more were from Germany, Italy, Poland, France and Spain. Nearly all these people were White, ranging from 95 per cent of those born in France to over 99 per cent of those born in Poland. There were over 13,000 people who were born in Portugal living in London in 1991, twice as many as from the next largest country (7,120 from Greece). The smallest number of migrants from the European countries listed was 71 people born in Albania – although the recent political situation has caused many more people to leave Albania for the UK.

Almost 13,000 people (12,947) in London were White people born in New Commonwealth African countries – mainly Zimbabwe (3,414), Kenya (3,384) and Nigeria (1,389). However, more than double that number were born in Non-Commonwealth African countries (28,023) – mainly South Africa which was not part of the Commonwealth in 1991 (14,721), and Egypt (5,892). Daley (1996) suggests that the White populations born in Egypt and Libya would include children born to British forces stationed there.

Over 58,000 (58,317) White people living in London in 1991 were born in Asia. The largest proportion of these people were born in the Middle East. Just over half of all people born in the Middle East living in London in 1991 recorded themselves as White – 27,516 people. People born in Israel and the Lebanon were more likely to record themselves as White, compared with people born in Saudi Arabia and Iraq. Of those White people born in South Asia (17,371), most were born in India (14,065). There were also 7,882 White people born in New Commonwealth SE Asia – split evenly between Hong Kong, Malaysia and Singapore. Other large Asian White groups included 1,326 born in Myanmar (Burma), 945 born in Japan, 837 born in the Philippines and 823 born in China.

**Table 2.5  Numbers of people, White people, and percentage of Whites born in European countries, living in London**

| Country of birth | Total people born in each country | White people born in each country | |
|---|---|---|---|
| | No. | No. | % |
| Germany | 32,027 | 31,062 | 97 |
| Italy | 30,052 | 29,648 | 99 |
| Poland | 21,823 | 21,628 | 99 |
| France | 20,923 | 19,941 | 95 |
| Spain | 19,047 | 18,737 | 98 |
| Portugal | 13,125 | 12,823 | 98 |
| Greece | 7,120 | 6,993 | 98 |
| Austria | 6,445 | 6,322 | 98 |
| Netherlands | 5,974 | 5,671 | 95 |
| Yugoslavia | 4,685 | 4,610 | 98 |
| Hungary | 4,451 | 4,369 | 98 |
| Denmark | 4,250 | 4,124 | 97 |
| Switzerland | 4,188 | 4,047 | 97 |
| Belgium | 4,112 | 3,927 | 96 |
| Sweden | 4,081 | 3,982 | 98 |
| Czechoslovakia | 3,412 | 3,362 | 99 |
| Norway | 2,118 | 2,011 | 95 |
| Finland | 1,954 | 1,912 | 98 |
| Romania | 1,774 | 1,731 | 98 |
| Bulgaria | 867 | 833 | 96 |
| Other Europe | 325 | 301 | 93 |
| Luxembourg | 229 | 221 | 97 |
| Albania | 71 | 66 | 93 |

*Source: 1991 Census, LRC Commissioned Table LRCT14*

The main other large White community in London not mentioned above are Cypriots. There were 48,897 White people born in Cyprus in London in 1991. Of course the total Cypriot community numbers much more than this as many Cypriots were born in the UK, and in other countries, and not all Cypriots identified themselves as White. It is also true to say that not all

White people born in Cyprus are Cypriots, but the majority are likely to be. Previous work (Storkey 1993) has estimated the total Cypriot community to be double the number who were counted as being born in Cyprus in the 1991 Census. There were a number of people who ticked the 'any other group' box and wrote in that they were Greek or Greek Cypriot, Turkish or

Turkish Cypriot. Altogether there were 31,159 in this category in London, of whom 16,621 were Turkish or Turkish Cypriot, and 14,538 were Greek or Greek Cypriot. The majority of the Greek community are likely to be Greek Cypriot as there were only 7,120 people living in London who were born in Greece compared with 50,684 born in Cyprus. However there is a large Turkish community in London with 20,426 people born in Turkey, so it is more difficult to say how many of those in the Turkish/Turkish Cypriot category were Turkish, and how many Turkish Cypriot. Although those who wrote in their response do not act as a good count of the overall size of the community, the comparable numbers in each borough may act as an indicator of the split within the borough of these two groups (assuming that both groups had equal tendencies to write in an answer rather than ticking one of the individual group boxes). For example, in Barnet three times as many people wrote in that they were Greek/Greek Cypriot, whilst in Southwark three times as many wrote in that they were Turkish/Turkish Cypriot.

There were over 5,000 White people born in New Commonwealth Caribbean (5,293) in London in 1991. Overall in London, less than four per cent of the Caribbean-born population was White, but in some boroughs this was much higher. In Richmond a third of the Caribbean-born population was White and in Kingston a fifth was White. This was not due particularly to one island group – White people from all Caribbean islands tended to live in these boroughs.

One of the other categories which was included within the White group was those people who said they were of mixed ethnic origin and were White. This included people who were, for example, Polish/British, or Scottish/German, and these were assumed by ONS to be White mixes. There were 1,558 people in this category in London, just over half (55 per cent) of whom were born in the UK. Of those born outside the UK, half were born in New Commonwealth countries – particularly Malta and Gozo (188), India (50) and

Cyprus (48). The other half were born in countries scattered around the world, with 58 born in the Middle East, 41 in the Irish Republic and 34 in the European Community.

**Black Caribbean**
Caribbean people belong to many different ethnic groups, including White, Indian and African. However by far the majority, (87 per cent) of people born in the Caribbean, recorded themselves as Black Caribbean. In London the Black Caribbean ethnic group constituted 4.4 per cent of the total population in 1991. The community is concentrated more in Inner London boroughs (7.1 per cent of the total Inner London population), than Outer London boroughs (2.7 per cent of the total Outer London population). Within Inner London there are further concentrations in a few boroughs, mainly Lambeth (12.6 per cent of the borough population), Hackney (11.2 per cent), Brent (10.2 per cent) and Lewisham (10.1 per cent).

Just over half – 53 per cent – of the Black Caribbean population was born in the UK, a figure similar for both Inner and Outer London boroughs. Brent, with the second largest Caribbean-born population had less than half of its Black Caribbean population born in the UK, therefore attracting a higher proportion of migrants.

The tables commissioned for London from the 1991 Census allow us to look in much greater detail than the standard tables at the areas within the Caribbean where many of London's Black Caribbean community have migrated from.

Of the Caribbean islands named in the 1991 Census, the largest migrant community came from Jamaica. There were over 76,000 people living in London in 1991 who migrated from Jamaica. Over 94 per cent of these people were Black Caribbeans. There were a number of boroughs with a few thousand Black Caribbean Jamaican-born migrants, but the largest concentrations were in Lambeth (9,703), Brent (7,530) and Lewisham (6,964).

Over 14,000 people (14,662) people were born in Guyana which is included as part of the Caribbean. Just over half of these (52 per cent) were recorded as Black Caribbean, with 14 per cent Indian, ten per cent in both the Other and Black Other ethnic groups, and six per cent White. It is impossible to know how ethnically diverse these people are, or how much is due to people recording their ethnicity in different ways given the categories available. There was quite an even spread of the 7,593 Black Caribbean Guyana-born people across London, with slightly larger concentrations in Wandsworth (705), Croydon (679) and Lambeth (653).

There were 13,466 Barbados-born people living in London in 1991. As with Jamaica-born people, most (94 per cent) recorded themselves as Black Caribbean. There was also quite an even spread across Inner and Outer London boroughs, with the largest communities of over 1,000 in Brent and Lambeth.

Just over ten thousand (10,184) people in the Census were recorded as born in Trinidad and Tobago. The range of ethnic groups recorded for Trinidad and Tobago-born people was much wider than for the other Caribbean islands named. Only 66 per cent of this group was Black Caribbean with nine per cent White, eight per cent from Other groups and eight per cent Indian.

There was a small group of people (230) who had migrated from Belize to London, recorded in the 1991 Census. There were more Belize-born migrants who were White (37 per cent) than Black Caribbean (27 per cent), and 14 per cent were within the Other group. It is possible that the Whites are linked to the British Army who have advised the Belize Army for a number of years. All boroughs had a few migrants from Belize in 1991, with Barnet having the most residents at just 19 people.

There were a sizeable number of people (27,756) born in other independent states in the New Commonwealth Caribbean. These include Antigua and Barbuda, Bahamas, Dominica, Grenada, Grenadines, St. Kitts-Nevis, St. Lucia and St. Vincent. There were also a further 2,841 people from New Commonwealth Caribbean Dependent territories which include Anguilla, Bermuda, Cayman Islands, Montserrat, Turks and Caicos Islands, and the British Virgin Islands. An additional 5,161 people said they were born in the West Indies or the British Windward or Leeward Islands, but didn't state the island name. Peach (1996) estimates that in Britain as a whole, these aggregate groups of other Caribbeans, numbering around 35,000 people, can be split roughly into a third from the Leeward Islands (Antigua, St. Kitts-Nevis and Anguilla) and two thirds from the Windwards (Dominica, Grenada, St Lucia and St. Vincent).

A further 660 people were born in other Caribbean islands such as Cuba, Dominican Republic, US Virgin Islands, Dutch, French, and Portuguese Windward Islands.

Other significant countries of birth for London's Black Caribbeans included the Irish Republic (790 people), New Commonwealth Africa (625 people) – particularly Ghana and Nigeria, and European Community countries (406 people).

In the 1991 Census there were 1,538 people who did not tick the Black Caribbean box, but who said they were Black and from the Caribbean. These people were transferred by ONS from the Black Other category into the Black Caribbean category. There were also 2,016 people who ticked 'any other ethnic group' and wrote in the free text field at the end of the options, that they were from the Caribbean. These people were also transferred by ONS back into the Black Caribbean category, although it seems less obvious that these people were black.

*Statistical representation of African makeup of pops in London*

## Black African

As with Caribbean people, African people come from a range of different ethnic groups, a result of colonial occupation, and substantial in and out migration of Europeans, Asians and people from other ethnic groups. Also, the term 'African' is sometimes seen as a political term identifying the original birthplace of many black peoples' ancestors – also incorporated into the term Afro-Caribbean. In the 1991 Census the term Black African is used – therefore separating out black Africans from Africans of other ethnic groups, and also from black Caribbean people. Altogether there were 246,025 people who were born in Africa living in London in 1991. Of these 41 per cent were Black, 33 per cent were Indian, and 17 per cent were White.

Of people belonging to the Black African ethnic group (163,635), one third were born within the UK – almost all in England. Of those born outside the UK, 95 per cent (99,984 people) were born in Africa.

The boroughs with the largest Black African populations were Lambeth (16,021), Southwark (15,713), Hackney (12,240), Newham (11,861) and Haringey (11,085).

Over half (56 per cent) of Black Africans living in London who were born outside the UK came from two West African countries – Nigeria and Ghana. There were 33,573 people born in Nigeria living in London in 1991 and 25,417 born in Ghana. Black African migrants from Nigeria mainly settled in Southwark (5,189), Lambeth (3,954) and Hackney (3,839). Those from Ghana were largely in Lambeth (2,536), Haringey (1,861), Newham (1,834), Brent (1,809) and Southwark (1,783).

The next largest group of Black Africans were in an amalgamated group called 'Other Africa'. There were 19,510 Black Africans here who were born in a number of countries including those in the Horn of Africa, ex-French colonies of Central Africa such as Zaire, and all other Non-Commonwealth countries excluding

northern and southern Africa. It is impossible to get more detail about this group, and frustrating as the numbers are so significant. ONS has been asked if possible to code all countries in the next Census to enable communities such as Somali migrants, for example, to be identified.

Other significant Black African communities included 7,545 people born in Uganda, and 4,264 born in Sierra Leone. Uganda-born people were concentrated in Newham (1,052) and Haringey (641), whilst the boroughs with the largest Sierra Leone-born populations were Southwark (575) and Lambeth (494).

Following these there were a number of other Black African groups which numbered between one and two thousand people. These included Black Africans who were Zimbabwe-born (1,934), Kenya-born (1,634), Zambia-born (1,526) and South Africa-born (1,402).

## Black Other

Some Census tables use a more detailed breakdown, identifying 35 ethnic groups. Four of these groups were added together to produce totals for the Black Other group. These included people who recorded themselves as Black British, any other non Caribbean, African, Asian or British Black group, of Black/White mixed origin, or who were Black, of mixed origin but not Black/White or Asian/White.

Most of the people (84 per cent of the total 80,613) in the Black Other group were born in the UK, and almost all of these in England. There was a wide range of countries/regions of birth for those 12,813 born outside the UK. There were a number of people (3,446) born in Caribbean islands who were black but not Black Caribbean. These included 1,394 born in Guyana, and 1,043 born in Jamaica. There were 1,555 Black people born in North and South America – around half (717) of whom were born in the USA.

There were 2,247 black people born in African countries who were not Black African. These included over 300 from both Nigeria and Ghana, and over 200 from both Kenya and South Africa. Almost two thousand (1,941) people in the Black Other group were born in Asia including 950 born in South Asia (India, Pakistan, Bangladesh and Sri Lanka), and 348 people born in the Philippines. There were a further 840 people who were born in Cyprus who classified themselves in the Black Other group, as well as 602 born in Mauritius and 338 born in Turkey.

The number of people recording themselves as Black British in London was 36,228. The boroughs with the largest numbers were Hackney (4,266), Brent (2,999) Lewisham (2,961) and Lambeth (2,877). Of these Black British people 96 per cent were born in the UK. There has been a lot of debate about the inclusion of a specific category for Black British people in the 2001 Census. Everybody agrees that the inclusion of a specific category would increase the number of people who would state that they were Black British. By not having a specific category in 1991, many Black British people are likely to have ticked one of the other boxes such as Black Caribbean – perhaps giving their family roots rather than the ethnic group they felt part of. Therefore the count of 36,000 Black British people in London will be an underestimate of the true size of this group.

As mentioned above, the vast majority of Black British people were born in the UK and almost all in England. There were 1,556 Black British born outside the UK, mostly in the New Commonwealth countries. Over 600 Black British people were born in the Caribbean (622), including 335 in Jamaica and 87 in Guyana. A further 405 were born in New Commonwealth Africa – mostly West Africa, including 136 in Nigeria and 124 in Ghana. There were also 73 Black British born in India and 50 in the Irish Republic.

The more detailed ethnic classification is particularly helpful when identifying people of non-mixed ethnicity who said they were Black but not Caribbean, African, Asian or British. In London there were a large number,

20,486, in this category. There were over a thousand people in this group in six boroughs in London – Hackney (1,528), Lambeth (1,483), Haringey (1,400) Brent (1,277), Lewisham (1,128) and Southwark (1,001). Almost 60 per cent (58 per cent) of this group were born in the UK – again, 98 per cent in England. We do not have any more information about this group, but examples of people in this category could include Black British people who ticked the Black Other box but who did not write in an answer, or for example, the children of Black people from any European country or of Black American parents. Of the 8,524 born outside the UK, nearly a quarter were born in the Caribbean, particularly Guyana (993) and Jamaica (527). Over 800 were born in Cyprus (811), and it has been suggested that some of these people might be the children of black members of the British armed forces stationed there (Owen 1996). The variety of other countries of birth in this category was large. Other countries of note included 514 born in the Irish Republic, 453 born in Mauritius, 430 born in the USA, 319 in Turkey, and 296 in the Philippines.

The total number of Black people of mixed Black/White origin recorded in the 1991 Census in London was 6,515. Just over half of these people lived in Inner London boroughs. Lambeth had the most people recorded in this category (506). The vast majority (90 per cent) of these people were born in the UK. Of the 663 people born outside the UK, 166 were born in the USA, 144 in New Commonwealth Africa, and 141 in the New Commonwealth Caribbean. Owen (1996) analyses the parents of children in the Black Other category using the one per cent household Sample of Anonymised Records (SAR). He shows that almost half of all Black Other children lived in households with one Black and one White partner. Black Caribbeans were the most likely Black group to have a White partner. A fifth of Black Other children lived in households with two Black partners – mainly both Black Caribbean or both Black Other. Over a quarter of Black Other children lived in households where the two partners were White. This may be due to adoption of black children by white people, or may be due to partnership break up where one of the white people is not the child's biological parent.

The final category making up the Black Other population was the Other mixed group, totalling 17,384. Two thirds of this group lived in Inner London boroughs, particularly Lambeth and Lewisham. The majority of these people (88 per cent) were born in the UK. From analysis by Owen (1996) referred to above, it seems as if many of these could be children whose parents were both Black and the children could be, for example, Jamaican/British or Nigerian/British or Tanzanian/Mauritian. Of the two thousand or so who were born outside the UK, nearly 700 were born in the New Commonwealth Caribbean, mainly Guyana (280), Trinidad and Tobago (169) and Jamaica (127); with 312 in New Commonwealth Africa, and 152 in New Commonwealth Asia. Around one hundred people were born in each of Mauritius (116), Iraq (102), USA (99) and South Africa (98).

**Indian**

When looking at the composition of the Indian ethnic group, it is again apparent that the group contains great diversity. It has been noted elsewhere that many Indians abroad share a set of values, beliefs, aspirations and a clear sense of identity (Clarke, Peach and Vertovec (1990) reported in Robinson (1996)). However, Indians in London practise different religions, speak a number of different languages, come from a range of different socio-economic groups, and could have been born in any of the world's continents.

In London, the Indian ethnic group was the largest ethnic minority group in 1991, other than the Irish for whom we have a count only of those born in Ireland and not the ethnic group as a whole. There were 347,091 people in the Indian ethnic category, of whom around a third were born in the UK. Of these, (126,297), 99 per cent were born in England, and the majority probably in London itself.

The proportion of UK-born Indians varied across the boroughs but was the same for both Inner and Outer London. Of those boroughs with large Indian populations, Redbridge, Newham and Ealing all had 41 per cent of their Indian populations born in the UK, compared with 32 per cent for Harrow and 34 per cent for Brent. This is likely to be partly a function of the age structure of the Indian group in different boroughs. A younger age structure means more women of childbearing age and therefore more UK-born children, and partly a difference in fertility rates between the Indian group in different boroughs.

Just over a third of the total group (35 per cent – 121,247 people) were born in India itself, although this percentage varied across boroughs. Comparing two boroughs with two of the largest Indian populations, 41 per cent of Newham's Indian population was born in India whilst only 26 per cent of Harrow's Indian population was India-born. A further 2,186 Indians in London were born in Pakistan, and 1,489 born in Sri Lanka.

Just less than a quarter of Indians in London (22 per cent – 77,956 people) were born in East Africa. Harrow (12,500) and Brent (11,901) had by far the largest populations of Indians born in East Africa. In fact 39 per cent of Harrow's Indians were born in East Africa compared to an average of 18 per cent in all London boroughs, and a low of 7 per cent for Indians in Hackney. Over half (58 per cent – 45,352 people) of Indians born in East Africa were from Kenya. There were a further 17,521 Indians born in Uganda, and 11,823 Indians born in Tanzania, with much smaller communities of less than 2,000 Indians born in Malawi and Zambia. Harrow and Brent had very similar sizes of all these groups with over 7,000 Kenya-born Indians, around 1,600 Tanzania-born, and 3,000 Uganda-born.

As well as Indians born in the UK, India and East Africa, there were also 3,508 Indians born in Commonwealth SE Asia – in Malaysia and Singapore rather than Hong Kong. Another Commonwealth country of origin for Indians is Mauritius, and nearly 3,000 Indians living in London in 1991 were born there.

There were 3,294 Indians who were born in the Caribbean – mostly Guyana. These were spread across London, with just over two hundred in each of Croydon, Enfield and Brent.

The final significant country which provides a place of origin for Indians in London is South Africa where 1,186 Indian residents in London were born.

## Pakistani

The Pakistani group may at first seem to be one of the more homogeneous ethnic group categories in the 1991 Census, as it includes people who identify themselves with one particular firmly established state. However there are a number of complexities even for this ethnic group. Pakistan only came into existence in 1947 when the Indian sub-continent was partitioned following independence from British rule. It was made up from regions where Muslims formed the majority, and had two wings, West Pakistan and East Bengal, which later became Bangladesh. As a consequence of this partition, many people migrated from India into Pakistan, and from Pakistan into India. Also, within present day Pakistan there are large ethnic divisions particularly between people living in the different regions, however these divisions are not seen so much in Britain as the majority of Pakistanis are Punjabis. Furthermore Kashmir is still disputed territory and some is under Pakistani authority rather than Indian. These factors highlight that there may be some overlap between the Pakistani, Indian and Bangladeshi groups, for example someone who was born pre-1947 in what was then India, but is now Pakistan may have recorded either on the Census form.

The Pakistani community numbered 87,816 in London in 1991. Unlike almost all the other ethnic groups, there were around the same proportions of

Pakistanis in Inner and Outer London. Waltham Forest had the largest Pakistani population with eight per cent of the borough's population being Pakistani, and Newham came next with six per cent.

Of all Pakistanis in London, 45 per cent were born in the UK, by far the majority in England. In the biggest communities in Waltham Forest and Newham, this proportion increased to half, which is likely to be a result of more settled communities with more children who have been born in the UK.

Half the Pakistani population were born in South Asia (44,030), and most of these people (38,593) were born in Pakistan. Over five thousand (5,164) were born in India, which may relate to some older people who were born before Pakistan became independent from India as discussed above. However, more India-born Pakistanis lived in boroughs with the largest Indian communities such as Ealing and Brent, than in boroughs with the largest Pakistani populations such as Waltham Forest and Newham. In contrast, only 234 Pakistanis were born in Bangladesh.

Again, as with other groups, not all those born in Pakistan were Pakistani, in fact 14 per cent came from other ethnic groups. This varied by borough and in Richmond for example, a third of the 280 Pakistan-born people were White. The only other significant countries of birth for Pakistani migrants were Kenya where 1,943 Pakistanis were born – now living mostly in Ealing and Hounslow, and Uganda where 430 were born.

## Bangladeshi

Of all the ethnic groups named in the 1991 Census, the Bangladeshi group is perhaps the most homogeneous. Bangladesh become an independent country in 1971 when it separated from the rest of Pakistan, and was recognised by the UK in 1972. The Bangladeshi population in London originates overwhelmingly from Sylhet, a district in the north east of Bangladesh. Although people began migrating from what is now Bangladesh in the 18th and 19th centuries, the current Bangladeshi community is of recent origin, with the bulk of the migration occurring during the 1980s.

There were 85,738 Bangladeshis in London in 1991, similar in size to the Pakistani population. Of these, 35 per cent were born in the UK, and all but 200 of those were born in England.

Of those born outside the UK (55,688), 98 per cent (54,533) were born in Bangladesh, making up 64 per cent of the whole Bangladeshi population. This very high proportion, compared with the spread of countries from which migrants of other ethnic groups have come to London, is mostly explained by the relatively recent emergence of Bangladesh itself, as most people migrated in the 1980s when Bangladesh was established as a country. Only 291 Bangladeshis were born in India, and 327 born in Pakistan, showing that people obviously identify with Bangladesh itself and not India or Pakistan which the country was once part of. This perhaps also reflects the young age structure of the group, with younger people tending to be the migrants, and not those who had lived for many years as part of another country.

There was a slight difference between boroughs in the proportions of Bangladeshis actually born in Bangladesh. Just including those with larger populations, the proportions varied from 62 per cent born in Bangladesh in Newham, to 71 per cent in Westminster.

There was a small number of Bangladeshis from some other countries around the world, but they only numbered more than 50 in three countries – Scotland (83), Irish Republic (81), and Wales (56).

As documented in many other places, Bangladeshis are particularly concentrated in Tower Hamlets where there were 36,955 in 1991. However, more than half (57 per cent) of London's Bangladeshis live in other boroughs, and those with particular concentrations include Newham with 8,152, Camden with 6,021, and Westminster with 3,997.

**Chinese**

The 1991 Census records the number of Chinese in London at 56,579 making it the smallest ethnic minority group of the ten named in the Census. Although it is an ethnic group category linked to a country, only a small proportion of Chinese migrants come from China. However, people seem to adhere to the concept of Chinese ethnicity. There are large Chinese communities in many other countries, particularly countries in SE Asia.

Chinese seamen had migrated to Britain during the second half of the 19th century, when they had stayed to work in British ports. Towards the end of the 19th century the Chinese communities began to grow and people set up laundries and catering businesses. However up until the end of the second World War, it is estimated that there were still fewer than 5,000 Chinese in Britain (Shang 1984). The next main wave of migration, which occurred in the 1960s, brought the majority of today's population into Britain.

Only a quarter (26 per cent) of Chinese in London were born in the UK, 98 per cent of whom were born in England.

For those migrating to London, Hong Kong is the country of origin of the largest number (14,772, or 26 per cent) of all Chinese in London. Next come Chinese who were born in Malaysia who number 7,979. Ten per cent of Chinese were born in China itself (5,871) and another ten per cent in Vietnam (5,773).

The remaining Chinese were born in other countries including Singapore (2,166), Mauritius (1,044), Taiwan (634), and the Caribbean (577).

## Other Asian

This should not be called an ethnic group. It shows much more heterogeneity than the other ethnic groups apart from the Black Other and Other groups which are similar aggregates, and there is no cultural bond which holds all the communities it contains together. There was no 'Other Asian' category in the Census, it has been composed of people who wrote in answers in the Other and Black Other categories, which had an Asian influence. This included people in the categories listed in Table 2.6.

In all there were 112,807 people in the Other Asian category in London. Of these, only a fifth were born in the UK. Of those born outside the UK, the main areas where people were born include Far East Asia (40,694, particularly Japan, the Philippines and Vietnam), Sri Lanka (21,578), Mauritius (6,846) and East Africa (6,190).

People born in Sri Lanka constituted the largest group in this Other Asian category. Most people (84 per cent) born in Sri Lanka categorised themselves as an ethnic group which was included within the Other Asian group. Other Asians born in Sri Lanka tended to live in the west of London in 1991, in Brent (2,627), Ealing (1,671), Merton (1,579) and Harrow (1,535).

Almost all (92 per cent) of the 17,192 people born in Japan were included within the Other Asian category, which they would have been had they written in

Japanese in the write in box. The largest number of Other Asians born in Japan was in Barnet (3,884), followed by Ealing (1,581) and Brent (1,528).

There were 13,429 people born in the Philippines living in London in 1991. Over four fifths (84 per cent) were classified in the Other Asian group. Other Asians born in the Philippines tended to live in central areas of London such as Newham (1,430), Kensington and Chelsea (1,229) and Westminster (1,144).

There were nearly 12,000 people born in Vietnam living in London in 1991. The Vietnamese in London are not a homogeneous community, coming from both Vietnamese and Chinese backgrounds, mainly from North and South Vietnam, but also from Cambodia and Laos. Many of the Chinese people born in Vietnam came from North Vietnam, where their families had been settled for several generations. Of those who were born in Vietnam, half were recorded in the Census as Chinese, and half wrote in an answer which was recoded into the Other Asian category, as would have happened if people had written Vietnamese. Other Asians born in Vietnam lived mostly in Hackney (742), Southwark (695) and Greenwich (620), whilst Chinese people born in Vietnam lived mostly in Southwark (1,041), Lambeth (882), and Lewisham (806).

People born in Mauritius (13,907) were recorded in a number of different ethnic groups in the Census. Half (6,846) were recorded as Other Asian.

The Other Asian group contained people of non-mixed ethnic origin who were not Indian, Pakistani or Bangladeshi.

The smallest number of people in the Other Asian group from the six categories comprising the group, as set out above in Table 2.6, were the number of East African Asians or Indo Caribbeans who were Black (705). These are people of non-mixed ethnic origin, and would include, for example, East African Asians

**Table 2.6  Ethnic group answers of people living in London recoded into the Other Asian category**

| | |
|---|---:|
| Black Other: | |
| East African Asian or Indo-Caribbean | 705 |
| Indian sub-continent | 2,280 |
| Other Asian | 11,930 |
| Other ethnic group: | |
| East African Asian or Indo-Caribbean | 3,468 |
| Indian sub-continent | 27,226 |
| Other Asian | 67,198 |
| Total | 112,807 |

*Source: 1991 Census, LRC Commissioned Table LRCT64*

who, unlike the majority, were not included within the Indian category, or Indo-Caribbeans who chose not to be included within the Indian or Caribbean categories. Within this group around a third were born in the New Commonwealth Caribbean, particularly Trinidad and Tobago and Guyana, a third were born in East Africa, particularly Kenya, and a third were born in the UK.

The next category was larger (2,280), and contained people who chose to record themselves as Black and with an ethnic group related to the Indian sub-continent, and who did not chose the Indian, Pakistani or Bangladeshi categories. This might include, for example, someone who was black Asian Sinhalese. Two thirds of the people in this group were born in Sri Lanka. As people from Sri Lanka often have dark skins compared with other people in South Asia and Far East Asia, they may have been more likely than other Asians to record themselves as Black. A further 19 per cent of this group were born in the UK.

The final Black category making up the Other Asian group were people of non-mixed origin who ticked the Black Other category and wrote in an ethnic origin relating to Asia excluding those already mentioned. Examples of this might include black Afghanis, or black Asian Mauritians. This was a large category with 11,930 people in London in this group, half in Inner London and half in Outer London. A third were born in the UK (3,854), but we do not have any other information about these people in terms of their ethnicity. Around half were born in the New Commonwealth. The main countries of birth for those born outside the UK were Sri Lanka (1,533), the Philippines (1,130), New Commonwealth East Africa (955), and Vietnam (310).

The remaining three categories of people included in the Other Asian group were people who were of non-mixed origin who said that none of the written categories suited them and who wrote in answers in the 'any other ethnic group' category. The categories are the same as those described above, but relate to those who did not say that they were Black.

The first of the three groups was comprised of people who were East African Asian or Indo-Caribbean, but not Black or Indian or Caribbean, or at least who did not choose one of those categories. This would include, for example, someone who wrote in that they were Ugandan Asian. There were 3,468 people in this category, and less than a quarter (22 per cent) were born in the UK. The majority (72 per cent) were born in the New Commonwealth, particularly East Africa (1,705) and the Caribbean (580).

The second category was for people who ticked any other ethnic group and who wrote in an answer relating to the Indian sub-continent. The number in this group in London was large – 27,226 people. Again, a large proportion (64 per cent) were born in Sri Lanka, in fact more than two thirds of all people born in Sri Lanka were in this category as they would have been if they had ticked the Other ethnic group box and had written in Sri Lankan or Tamil for example. (As noted above, a number of people born in Sri Lanka also ticked the Black Other box and wrote in an answer which was also recoded back into the Other Asian category). As well as people in this category including migrants from Sri Lanka, there were 5,895 born in the UK, and 1,266 born in Africa.

The final category making up the Other Asian group were those people who ticked the Other ethnic group box and who wrote in an answer which was related to Asian ethnicity, but could not be coded to any of the other codes given. This was the largest sub-group within the Other Asian category with 67,198 people. The majority of people in this category were those born in countries in the Far East such as Japan (15,581), the Philippines (10,101), Vietnam (5,227), Mauritius (5,165), Malaysia (2,698) and Myanmar (Burma – 923), as well as others from South Asia (2,864), and East Africa (2,049).

## Other

The 'Other' ethnic group is a residual category containing all people not included in the other nine main ethnic categories. It aggregates many different communities and some have gone as far as labelling it a category of desperation (Al-Rasheed 1996). Two per cent of London's population were in this category – numbering 120,872 people. Over half (53 per cent) of this group were born in the UK. The countries of birth of those born outside the UK are shown in Table 2.7.

Almost half of those born outside the UK were born in the Middle East or North Africa (25,402), and many believe that the majority of these people are Arabs. From the more detailed ethnic breakdown we know that 32,143 people in the 'Other' category stated an ethnic origin which was Arab, North African or Iranian. For many Arab people, the categories of White, Black and Asian would not have been obviously appropriate to record their ethnicity. Al-Rasheed (1996) states that the majority of Arabs would regard themselves as white, but that some, knowing that in Britain the White category has implications of European whiteness, would have chosen to tick the 'Other' category in order to record their Arab origins, even though they would still consider themselves to be white. Although people from Arab countries are found within the 'Other' group, many people born in this part of the world were recorded as White on the Census forms, for example, 54 per cent of those born in the Middle East were White. A minority would have been European Whites born in these countries to parents working in the oil business, or on military bases or for colonial administrations. Just under a thousand (955) were born in Israel and might include a number of Jewish people. It seems that around half of all Arab people were recorded within the White category, and half within the Other category. If we estimate that half the Arab community were within the Other group and stated their Arab origins, and half were hidden within the White group, it gives us a figure of around 64,000 for the Arab population in London.

**Table 2.7 The countries of birth given within the Other ethnic category with more than 500 people living in London**

| Country of birth | Number of people |
| --- | --- |
| Colombia | 1,216 |
| Egypt | 2,761 |
| Guyana | 1,524 |
| India | 7,321 |
| Iran | 7,182 |
| Iraq | 4,094 |
| Irish Republic | 559 |
| Israel | 955 |
| Jamaica | 672 |
| Kenya | 921 |
| Lebanon | 1,791 |
| Libya | 551 |
| Malaysia | 662 |
| Mauritius | 923 |
| Morocco | 2,771 |
| Myanmar ~~it's called Burma actually~~ | 929 |
| Pakistan | 869 |
| Philippines | 602 |
| South Africa | 545 |
| Sri Lanka | 890 |
| Syria | 588 |
| Trinidad and Tobago | 856 |
| Turkey | 1,473 |
| USA | 828 |
| USSR | 682 |

*Source: 1991 Census, LRC Commissioned Table LRCT14*

The other half of people within the 'Other' group who were born outside the UK, came from a variety of countries, some of which were areas of the world not covered by any of the other categories, such as South

America. Others were from countries where ethnicity is a complex issue – perhaps because of influences from a number of different ethnic groups, and where people from those countries seemed to respond in a number of different ways to the Census question categories, for example Guyana, Mauritius, and Trinidad and Tobago. There was a large number of people born in India in the 'Other' category (7,321), which Al-Rasheed (1996) suggests could include for example, Parsis who originate from Iran and who therefore may not identify with the Indian ethnic group itself. The final group which is included in the 'Other' category is people of mixed ethnic origin who were not Black.

From the full 35 code breakdown, nine of the codes were aggregated to form the 'Other' ethnic group. These included two categories of people who ticked the Black Other category, and wrote in an answer which was then recoded into the 'Other' ethnic group category. The full list of the nine categories is shown in Table 2.8.

The total number of people recording a mixed ethnic origin in the Other ethnic group was 56,639. People of mixed White ethnic origin were recoded back into the White group, and people who ticked the Black Other box and had mixed ethnic origins remained within the Black Other group. The total combined of all these mixed ethnic origin categories was 82,096. The number may well have been larger had there been a separate category for those of mixed ethnic origin, as many may have ticked a category representing just one of the groups they identified with.

There were only a handful in the Asian/White mixed category (52 people), who ticked the Black Other box in the Census question, almost all recorded themselves in the 'Other ethnic group' category. Of the 22,437 in this group, over half (57 per cent) were born in the UK. These may be the children of one Asian and one White parent, or could be the children of Anglo-Asian parents. It is interesting to note that Berrington (1996) shows that the number of inter-ethnic unions in

**Table 2.8 Ethnic group answers of people living in London aggregated to form the Other category**

| | |
|---|---:|
| Black Other: | |
| North African, Arab or Iranian | 2,810 |
| Asian/White mixed origin | 52 |
| | |
| Other ethnic group: | |
| British – ethnic minority indicated | 6,855 |
| British – ethnic minority not indicated | 5,775 |
| North African, Arab or Iranian | 29,333 |
| Other answers | 19,460 |
| Black/ White mixed origin | 9,665 |
| Asian/White mixed origin | 22,437 |
| Other mixed origin | 24,485 |
| | |
| Total | 120,872 |

*Source: 1991 Census, LRC Commissioned Table LRCT64*

London between Indians and Whites is small with only five per cent of Indians in partnerships having a White partner. Of those born abroad (9,538), nearly eight thousand were born in the New Commonwealth, and 6,488 of those in South Asia and particularly India. Some of these people may be the children of Anglo/Indian partnerships who were born abroad themselves, or from partnerships formed between Indians and people from other White groups in India. A further 828 Asian/White people were born in New Commonwealth SE Asia in the combined region of Hong Kong, Malaysia and Singapore.

There were nearly ten thousand people (9,665) who stated that they were of mixed ethnic origin with a Black/White ethnicity, and who did not tick the Black other box. These people were counted within the Other ethnic group. Of those, almost all (8,403 people) were born in the UK, and many are likely to be the children of one Black parent and one White parent. Berrington (1996) shows that there are more inter-ethnic unions between the Black and White groups than between any other, and that this is particularly true for younger people, with 40 per cent of Black Caribbean men aged 16-34 who were married or cohabiting in 1991 having a White partner.

The final category in the Other group were people of mixed ethnic origin who were not of Black/White,

Asian/White or White mixed ethnic origin. There were 24,485 in this category. A high proportion of the people in this group (74 per cent) were born in the UK, so we have no further clues about their ethnicity. Given the diversity of London's population, people in this group could identify with a large range of different ethnic groups. Of those born outside the UK (6,335), most were born in the New Commonwealth (4,072) with nearly two thousand born in the Caribbean, particularly Guyana, and nearly one thousand born in Asia. Other significant origins for those in this group were New Commonwealth Africa (588), Mauritius (341), Middle East (324), and South Africa (255).

**Gender patterns**

Overall in London there were more females than males, with a sex ratio of 93 males for every 100 females. This constitutes a large change from the sex ratio at birth which is 105 boys to 100 girls. The gender structure of a community is affected by its age structure. As women generally have a longer life expectancy than men, the older the age structure, the more likely there are to be more females than males in the population. At birth in the UK there are more boys than girls, and up until age 50 there are more males than females although the differences can be quite small. However from age 50 onwards there are more females than males, and at the oldest age groups the differences can be very large, hence producing population totals with more females than males in the population. The pattern of more females than males existed for every London borough apart from the City where there were more males than females.

**Gender by country of birth**

There were more females than males for both those born in the UK and outside the UK. However there were a number of countries of birth for which there were more males than females. These included Scotland, Northern Ireland, East Africa, Bangladesh, Pakistan, Sri Lanka, Cyprus, Gibraltar, Malta and Gozo, Turkey, Non-New Commonwealth Africa and Rest of World, as shown in Table 2.9.

Interesting points to note are the fact that the ratio for people born in India reflects more females than males, whereas the ratios for the other South Asian countries of Bangladesh, Pakistan and Sri Lanka reflect more males than females. This is particularly so for people born in Sri Lanka – with 29 per cent more males than females in the population. Perhaps this is because males tended to migrate first and the Indian community is well settled in London and wives and families have followed and been united. The other communities are newer and perhaps fewer women have migrated.

Of people born in Turkey living in London there were 25 per cent more males than females.

Those born in Scotland and Northern Ireland also had more males than females in the population compared with England and Wales and the Irish Republic where there were more females than males. This could reflect a younger age structure in the migrant groups from Scotland and Northern Ireland.

Migrants who were born in Europe (outside the UK and Ireland) had considerably more females in their communities than males with around 70 males per 100 females.

Borough data reveal some unusual features – however this is often in communities with very small numbers. Borough variations are also more often seen in specific country of birth data rather than in those figures where a number of countries have been aggregated to form a region such as SE Asia. Of those larger communities – some of the boroughs with large gender imbalances for particular countries of birth are as follows:

*Born in Scotland* – Those in Tower Hamlets and Newham had 25 per cent more males than females.

*Born in Northern Ireland* – Those in Newham, Tower Hamlets, and Barking and Dagenham had significantly more males than females (31 per cent, 33 per cent and 41 per cent respectively).

**Table 2.9  Gender ratio (males per 100 females) by country/area of birth of people living in London**

| Country of birth | Females excess gender ratio | Country of birth | Males excess gender ratio |
|---|---|---|---|
| UK | 93 | Scotland | 104 |
| England | 93 | N Ireland | 101 |
| Wales | 88 | East Africa (New Commonwealth) | 106 |
| Outside UK | 90 | Bangladesh | 110 |
| Irish Republic | 85 | Pakistan | 110 |
| Old Commonwealth | 81 | Sri Lanka | 129 |
| New Commonwealth | 96 | Cyprus, Gibraltar, Malta and Gozo | 106 |
| Other Africa (New Commonwealth) | 89 | Turkey | 125 |
| Caribbean (New Commonwealth) | 82 | Africa not New Commonwealth | 112 |
| India | 92 | Rest of World | 101 |
| SE Asia (New Commonwealth) | 93 | | |
| Other New Commonwealth | 98 | | |
| European Community | 73 | | |
| Remainder of Europe | 70 | | |
| USSR | 83 | | |
| North and South America | 78 | | |
| Asia not New Commonwealth | 92 | | |

*Source: 1991 Census, LRC Commissioned Table LRCT13*

*Born in the Irish Republic* – Two areas in London had distinctly fewer males than females. These included Bexley (74 per cent), Havering (73 per cent) and Bromley (68 per cent) in eastern and south eastern London, and Kingston (71 per cent), Richmond (74 per cent) and Sutton (71 per cent) in South West London.

*Born in Bangladesh* – A number of boroughs had significantly more males than females in their Bangladesh-born populations, but the more extreme cases were those boroughs with small Bangladeshi communities.

*Born in India* – Most boroughs fell very close to the average of 92 males for every 100 females. The borough which stood apart was Tower Hamlets which as well as having the smallest Indian-born community of any London borough, also had 20 per cent more males than females.

*Born in Pakistan* – As with people born in Bangladesh, a number of boroughs had significantly more males than females in their Pakistan-born populations. Hammersmith and Fulham had 39 per cent more males than females and Camden 50 per cent.

*Born in Sri Lanka* – There were large excesses of males over females in all boroughs except Kensington and Chelsea, Westminster, Bromley and Sutton. Some boroughs had extremely large excesses of males – with

Newham's large Sri-Lankan born population having 78 per cent more males than females, and Waltham Forest having 89 per cent more males.

*Born in the European Community* – Nearly all boroughs had fewer males than females – but Bromley only had half as many males as females. Tower Hamlets went against the trend with more males than females, particularly due to its male dominated Poland-born population.

*Born in Turkey* – Nearly all boroughs had more males than females but Haringey with the second largest Turkish-born population in London had 50 per cent more males than females in its population.

*Born in Non-Commonwealth Africa* – Haringey and Newham both had quite large populations of this group, with many more males than females (44 per cent and 56 per cent respectively).

## Age

One of the ways of simplifying age data is to break the population down into groups of people in order to compare the proportions of children, people of working age, and older people.

Overall in London, 22 per cent of the residents in 1991 were under 18, 59 per cent were between 18 and 59, and the remaining 19 per cent were 60 and over. There was little difference between Inner and Outer London, but there were wider differentials between boroughs. The Central London boroughs of the City, Westminster, and Kensington and Chelsea had the smallest proportion of children aged 0-17 in their populations. The City had just 7 per cent at these ages, whilst the other two boroughs had around 15 per cent, compared with Tower Hamlets with over 28 per cent. Haringey, Hackney, Newham, Lambeth and Brent all had the lowest proportions of older people in their populations with less than 17 per cent at those ages. This compares with Barking and Dagenham with more than 23 per cent aged 60 and over.

## Age by gender

In London there were around 1.5 million children, four million people aged 18-59, and 1.3 million older people aged 60 and over. The split by gender is shown in Table 2.10

There are more male children than female as expected in London. Females in England live on average five years longer than males, and this accounts for the higher proportion of women aged 60 and over in London (22 per cent of the female population) compared with men (17 per cent of the male population). Consequently there are slightly smaller proportions of women aged 18-59, compared with males at those ages (but more in actual numbers).

## Country of birth by age

The proportions of the population in each of the broad age groups for a number of different country of birth groups are set out in Table 2.11.

The table shows that there are quite large differences in the age structure of migrants who were born outside the UK, and those people born inside the UK. The main difference is that there were far fewer children aged 0-17 who had migrated. This is perhaps not surprising as many migrants move in their early adult years before they have children, and once they are settled they then start families, and therefore the children are UK born. As well as differences between UK and non-UK born people, there are also differences in age structure between different migrant groups. Migrants from the USSR had the oldest age structure with nearly two thirds of the population aged 60 or over. This compares with Commonwealth Africa

**Table 2.10  Total population by age and gender, London**

| Age group | male | female |
|---|---|---|
| 0-17 | 741,600 | 709,200 |
| 18-59 | 1,933,100 | 2,024,600 |
| 60+ | 530,900 | 740,400 |

*Source: 1991 Census, LRC Commissioned Table LRCT13*

(excluding East Africa) where only three per cent were aged 60 or older. Other migrant groups had lower proportions of children, such as migrants from the Irish Republic, India and the Commonwealth Caribbean. The group of migrants from Commonwealth East Africa were unusual in having low proportions of children and older people, and a very high proportion of people of working age (90 per cent).

There were also considerable differences between boroughs, which was partly due to the different ethnic groups living in each area. For example, Tower Hamlets had the highest proportion of children aged 0-17 of any borough, and a particularly high proportion of children born outside the UK (22 per cent), which was influenced by the large number of Bangladesh-born children (7,932). There were also some differences in the age structures of the same migrant group between different boroughs. For example, in Westminster 40 per cent of Irish-born were 60 or over, whereas in Waltham Forest only 17 per cent of migrants from the Irish Republic were in this age group.

**UK-born and those born outside of the UK**
The population pyramids for these groups shown in Figures 2.1 to 2.6 immediately highlight the differences in age structure between migrants and those who were born in the UK. The UK-born age structure shows large proportions of older people with more women than men as expected, as the life expectancy of women is greater than that of men. It also shows fairly even numbers of people in each of the age bands apart from young adult ages of 20-29 where there are slightly more people (partly due to the baby-boom as these are the babies of the 1960s, and partly due to young people moving into London from the rest of the UK for work). This is a typical population pyramid of a developed population with long life expectancy and low fertility rates.

In contrast, the pyramid for those born outside the UK shows a very different pattern. This shows a high

**Table 2.11 The proportions of the population living in London by age group and country of birth**

| Country/region of birth | 0-17 | 18-59 | 60 plus |
| --- | --- | --- | --- |
| Total | 21.72 | 59.25 | 19.03 |
| Inside the UK | 25.50 | 54.54 | 19.96 |
| Outside the UK | 8.07 | 76.27 | 15.66 |
| Irish Republic | 3.85 | 69.80 | 26.36 |
| Old Commonwealth | 6.01 | 84.56 | 9.43 |
| New Commonwealth | 7.32 | 80.12 | 12.56 |
| Bangladesh | 32.11 | 62.89 | 5.00 |
| India | 3.67 | 76.46 | 19.87 |
| Pakistan | 8.96 | 83.35 | 7.70 |
| Sri Lanka | 8.49 | 83.64 | 7.87 |
| NC East Africa | 5.66 | 90.42 | 3.93 |
| NC Other Africa | 12.13 | 84.77 | 3.10 |
| NC Caribbean | 2.13 | 77.38 | 20.50 |
| SE Asia | 7.45 | 87.39 | 5.15 |
| Cyprus, Gibraltar, etc | 2.08 | 77.74 | 20.18 |
| Turkey | 19.55 | 75.54 | 4.91 |
| USSR | 5.45 | 31.79 | 62.76 |
| European Community | 7.23 | 73.33 | 19.44 |
| Remainder of Europe | 4.74 | 54.66 | 40.61 |
| Non NC Africa | 14.08 | 75.45 | 10.47 |
| America not incl. Canada | 14.69 | 77.80 | 7.51 |

*Source: 1991 Census, LRC Commissioned Table LRCT13*
*Note: NC = New Commonwealth*

proportion of people aged 20-59. The 20 year olds are likely to be more recent migrants, whereas those in their 40s and 50s are more likely to have migrated in the 1960s and '70s. Of course people can migrate at any age, and older people often do move for family re-unification, but in general most migrants tend to be young adults. The proportion of children in the migrant group is very small compared with the UK born population, as young migrants are more likely to

**Figure 2.1 Age pyramid of people born in the UK**

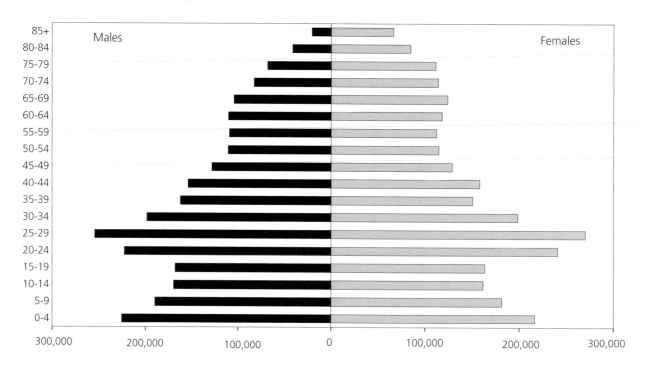

**Figure 2.2 Age pyramid of people born outside the UK**

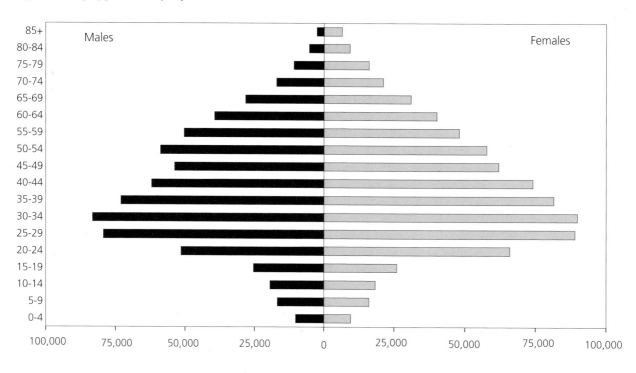

*Source: 1991 Census, LRC Commissioned Table LRCT13*

have children once they are settled, rather than bring in young children with them (unless they are refugees and have been forced to move). The proportion of migrants aged 70 and over is also relatively small, although the numbers are still significant, partly reflecting the low levels of overseas migration into the UK before the second world war.

## UK-born

Brent, Newham and Tower Hamlets have the youngest age structures in this group, with around a third of their populations aged under 18. Westminster (20 per cent) and the City (8 per cent) have the smallest proportions of children. The City (67 per cent), Hammersmith and Fulham (61 per cent), and Wandsworth (60 per cent) have the largest proportions of people of aged 18-59. The range of proportions of boroughs' populations aged 60 and over were small with all boroughs having between 16 per cent and 25 per cent of their UK-born populations at that age. Haringey had the smallest proportion of older people at 16 per cent. Overall there were 44 per cent more UK-born women than men aged 60 or over in London.

## People born outside the UK

Of all London residents born outside the UK, 8 per cent were 0-17, 76 per cent were 18-59 and 16 per cent were aged 60 or over. Particular differences by borough were the high proportion of migrant children in Tower Hamlets (22 per cent of all migrants), and the high proportion of those of working age in Waltham Forest (82 per cent of all migrants). Newham and Havering showed the difference in proportions of older migrants – Newham had less than 10 per cent of migrants aged 60 or over, whilst 23 per cent of migrants in Havering were in this age group.

Population pyramids for four countries of birth are shown to highlight differences in age structure between different migrant groups.

## Migrants born in India and Bangladesh

These two pyramids (Figures 2.3 and 2.4) show the differences in age structure between sets of migrants from two South Asian countries. The India-born pyramid matches that of all people born outside of the UK quite closely, but shows a slightly older age structure as if the whole pattern has shifted up slightly. There are fairly even numbers of males and females. This represents a well established community in London. The Bangladesh-born pyramid is a very different shape. It reflects the structure of a much newer migrant community. There are more children aged 10-14 and 15-19 than in any other age band which is very unusual for a migrant group. This could be explained by high fertility rates, and a high likelihood of migrating with young children.

There is also a greater difference in this pyramid between the numbers of males and females in each age band. This can be seen particularly for people in their 40s. There were less than 2,000 men in their 40s compared with nearly 3,400 women. The seemingly low number of men in their 40s could be a consequence of stricter immigration controls which came into force when these men would have been in their early 20s. It has also been suggested that the imbalance between men and women could be a result of the men who arrived in the 1960s taking wives who were much younger than themselves. The Samples of Anonymised records show that the average age of Bangladeshi husbands is ten years older than Bangladeshi wives (Eade et al 1996). The final large difference between the two pyramids is in the numbers of older people. There were under 3,000 Bangladesh-born people aged 60 and over in 1991 compared with over 30,000 born in India.

## Born in Cyprus, Gibraltar, Malta and Gozo, and in Turkey

Again, these two communities are very close geographically, but show very different patterns in their age structures. The group of people born in Cyprus, Gibraltar, Malta and Gozo is dominated by those born

**Figure 2.3 Age pyramid of people born in India**

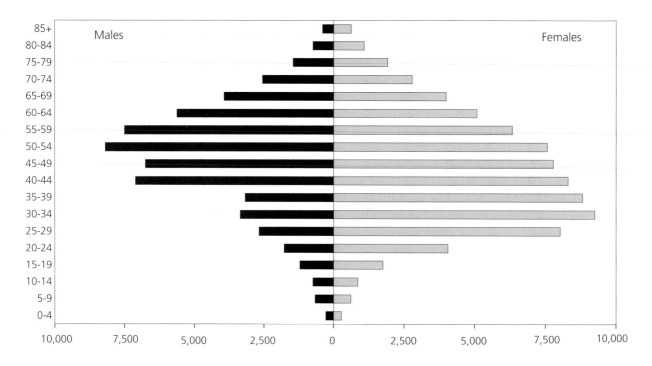

**Figure 2.4 Age pyramid of people born in Bangladesh**

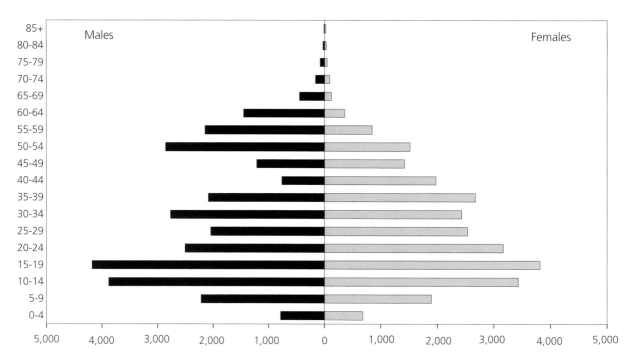

*Source: 1991 Census, LRC Commissioned Table LRCT13*

**Figure 2.5 Age pyramid of people born in Cyprus, Gibraltar, Malta and Gozo**

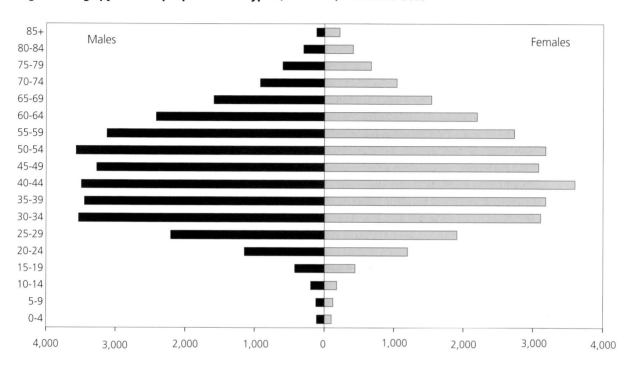

**Figure 2.6 Age pyramid of people born in Turkey**

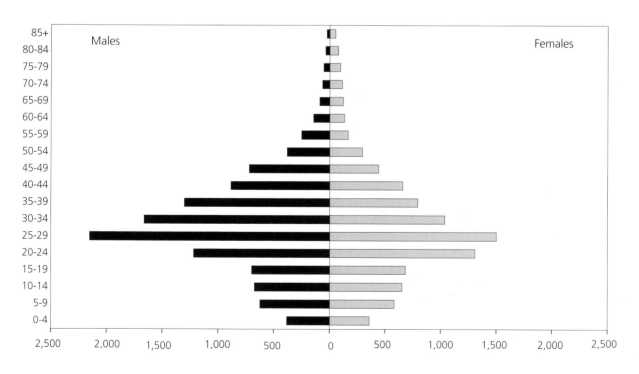

*Source: 1991 Census, LRC Commissioned Table LRCT13*

in Cyprus, (85 per cent). This pyramid (Figure 2.5) shows an older age structure than those born in Turkey (Figure 2.6), with 20 per cent of the population aged 60 and over compared with five per cent of those born in Turkey. In contrast, only two per cent of those born in Cyprus, Gibraltar, Malta and Gozo were aged 0-17 compared with 20 per cent of those born in Turkey. The Cyprus, Gibraltar, Malta and Gozo born group is distinctive in that there are fairly even numbers in all age bands from 30 to 60.

The age profiles of these groups can contribute to our knowledge of how these populations might grow in the future. Because these people were born abroad, they may have particular needs in terms of services provided by those working in the public and voluntary sectors. However, the full communities will also include UK-born people and those born in other countries, so analysing just these data will only contribute a partial picture.

Whilst these pyramids can provide clues as to past migration patterns, they cannot tell us about future patterns of migration which will depend upon external factors such as the socio-economic and political situation both in the countries of origin and in the UK. What they can show is the demographic changes which occur through the population ageing. For example, adequate support services for children born in Turkey who may not have English as a first language must be provided. It should also be ensured, for example, that the large numbers of Cypriot pensioners are adequately provided for by the existing range of services offered for older people.

**References**

M Al-Rasheed, 'The Other-Others: hidden Arabs?' in *Ethnicity in the Census, Volume Two – The ethnic minority populations of Great Britain*, ONS, 1996

A Berrington, 'Marriage Patterns and inter-ethnic unions' in *Ethnicity in the Census. Volume One – Demographic characteristics of the ethnic minority populations*, ONS, 1996

C Clarke, C Peach and S Vertovec, *South Asians Overseas: Migration and Ethnicity*, Cambridge University Press, 1990

P Daley, 'Black Africans: students who stayed' in *Ethnicity in the Census, Volume Two – The ethnic minority populations of Great Britain*, ONS, 1996

J Eade et al, 'The Bangladeshis: the encapsulated community' in *Ethnicity in the Census, Volume Two – The ethnic minority populations of Great Britain*, ONS, 1996

D Owen, 'Black-Other: the melting pot' in *Ethnicity in the Census, Volume Two – The ethnic minority populations of Great Britain*, ONS, 1996

C Peach, 'Black-Caribbeans: class, gender and geography' in *Ethnicity in the Census, Volume Two – The ethnic minority populations of Great Britain*, ONS, 1996

V Robinson, 'The Indians: onward and upward' in *Ethnicity in the Census, Volume Two – The ethnic minority populations of Great Britain*, ONS, 1996

A Shang, *The Chinese in Britain*, Batsford Academic and Educational, 1984

M Storkey, *Identifying the Cypriot Community from the 1991 Census*, London Research Centre, 1993

# Chapter 3
# Migration

# Migration

## Introduction

London's population peaked this century in 1939 at the time of National Registration when 8.6 million residents were recorded. Since that time the population has fallen, with the decline being particularly rapid during the 1960s and 1970s. However this decline was halted in 1984 when the population of London began to grow again. The main reason for this growth was a change in migration flows. During the 1960s and 1970s London had a net migration loss of as many as 100,000 people a year. Since 1984 the net migration losses have been much smaller, and have been less than natural growth hence the increase in population.

This highlights the enormous importance of migration patterns to London. There are a number of data sources which provide information about migration patterns. They include the 1991 Census which provides an extraordinary amount of migration data enabling examination of how people move within, into and out of London. The advantage of the Census is that the coverage is so large that the data give us a very clear picture of migration patterns in 1991, and Census data can be also be used as a check against other data sources. Other than the Census, the main migration sources for London are National Health Service data which show movements of people when they re-register with a doctor, the International Passenger Survey (IPS) which gives details of international flows, and asylum seeker and visitor switcher data from the Home Office.

This chapter aims to describe migration in London in 1990/91, by looking at the overall patterns of migration and then looking at migration by age, gender and ethnicity. A description of the commissioned data is contained within Appendix 2 together with an outline of adjustments made.

## Overall patterns of migration in London

The Census showed that three quarters of a million (758,210) people who were resident in London had a different address a year before. This includes all people who moved, however short the distance travelled, and is a count of people moving into London as well as those moving within London.

There was a net movement of 34,000 people out of London boroughs over the period 1990-1991, the difference between the number of people moving into London boroughs (456,000) and the number moving out of London boroughs (490,000). These figures of course will double count a third of all movers resident in London in 1991, as they moved from one London borough to another, and therefore would be in-migrants to one area and out-migrants from another.

## Migration patterns by ethnicity in London

In 1990-1991 ethnic groups in London differed substantially in their propensity to migrate. The Black African group was the most mobile with a quarter moving in the year before the Census. The two largest minority groups in London, the Indian and Black Caribbean groups were the least mobile with less than ten per cent of people moving over that time. Table 3.1 shows the percentage of each ethnic group who migrated in the year previous to the Census.

The ethnic group migration data, with the adjustments

**Table 3.1 Percentage of each ethnic group moving in the year preceding the 1991 Census.**

| | |
|---|---|
| Black African | 25 |
| Other Asian | 21 |
| Chinese | 17 |
| Other | 17 |
| Black Other | 13 |
| Bangladeshi | 12 |
| Pakistani | 11 |
| White | 11 |
| Black Caribbean | 9 |
| Indian | 8 |

*Source: 1991 Census, Local Base Statistics Table 17*
*Note: Migrants in this case includes those who moved within an area*

made to reallocate those who did not state their original address, and including an estimate of international out-migration (as described in Appendix 2), showed that overall the net balance of migration in London was a loss of 34,000 people. This was composed of a net loss of 53,000 White people, and a net gain of 19,000 people from ethnic minority groups. The full breakdown is shown in Table 3.2.

In all ethnic minority groups, flows of people out of London were compensated by flows of people into London.  For example, the second largest ethnic minority group in London, the Black Caribbean community, had over eleven thousand people who moved into London boroughs almost completely compensated by over ten thousand other people who moved out of London boroughs during the year 1990/91.

## Migration by gender
Overall in the population there was little difference in the proportions of each sex migrating. Seven per cent

**Table 3.2 Total in-migration, out-migration and net migration in London, by ethnic group**

| Ethnic group | In-migrants | Out-migrants | Net migration |
|---|---|---|---|
| White | 347,727 | 400,970 | -53,243 |
| Black Caribbean | 11,748 | 10,981 | 766 |
| Black African | 26,705 | 19,823 | 6,883 |
| Black Other | 4,895 | 4,464 | 431 |
| Indian | 16,622 | 13,178 | 3,445 |
| Pakistani | 5,369 | 3,695 | 1,673 |
| Bangladeshi | 6,043 | 5,050 | 993 |
| Chinese | 6,925 | 6,109 | 816 |
| Other Asian | 16,859 | 14,074 | 2,785 |
| Other | 13,372 | 11,930 | 1,441 |
| Total | 456,264 | 490,275 | -34,010 |

*Source: 1991 Census, LRC Commissioned Table LRCT49*

of females in each borough in 1991 had moved in over the past year, and seven per cent of the 1991 female population also moved out.  This compares with seven per cent of males who moved in to a London borough and eight per cent of males who moved out. However, it is known that males were more likely to be missed from the Census than females, and the effect of this differential undercount is explored later.

## Migration by age and gender
In London as a whole, levels of migration by age for males and females were quite similar although women had higher levels moving in and out in their late teens and 20s and lower levels moving in their 30s and 40s. This may be because more young women move for work or to join partners in their twenties, whereas they are less mobile in their 30s and 40s, with family responsibilities and being less likely to move for work purposes.

The age profile of movers, shown in Figure 3.1 mirrors that of numerous other analyses showing very large number of movers at young adult ages, particularly people in their 20s. An interesting feature is that the number of female out-migrants is similar for ages 45 up to pensionable age, and over pensionable age, whereas the male numbers drop significantly at pensionable age. The longer life expectancy of females coupled with the earlier pensionable age means that this does not necessarily show an increased propensity to migrate.

The figures shown do not reflect the propensity to move, they show the level of migration. Some of the differences in levels of migration can be explained by the difference in the sex balance within the population in particular age bands. For example there were three per cent more male than female movers in the 5-15 year age group, yet in the population in that age group there were five per cent more males than females, so the migration rates may be more similar than at first suggested. Figure 3.2 shows a comparison of out-migration rates calculated for males and females.

**Figure 3.1  The total level of migration in and out of London boroughs by age and sex, 1990-1991**

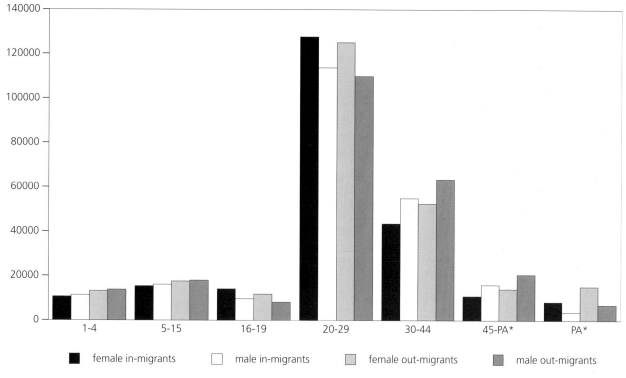

* Pensionable Age

*Source: 1991 Census, LRC Commissioned Table LRCT49*
*Note: The age groups are not even in size*

## Migration rates

Calculating migration rates is a good way of comparing migration characteristics of males and females. The most accurate way of doing this would be to relate the migrants to the true populations at risk of moving (the exposed population). For out-migrants the exposed population is those people in the relevant age/sex/ethnic group who were in each borough in April 1990, and who were still alive in April 1991. In this analysis the 1991 Census population has been used. Calculating in-migration rates is far more difficult as the exposed population at risk of migrating into each borough is, in theory, all the people of that ethnicity in other London boroughs, the rest of Great Britain and overseas, between 21 April 1990 and 21 April 1991. Out-migration rates were calculated by applying the numbers of people who moved to those at risk of moving. (In the LRC projections model, the in-migration flows generated by the rates in 1991 are held

constant over time). The number of people in each age/sex/ethnic group in 1991 was taken to represent the exposed population.

Overall out-migration rates by age and sex are shown in Figure 3.2. The figure shows that the overall pattern shown in Figure 3.1 is maintained with females more likely than males to move out of an area in their late teens, whilst males were more likely than females to move between ages 30 and 44. The calculation of rates makes comparisons of the 45 to pensionable age and the pensionable age category far more meaningful as it makes allowance for the different age bands for men and women caused by the different retirement ages.

One problem with interpreting these data is that they do not include any adjustments for under-enumeration. We know that under-enumeration varied by age, gender and location, although as yet it has been

**Figure 3.2  Out-migrants per 100 people for males and females from London boroughs 1990-1991**

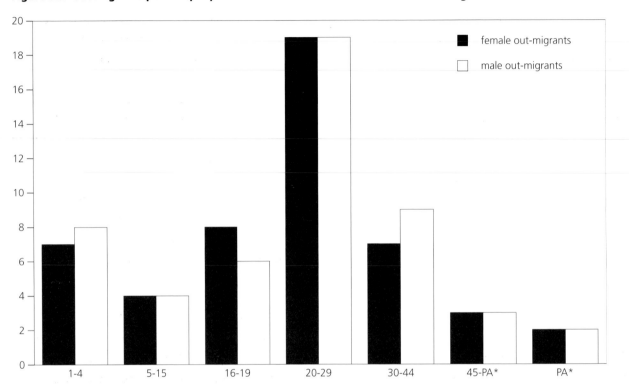

\* Pensionable Age

*Source:  1991 Census, LRC Commissioned Table LRCT49*

impossible to quantify any additional differentials by ethnic group.  It may be possible that some of the differences in movement by sex could be accounted for by differential under-enumeration. In order to examine this the migration data were adjusted using the ONS boost factors by age and sex for Inner and Outer London, and the sex ratios from this analysis compared with ratios calculated without adjusting for under-enumeration.  The two sets of ratios showing male movers per 100 females for Greater London are shown in Table 3.3.

From Table 3.3 it can be seen that incorporating the boost factors removes the previously seen pattern of more female migrants than male. This is almost entirely due to the fact that the Census is thought to have missed significantly more men in their 20s than women, and if the male flows are increased to reflect this disproportionate loss, they almost match the levels of female migrants. Of course, the critical assumption

made here is that the migration patterns of those people recorded by the Census was similar to those who were missed. Realistically this assumption cannot

**Table 3.3  Number of male migrants per 100 female migrants**

| | without adjustment for under-enumeration | | with adjustment for under-enumeration | |
| --- | --- | --- | --- | --- |
| | **in** | **out** | **in** | **out** |
| 1-4 | 107 | 105 | 108 | 106 |
| 5-15 | 104 | 103 | 105 | 104 |
| 16-19 | 68 | 69 | 69 | 71 |
| 20-29 | 89 | 88 | 98 | 96 |
| 30-44 | 126 | 121 | 129 | 123 |
| 45-pensionable age | 147 | 146 | 147 | 146 |
| Pensionable age | 45 | 47 | 43 | 45 |
| All ages | 98 | 97 | 101 | 100 |

*Source: 1991 Census, LRC Commissioned Table LRCT49*

be made as we have no information about the migration patterns of people missed by the Census, although it is believed that those missed by the Census may well have had higher mobility than those recorded by enumerators.

## Migration patterns by gender and ethnicity

The migration out of London boroughs of males and females in different ethnic groups can be examined by calculating out-migration rates. Migration rates for males and females were very similar for all ethnic groups. From Table 3.4 it can be seen that males had the same or slightly higher out-migration rates in all ethnic groups.

As Table 3.4 shows, the two biggest ethnic minority groups in London, the Caribbean and Indian groups had the lowest out-migration rates. If this pattern continues it will have particular implications for the future composition of London's population as these groups will not be leaving London in the same way that White people do. White people have traditionally left London at different life stages such as when

children are born, perhaps returning back to home towns after working in London for a spell, and at retirement ages. The low out-migration rates for the two biggest ethnic minority groups will serve to increase the ethnic minority population of London, whereas if people from these ethnic groups do begin to move out of London at the same rates as the White population, it will serve to decrease the ethnic minority population of London.

As in-migration rates are problematic to calculate, an alternative approach was used to compare inflows for different ethnic groups. The sex ratios of the numbers of in-migrants were calculated and are shown in Table 3.5.

Table 3.5 shows that in the White, Other Asian, Black Other, Indian, Chinese, and Black Caribbean groups there were slightly more females than males moving into London boroughs, whereas the Pakistani, Other, Black African and Bangladeshi groups had slightly more males than females. The biggest difference was for the Pakistani population where there were 21 per

**Table 3.4  Out-migration rates of ethnic groups from London boroughs by gender (out-migrants per 100 population)**

|  | Females | Males |
| --- | --- | --- |
| Pakistani | 4 | 5 |
| Other | 10 | 11 |
| Black African | 12 | 14 |
| Bangladeshi | 6 | 6 |
| White | 8 | 8 |
| Other Asian | 13 | 14 |
| Black Other | 6 | 6 |
| Indian | 4 | 4 |
| Chinese | 11 | 11 |
| Black Caribbean | 4 | 4 |
| All ethnic groups | 7 | 8 |

*Source: 1991 Census, LRC Commissioned Table LRCT49*

**Table 3.5  The number of male in-migrants per 100 female in-migrants**

| Ethnic group | Sex ratio |
| --- | --- |
| Pakistani | 121 |
| Other | 108 |
| Black African | 103 |
| Bangladeshi | 101 |
| White | 97 |
| Other Asian | 97 |
| Black Other | 94 |
| Indian | 93 |
| Chinese | 93 |
| Black Caribbean | 87 |
| All ethnic groups | 98 |

*Source: 1991 Census, LRC Commissioned Table LRCT49*

cent more male in-migrants than female.

## Migration patterns by age, gender and ethnicity in London

Having established that migration varies by ethnicity and also by gender and age, migration patterns by age, gender and ethnicity can also be examined. Out-migration rates by these three variables are set out in

Table 3.6

We have already seen in Table 3.4 that the Black Caribbean, Black Other and South Asian groups all have low overall out-migration rates. The analysis by age in Table 3.6 allows us to see that the main cause of this is the low rates for both males and females in their 20s which are only half those of other ethnic groups.

**Table 3.6 Out-migration rates by age, gender and ethnic group (percentage of population at risk)**

|  | 1-4 | 5-15 | 16-19 | 20-29 | 30-44 | 45-PA | PA and over | Total |
|---|---|---|---|---|---|---|---|---|
| White females | 8 | 4 | 8 | 21 | 7 | 3 | 2 | 8 |
| White males | 8 | 4 | 5 | 20 | 9 | 3 | 2 | 8 |
| Black Caribbean females | 4 | 3 | 6 | 8 | 4 | 1 | 1 | 4 |
| Black Caribbean males | 4 | 3 | 4 | 8 | 5 | 1 | 1 | 4 |
| Black African females | 11 | 9 | 14 | 20 | 10 | 5 | 9 | 12 |
| Black African males | 12 | 9 | 12 | 22 | 14 | 5 | 5 | 14 |
| Black Other females | 5 | 3 | 6 | 9 | 6 | 2 | 3 | 6 |
| Black Other males | 6 | 3 | 4 | 11 | 8 | 3 | 3 | 6 |
| Indian females | 4 | 2 | 4 | 9 | 3 | 2 | 3 | 4 |
| Indian males | 4 | 2 | 3 | 9 | 4 | 2 | 2 | 4 |
| Pakistani females | 5 | 3 | 4 | 9 | 3 | 2 | 4 | 4 |
| Pakistani males | 5 | 2 | 3 | 10 | 6 | 2 | 2 | 5 |
| Bangladeshi females | 6 | 5 | 8 | 8 | 6 | 5 | 5 | 6 |
| Bangladeshi males | 6 | 5 | 7 | 10 | 7 | 5 | 6 | 6 |
| Chinese females | 8 | 4 | 10 | 24 | 10 | 4 | 4 | 11 |
| Chinese males | 7 | 5 | 8 | 24 | 12 | 4 | 4 | 11 |
| Other Asian females | 12 | 10 | 12 | 24 | 11 | 5 | 6 | 13 |
| Other Asian males | 12 | 10 | 12 | 23 | 14 | 7 | 5 | 14 |
| Other females | 9 | 7 | 9 | 18 | 10 | 5 | 4 | 10 |
| Other males | 10 | 6 | 8 | 21 | 13 | 5 | 4 | 11 |
| All females | 7 | 4 | 8 | 19 | 7 | 3 | 2 | 7 |
| All males | 8 | 4 | 6 | 19 | 9 | 3 | 2 | 8 |

*Source: 1991 Census, LRC Commissioned Table LRCT49*
*Note: PA = Pensionable Age*

Gender differences by age and ethnic group for in-migrants are compared in Table 3.7. The gender differences seen in the flows of in-migrants by age are very similar to those seen in the flows of out-migrants by age. The pattern of more males moving at the youngest ages followed by more females than males moving in their teens and 20s, then more males moving from their 30s up to pensionable age and finally more female pensioners moving than males is replicated for both in and out-migrants. This is perhaps not so surprising as the moves include a measure of double counting as mentioned above where an out-migrant from one borough becomes an in-migrant to another borough. In order to see any gender differences between the types of migrant flows we need to separate out the flows by the distance moved, and this analysis is set out in the following sections.

Distinctive patterns within the data in Table 3.7 include the Chinese group with low numbers of boys aged 1-4 moving, but high numbers of girls aged 5-15.

The Bangladeshi and Pakistani groups have high numbers of male migrants compared with females between 45 and pensionable age.

**Type of move**

Around two thirds of all people in London who had moved in the past year had moved from an area within London, and more than half of those had moved from the same borough. These data come from the national migration report which separates out people who had moved who did not state their original address (11 per cent of movers), and so are slightly different from the ethnic group data where those who did not state their original address have been reallocated. The full list of movements from the national migration report is set out in Table 3.8.

A small proportion (six per cent) of migrants had moved in from the rest of South East England (excl. London), and the same proportion moved in from the rest of Great Britain. One in seven people who stated

**Table 3.7  Sex ratios (males to 100 females) of in-migrants by age and ethnicity**

|  | 1-4 | 5-15 | 16-19 | 20-29 | 30-44 | 45-PA | PA and over | Total |
|---|---|---|---|---|---|---|---|---|
| White | 108 | 104 | 63 | 89 | 131 | 151 | 44 | 97 |
| Black Caribbean | 107 | 109 | 57 | 77 | 95 | 146 | 44 | 87 |
| Black African | 99 | 102 | 90 | 95 | 128 | 107 | 40 | 103 |
| Black Other | 118 | 111 | 54 | 86 | 103 | 143 | 61 | 94 |
| Indian | 98 | 99 | 82 | 79 | 116 | 124 | 61 | 93 |
| Pakistani | 122 | 109 | 97 | 107 | 157 | 194 | 45 | 121 |
| Bangladeshi | 124 | 104 | 69 | 85 | 82 | 189 | 106 | 101 |
| Chinese | 88 | 130 | 89 | 88 | 99 | 112 | 51 | 93 |
| Other Asian | 104 | 107 | 107 | 86 | 102 | 127 | 38 | 97 |
| Other | 104 | 99 | 78 | 106 | 128 | 139 | 47 | 108 |
| All ethnic groups | 107 | 104 | 68 | 89 | 126 | 147 | 45 | 98 |

Source: 1991 Census, LRC Commissioned Table LRCT49
Notes: The migration sex ratios include people moving from borough to borough within London as well as movers into London, but the ratios do not include people who moved within each borough
PA = Pensionable Age

**Table 3.8 Type of move of migrants in London**

| Type of move | number of migrants | % |
|---|---|---|
| Migrants resident in London | 758,206 | 100.0 |
| Migrants moving within London | 471,632 | 62.2 |
| *Includes migrants moving within boroughs* | *270,481* | *35.7* |
| Migrants moving to London from ROSE | 48,700 | 6.4 |
| Migrants moving to London from RGB | 47,921 | 6.3 |
| Migrants moving to London from OGB | 104,726 | 13.8 |
| Migrants moving to London from not stated | 85,227 | 11.2 |

*Source: 1991 Census, Migration Report Table 3*
*Notes:*
*ROSE = Rest of the South East*
*RGB = Rest of Great Britain*
*OGB = Outside Great Britain*

their previous address had moved from overseas. The figures by ethnic group which include the reallocation of those who did not state their origin are included within Table 3.9.

After reallocation of those who did not state their former address, over two thirds of moves were within London, 40 per cent being within the same borough, and 30 per cent being from one borough to another within London. This pattern did not vary substantially by ethnic group, although half the moves of Black Caribbeans and people in the Black Other category were within the same borough compared with Chinese and Other Asians who made a much lower number of moves (just over a quarter) within the same borough. One in six migrants into London were from outside Great Britain. This did vary substantially by ethnic group from Caribbeans with only 8 per cent of migrants from overseas, to the Other Asian group where 43 per cent of migrants in London had moved in from overseas. Finally, moves in from the rest of Great Britain constituted 14 per cent of the overall total. Bangladeshis and Black Africans had only 3 per cent of their migrants moving in from the rest of Britain, compared with nearly one in five Whites.

**Moves within London**

The figures in Table 3.8 show the large total number of short distance moves made by migrants in London. The number of moves within London where people

**Table 3.9 Percentage of type of move by ethnic group, London**

| | within Greater London | within boroughs | in from rest of GB | in from outside GB | Row total |
|---|---|---|---|---|---|
| White | 30 | 40 | 17 | 13 | 100 |
| Black Caribbean | 34 | 52 | 5 | 8 | 100 |
| Black African | 33 | 33 | 3 | 32 | 100 |
| Black Other | 33 | 50 | 6 | 10 | 100 |
| Indian | 29 | 42 | 11 | 18 | 100 |
| Pakistani | 24 | 44 | 9 | 23 | 100 |
| Bangladeshi | 38 | 42 | 3 | 18 | 100 |
| Chinese | 32 | 27 | 12 | 29 | 100 |
| Other Asian | 23 | 28 | 6 | 43 | 100 |
| Other | 28 | 34 | 8 | 30 | 100 |
| All ethnic groups | 30 | 40 | 14 | 16 | 100 |

*Source: 1991 Census, LRC Commissioned Table LRCT49*

either remained within their borough or moved to another borough within London varied between different ethnic groups, as shown in Table 3.10.

As with all the migration data, the flows were dominated by those of the White group. Over three quarters of migrants moving within London were White. The number of male and female migrants was quite similar for each ethnic group, apart from the Black Caribbean group where there were more female movers than male.

**Moves between London and the rest of Great Britain**

More people moved out of London to the rest of Great Britain than vice versa, as shown in Table 3.11. Overall there were slightly more males moving in, and slightly more females moving out. The comparison of males and females in each of the ethnic groups in Table 3.11 shows very similar numbers moving in each ethnic group except for Pakistani in-migrants where the equivalent of 145 males moved for every 100 females.

One in ten people moving into London from the rest of Britain were from ethnic minority groups, compared with 5.5 per cent of Britain's population in 1991. This means that ethnic minorities were more likely to move to London than the White population. However as 20 per cent of London's population belonged to (non-White) ethnic minority groups at that time, this flow of people had the impact of slightly decreasing the proportion of the capital's population who were ethnic minorities.

The pattern of movement out of London was quite different with only 7 per cent of migrants moving from London to the rest of Britain being ethnic minorities compared with 20 per cent in London as a whole. Therefore there were quite low levels of migration of ethnic minorities out of London (although higher estimated levels of international out-migration as seen later). We have already seen how the two biggest ethnic minority communities in London are also the least mobile. In this analysis we can see how the Black Caribbean group is particularly less likely to move out of London. They constitute 4.4 per cent of London's

**Table 3.10  Short distance moves by ethnic group and gender**

| | Moves within London from borough to borough | | Moves within boroughs | |
| --- | --- | --- | --- | --- |
| | Female | Male | Female | Male |
| White | 87,948 | 86,309 | 123,515 | 111,476 |
| Black Caribbean | 4,503 | 3,921 | 7,208 | 5,633 |
| Black African | 6,618 | 6,331 | 6,916 | 5,986 |
| Black Other | 1,716 | 1,555 | 2,672 | 2,198 |
| Indian | 4,228 | 4,126 | 5,923 | 6,006 |
| Pakistani | 1,019 | 1,253 | 1,961 | 2,298 |
| Bangladeshi | 1,899 | 2,000 | 2,110 | 2,178 |
| Chinese | 1,538 | 1,524 | 1,350 | 1,205 |
| Other Asian | 2,648 | 2,782 | 3,332 | 3,241 |
| Other | 2,648 | 3,067 | 3,332 | 3,447 |
| Total | 114,764 | 112,869 | 158,320 | 143,668 |

Source: 1991 Census, LRC Commissioned Table LRCT49

**Table 3.11  Gender of migrants moving in and out of London to and from the rest of Great Britain**

|  | Females in | Males in | Females out | Males out |
|---|---|---|---|---|
| White | 47,946 | 49,020 | 73,570 | 71,356 |
| Black Caribbean | 667 | 639 | 534 | 611 |
| Black African | 536 | 521 | 422 | 610 |
| Black Other | 300 | 318 | 335 | 345 |
| Indian | 1,577 | 1,465 | 1,652 | 1,708 |
| Pakistani | 361 | 520 | 368 | 428 |
| Bangladeshi | 133 | 158 | 223 | 408 |
| Chinese | 513 | 579 | 496 | 528 |
| Other Asian | 697 | 608 | 623 | 577 |
| Other | 775 | 810 | 838 | 946 |
| Total | 53,504 | 54,640 | 79,060 | 77,518 |

*Source: 1991 Census, LRC Commissioned Table LRCT49*

**Table 3.12  Gender of international in-migrants to London boroughs**

|  | Female in-migrants | | Male in-migrants | | Sex ratio (males per 100 females) |
|---|---|---|---|---|---|
|  | Number | % | Number | % |  |
| White | 40,257 | 64.6 | 36,247 | 62.5 | 90 |
| Black Caribbean | 1,114 | 1.8 | 903 | 1.6 | 81 |
| Black African | 6,019 | 9.7 | 6,680 | 11.5 | 111 |
| Black Other | 510 | 0.8 | 496 | 0.9 | 97 |
| Indian | 2,814 | 4.5 | 2,412 | 4.2 | 86 |
| Pakistani | 1,044 | 1.7 | 1,169 | 2.0 | 112 |
| Bangladeshi | 972 | 1.6 | 880 | 1.5 | 91 |
| Chinese | 1,533 | 2.5 | 1,238 | 2.1 | 81 |
| Other Asian | 5,010 | 8.0 | 4,914 | 8.5 | 98 |
| Other | 3,009 | 4.8 | 3,062 | 5.3 | 102 |
| Total | 62,282 | 100 | 58,001 | 100 | 93 |

*Source: 1991 Census, LRC Commissioned Table LRCT49*

population, yet only 0.7 per cent of total migrants moving out of London to the rest of Britain. The Indian group showed similar patterns with 5.2 per cent of London's population but only 2.1 per cent of migrants moving out to the rest of Britain. If this pattern continued, it would have the impact of increasing the ethnic minority population of London.

**Moves to London from overseas**

The Census is a very exciting source of international migration data as there are only two other sources, Home Office data and the International Passenger Survey (IPS) which give us information about this population, and both are only able to provide a very limited amount of data. Home Office data are not available for London, they only record information about migrants entering the UK as a whole, whilst the sample size of the IPS means that data for London are subject to large confidence intervals.

The Census shows 103,000 people living in London in 1991 who recorded addresses abroad a year before, (120,000 including the estimate of those who did not state their original address). There were more females than males moving to London, and the biggest age group were those in their 20s. The gender balance of international migrants moving into London is shown in Table 3.12. Almost two thirds (64 per cent) of the international in-migrants were in the White group (compared with 80 per cent of London's resident population). The second highest flow of international in-migration was for the Black African group which made up 11 per cent of migrants compared with 2 per cent of London's population.

Just over a third of international migrants were from ethnic minority groups compared with a fifth of the population in 1991. Therefore the flow of international migrants served to increase the proportion of people belonging to ethnic minority groups in London.

Overall more females than males moved into London from overseas, but there were three ethnic groups where the reverse was true. In the Other group the numbers were almost equal, but in the Black African and Pakistani groups just over ten per cent more males

**Table 3.13  International migrants by age**

|  | Number | %1-17 | %18-29 | %30-59 | %60+ |
|---|---|---|---|---|---|
| White | 65,275 | 12 | 58 | 28 | 2 |
| Black Caribbean | 1,664 | 21 | 41 | 32 | 6 |
| Black African | 10,515 | 29 | 42 | 28 | 2 |
| Black Other | 827 | 24 | 49 | 26 | 2 |
| Indian | 4,741 | 18 | 38 | 36 | 9 |
| Pakistani | 1,962 | 26 | 37 | 34 | 3 |
| Bangladeshi | 1,582 | 42 | 26 | 26 | 6 |
| Chinese | 2,430 | 14 | 50 | 33 | 2 |
| Other Asian | 8,859 | 24 | 35 | 39 | 2 |
| Other | 5,208 | 31 | 34 | 31 | 3 |
| Total | 103,063 | 17 | 51 | 30 | 2 |

Source: 1991 Census, LRC Commissioned Table LRCT25
Note: Figures do not include adjustment for those who did not state their original address

than females migrated.

More than four out of every five international in-migrants were of working age. Half of all international migrants into London in 1990-1991 were aged between 18 and 29. The next biggest age group were those aged 30-59, who constituted 30 per cent of all international in-migrants. Around one in six of those moving from overseas to London were children, and a small proportion – only 2 per cent – were aged 60 or over. Differences in these proportions by gender were very small, with more 18-29 year old females moving than males of that age, and more 30-59 year old males moving than females. A summary of the age profile of international migrants is shown in Table 3.13.

Some boroughs received far more international migrants than others. The borough receiving the highest number of international migrants in 1990-1991 was Westminster with 9,452, then Kensington and Chelsea with 7,770, whilst Barking and Dagenham received the least with 514. The totals for all boroughs are shown in Table 3.14. Map 3.1 shows clearly that the boroughs with the largest numbers of international migrants were generally towards the west and north, whereas boroughs with the smallest numbers were mainly towards the east.

### International migrants by country of birth

The Census also allows us to examine the country of birth of international migrants who moved to London in 1990-1991. There are 122 regions and countries which are named. The total figures for London are shown in Table 3.15. Of the 103,000 in-migrants recorded, 79 per cent were born outside the UK. The remaining 21 per cent (21,654) were people who were born in the UK but who had lived abroad and who had now returned and were resident at the time of the Census.

The main area of origin for international migrants was the European Community where nearly 40,000 migrants were born - 38 per cent of all the

**Table 3.14  Number of international migrants moving to London boroughs**

| | |
|---|---:|
| City of London | 121 |
| Barking & Dagenham | 514 |
| Barnet | 6,443 |
| Bexley | 575 |
| Brent | 5,552 |
| Bromley | 1,847 |
| Camden | 5,923 |
| Croydon | 2,843 |
| Ealing | 5,529 |
| Enfield | 2,059 |
| Greenwich | 1,859 |
| Hackney | 2,370 |
| Hammersmith & Fulham | 4,302 |
| Haringey | 4,328 |
| Harrow | 2,773 |
| Havering | 601 |
| Hillingdon | 2,141 |
| Hounslow | 2,871 |
| Islington | 2,559 |
| Kensington & Chelsea | 7,770 |
| Kingston upon Thames | 1,903 |
| Lambeth | 3,677 |
| Lewisham | 1,979 |
| Merton | 2,942 |
| Newham | 3,096 |
| Redbridge | 1,954 |
| Richmond upon Thames | 2,843 |
| Southwark | 2,378 |
| Sutton | 1,130 |
| Tower Hamlets | 1,639 |
| Waltham Forest | 2,282 |
| Wandsworth | 4,808 |
| Westminster | 9,452 |
| Inner London | 54,402 |
| Outer London | 48,661 |
| Greater London | 103,063 |

Source: 1991 Census, LRC Commissioned Table LRCT25

## Map 3.1 International migrants to London boroughs 1990/91

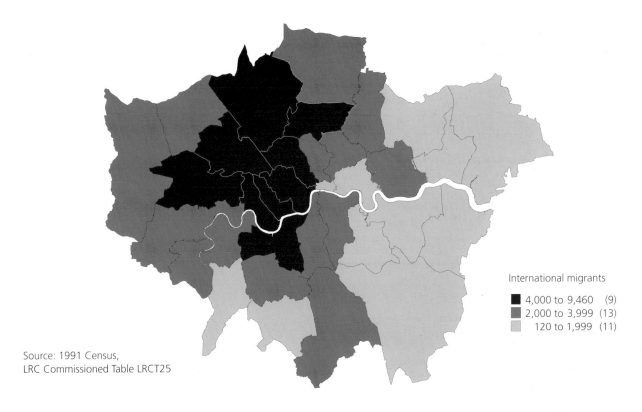

International migrants

■ 4,000 to 9,460 (9)
■ 2,000 to 3,999 (13)
▢ 120 to 1,999 (11)

Source: 1991 Census,
LRC Commissioned Table LRCT25

## Map 3.2 Net migration into/out of London boroughs 1990/91

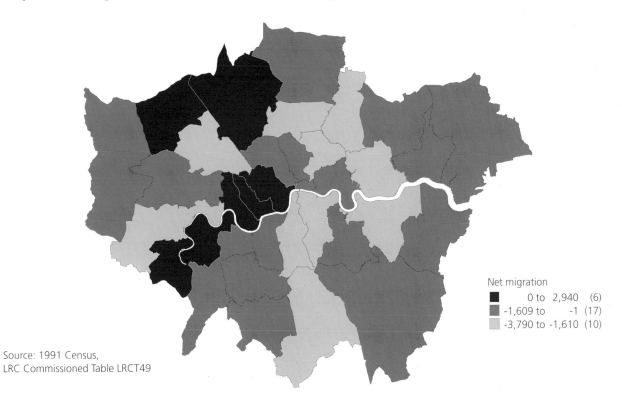

Net migration

■ 0 to 2,940 (6)
■ -1,609 to -1 (17)
▢ -3,790 to -1,610 (10)

Source: 1991 Census,
LRC Commissioned Table LRCT49

**Table 3.15 International migrants who moved to London during 1990-1991, by country of birth**

| | | | | | | | |
|---|---|---|---|---|---|---|---|
| Total persons | 103,063 | South Africa | 1,449 | Cyprus | 525 | Morocco | 173 |
| Born outside UK | 81,409 | Nigeria | 1,421 | Northern Ireland | 506 | Taiwan | 168 |
| Europe | 43,743 | Uganda | 1,419 | Philippines | 473 | Hungary | 166 |
| EC | 39,597 | Scotland | 1,147 | Switzerland | 472 | Guyana | 142 |
| UK | 21,654 | Canada | 1,068 | Romania | 434 | Jordan | 135 |
| England | 19,430 | Brazil | 1,043 | Trinidad & Tobago | 416 | Czechoslovakia | 131 |
| South Asia | 8,320 | Lebanon | 1,027 | Yugoslavia | 414 | Syria | 128 |
| Irish Republic | 6,321 | Malaysia | 959 | Singapore | 386 | Algeria | 123 |
| Middle East | 5,617 | Iraq | 944 | Norway | 377 | Libya | 92 |
| USA | 5,453 | Kenya | 910 | Zambia | 370 | Channel Islands | 89 |
| Australia | 5,330 | Denmark | 877 | USSR | 358 | Malta & Gozo | 82 |
| New Zealand | 4,168 | Iran | 811 | Mauritius | 346 | Barbados | 70 |
| Japan | 4,059 | Portugal | 783 | Egypt | 342 | Malawi | 68 |
| India | 3,128 | Hong Kong | 779 | Tanzania | 308 | Burma | 67 |
| East Africa | 3,075 | Ghana | 772 | Belgium | 300 | Gambia | 65 |
| France | 3,003 | Sweden | 706 | Bulgaria | 283 | Seychelles | 59 |
| West Africa | 2,460 | Netherlands | 693 | Thailand | 281 | Botswana/Les/Swaz | 52 |
| South East Asia | 2,124 | Greece | 660 | Colombia | 264 | Tunisia | 49 |
| Sri Lanka | 2,113 | Southern Africa | 648 | Central America | 228 | Gibraltar | 38 |
| Germany | 2,052 | Israel | 610 | Finland | 223 | Luxembourg | 28 |
| Turkey | 1,923 | Zimbabwe | 596 | Saudi Arabia | 221 | Isle of Man | 16 |
| Italy | 1,765 | Poland | 596 | Vietnam | 216 | Ireland (part not stated) | 12 |
| Pakistan | 1,614 | China | 577 | Sierra Leone | 202 | Belize | 10 |
| Bangladesh | 1,465 | Wales | 559 | Austria | 191 | Albania | 7 |
| Spain | 1,449 | Jamaica | 545 | | | | |

*Source: 1991 Census, LRC Commissioned Table LRCT68*

international migrants to London in that year. The individual country which was the origin for the most international migrants was the Irish Republic with 6,321 migrants. This flow is particularly useful to quantify as the IPS does not measure flows to and from the Irish Republic.

**Borough migration patterns**

Some boroughs had much higher proportions of migrants than others. The total number of in and out migrants in each borough is shown in Table 3.16. The boroughs with the smallest number of migrants, apart from the City of London, were the Outer London boroughs of Barking and Dagenham, Bexley, Havering, Sutton and Kingston, in the east and south west of London. Boroughs with the largest number of migrants included Westminster, Wandsworth, Lambeth, Kensington and Chelsea, Barnet, Camden and Ealing, in Central London and in a crescent from south to north west London.

Overall in London these figures show a net loss of 34,000 people out of London boroughs over the year 1990-1991. As Map 3.2 shows, the majority of boroughs had a net loss of population due to migration, although Westminster and Kensington and Chelsea had a gain of a few thousand people. The net migration loss of Inner and Outer London was fairly even with Inner London losing 14,000 people and Outer London losing 20,000. These figures include people moving from one borough to another, which we have seen above includes 30 per cent of all moves into London boroughs, and therefore a degree of double counting. In this analysis therefore, these people would be counted once as in-migrants to one borough, and once as out-migrants from another borough. However at borough level they provide a good indicator of size and comparative flows.

**Borough migration patterns by ethnicity**

The net migration flow of each ethnic group in each borough is shown in Table 3.17.

**White net migration**

Almost all London boroughs were losing more White people than they were gaining in 1990-1991. This pattern is not unusual as London was losing population from the end of the second World War to the mid-1980s, as people moved out when they had families and at older ages to retire. The exceptions to this pattern in the 1990-1991 data were Hammersmith and Fulham, Kensington and Chelsea, Westminster, and Richmond which all had a net gain in their White populations. The loss in terms of numbers was much greater in Outer London, but both Inner and Outer London lost around the same percentage of their White

**Table 3.16 Total number of in- and out-migrants and net migration by borough**

|  | Total in | Total out | Net |
| --- | --- | --- | --- |
| City of London | 667 | 775 | -108 |
| Barking & Dagenham | 4,877 | 5,882 | -1,005 |
| Barnet | 21,424 | 20,728 | 696 |
| Bexley | 7,591 | 8,863 | -1,272 |
| Brent | 18,091 | 19,703 | -1,612 |
| Bromley | 12,353 | 13,328 | -975 |
| Camden | 20,188 | 20,298 | -110 |
| Croydon | 14,698 | 17,119 | -2,421 |
| Ealing | 19,353 | 20,495 | -1,142 |
| Enfield | 11,895 | 13,250 | -1,355 |
| Greenwich | 10,275 | 12,904 | -2,629 |
| Hackney | 12,275 | 15,399 | -3,124 |
| Hammersmith & Fulham | 18,104 | 17,621 | 483 |
| Haringey | 18,060 | 21,144 | -3,084 |
| Harrow | 11,925 | 11,892 | 33 |
| Havering | 6,620 | 7,964 | -1,344 |
| Hillingdon | 11,665 | 12,972 | -1,307 |
| Hounslow | 13,283 | 14,953 | -1,670 |
| Islington | 13,597 | 14,085 | -488 |
| Kensington & Chelsea | 21,032 | 19,132 | 1,900 |
| Kingston upon Thames | 9,369 | 9,376 | -7 |
| Lambeth | 20,588 | 24,378 | -3,790 |
| Lewisham | 14,042 | 14,694 | -652 |
| Merton | 13,135 | 13,987 | -852 |
| Newham | 11,835 | 14,808 | -2,973 |
| Redbridge | 11,608 | 12,591 | -983 |
| Richmond upon Thames | 12,636 | 12,131 | 505 |
| Southwark | 13,884 | 16,585 | -2,701 |
| Sutton | 8,682 | 9,105 | -423 |
| Tower Hamlets | 9,254 | 10,217 | -963 |
| Waltham Forest | 11,216 | 13,314 | -2,098 |
| Wandsworth | 24,649 | 26,119 | -1,470 |
| Westminster | 27,392 | 24,461 | 2,931 |
| Inner London | 225,567 | 239,717 | -14,150 |
| Outer London | 230,697 | 250,558 | -19,861 |
| Greater London | 456,264 | 490,275 | -34,011 |

*Source: 1991 Census, LRC Commissioned Table LRCT49*

## Table 3.17 Net migration flow by ethnic group by borough

| | White | Black Caribbean | Black African | Black Other | Indian | Paki-stani | Bangla-deshi | Chinese | Other Asian | Other |
|---|---|---|---|---|---|---|---|---|---|---|
| City of London | -91 | -2 | -6 | -1 | -6 | -4 | -11 | 5 | 3 | 4 |
| Barking & Dagenham | -1,249 | 48 | 116 | 10 | 18 | 43 | 24 | -17 | 12 | -10 |
| Barnet | -1,178 | 63 | 441 | 21 | 384 | 87 | -12 | 189 | 695 | 7 |
| Bexley | -1,425 | -16 | 36 | -6 | 111 | 12 | 28 | 40 | -22 | -30 |
| Brent | -2,242 | -180 | 379 | 68 | -1 | 75 | -55 | 1 | 226 | 116 |
| Bromley | -1,411 | 49 | 87 | 30 | 110 | 15 | 17 | 21 | 53 | 53 |
| Camden | -955 | -27 | 245 | 19 | 55 | -8 | 200 | 49 | 170 | 142 |
| Croydon | -3,498 | 251 | 330 | 44 | 191 | 71 | 21 | 63 | 140 | -34 |
| Ealing | -2,221 | 147 | 376 | 25 | -78 | 121 | 21 | 42 | 225 | 200 |
| Enfield | -2,388 | 279 | 428 | 7 | 170 | 67 | -10 | 56 | -25 | 60 |
| Greenwich | -3,026 | 75 | 269 | 17 | -45 | 34 | 15 | -10 | 79 | -36 |
| Hackney | -2,209 | -102 | -236 | -103 | -80 | -16 | -136 | -75 | -40 | -123 |
| Hammersmith & Fulham | 287 | -112 | 39 | 26 | 13 | -14 | 8 | 22 | 61 | 152 |
| Haringey | -3,265 | -125 | 486 | 52 | -107 | -24 | -14 | -34 | -67 | 14 |
| Harrow | -1,830 | 59 | 255 | 26 | 1,058 | 63 | 42 | -1 | 194 | 166 |
| Havering | -1,452 | -7 | 32 | 6 | 55 | 22 | -23 | 51 | -1 | -26 |
| Hillingdon | -2,202 | 52 | 147 | 31 | 382 | 89 | 53 | 41 | 45 | 55 |
| Hounslow | -2,728 | 13 | 187 | 0 | 415 | 224 | 45 | 16 | 54 | 104 |
| Islington | -1,040 | 34 | 309 | 25 | 15 | -11 | 85 | 19 | 36 | 40 |
| Kensington & Chelsea | 1,520 | -2 | 164 | -4 | 43 | 56 | -40 | 27 | 34 | 103 |
| Kingston upon Thames | -576 | 35 | 88 | -1 | 93 | 51 | -4 | 48 | 205 | 53 |
| Lambeth | -3,536 | -120 | 215 | -50 | -44 | -37 | 19 | -70 | -68 | -99 |
| Lewisham | -1,587 | 288 | 438 | 116 | -12 | 41 | 7 | 18 | 59 | -20 |
| Merton | -1,521 | 64 | 233 | -7 | 80 | 53 | 29 | 65 | 194 | -42 |
| Newham | -3,830 | 60 | 729 | 27 | -368 | 103 | 344 | -33 | 96 | -102 |
| Redbridge | -2,397 | 105 | 277 | 25 | 507 | 170 | 153 | 31 | 96 | 50 |
| Richmond upon Thames | 260 | 16 | 4 | 1 | 121 | 14 | -16 | 6 | 61 | 39 |
| Southwark | -2,687 | -90 | 73 | -33 | 0 | 10 | 74 | 48 | -34 | -61 |
| Sutton | -714 | 25 | 61 | 19 | 41 | 11 | 12 | 22 | 42 | 59 |
| Tower Hamlets | -985 | -44 | 71 | 24 | -42 | 12 | 66 | -11 | -28 | -26 |
| Waltham Forest | -2,839 | 84 | 329 | 24 | 19 | 198 | -5 | 9 | 47 | 36 |
| Wandsworth | -1,413 | -177 | 138 | -36 | 93 | 33 | 16 | 39 | -100 | -62 |
| Westminster | 1,185 | 25 | 141 | 30 | 254 | 115 | 44 | 137 | 344 | 656 |
| Inner London | -18,607 | -396 | 2,807 | 91 | -187 | 255 | 658 | 143 | 466 | 620 |
| Outer London | -34,637 | 1,162 | 4,076 | 340 | 3,631 | 1,418 | 335 | 673 | 2,318 | 822 |
| Greater London | -53,243 | 766 | 6,883 | 431 | 3,445 | 1,673 | 993 | 816 | 2,785 | 1,441 |

*Source: 1991 Census, LRC Commissioned Table LRCT49*

populations. Overall in the year 1990-1991 London had a net loss of 53,000 White people. The boroughs losing the most White people were Newham (3,830), Lambeth (3,536), Croydon (3,498), and Haringey (3,265). If the differences between those boroughs gaining and those losing White people were maintained over a number of years, it would make a significant difference to the ethnic group composition of those boroughs.

**Black net migration**

Overall there were net gains of Black people across London. For the Black Caribbean and Black Other groups the gain was less than a thousand people (770 and 430 respectively), whereas the net gain for the Black African group was nearly 7,000 people. There was a net loss of Black Caribbeans in 13 boroughs and a net loss overall from Inner London. Black Africans only showed a net loss in the City of London, whilst the Black Other group showed a small net loss in nine boroughs. The Black Caribbean group had the biggest net gains from migration in Lewisham (288) and Enfield (279), and the biggest net losses from migration in Brent (-180) and Wandsworth (-177). Newham (729) and Haringey (486) had the largest net gains from Black African migration, with Hackney (-236) the only borough to show a significant loss. Gains and losses were very small for the Black Other group, with Lewisham the only borough to gain over 100 people through migration, and Hackney the only borough to lose over 100 people through migration.

**South Asian net migration (Indian, Pakistani and Bangladeshi)**

All three groups showed net gains in numbers through migration across London, although the Indian group showed a net loss in Inner London. The Indian group had the largest flows of numbers, with net gains in London of 3,445 people, compared with 1,676 Pakistanis and 997 Bangladeshis. The most striking migrant flow for South Asian groups in London was the net gain in Harrow of 1,058 Indians. This contrasted with a net loss of 368 Indians out of

Newham. The net loss of population in Inner London from the two biggest ethnic minority groups – Indian and Black Caribbean, reflects the patterns of movement seen generally in cities, which is a tendency for people to move into the centre when they first move to a city, and then move out from the centre over time.

Hounslow and Redbridge were significant for their gain in Pakistanis through migration, with Hounslow having a net gain of 224, and Redbridge 170. Newham (344) and Camden (200) showed the biggest migration gain of Bangladeshi people.

**Chinese and Other groups' net migration**

As with all other ethnic minority categories, these three groups also showed net migration gains across London. The Chinese had a net gain of 814 people, whilst the net gains for the Other Asian and Other categories were larger at 2,786 and 1,438 respectively. There was a split between those boroughs having net migration gains and losses for each of the groups, although the net losses were generally very small. There were only two net losses of more than 100 people, both in the Other category, – a loss of 123 people from Hackney, and 102 people from Newham. Net gains tended to be bigger with, for example, Barnet having a net gain of 695 people in the Other Asian category, and Westminster having a net gain of 656 people in the Other category.

# Chapter 4
# Households and families

# Households and families

## Introduction

This chapter deals with the two related concepts of households; that is single people or groups of people living together who may or may not be related, and families; couples with or without children or lone parents with children.

Previous reports – *London's Ethnic Minorities: One City Many Communities* and *Ethnic Group Data for London* – have presented some data for these topics, which is summarised here, but this report explores them more fully. All figures presented for ethnic groups are taken from the 1991 Census, since this is the only source of detailed statistics within London.

## Households

The ethnic group of the household is taken as that of the head of household in all Census data. Table 4.1 gives the total number and percentage of households and percentage of all residents in each ethnic group in London.

**Table 4.1 Ethnic group of households and residents in London**

|  | Households | | Residents |
|  | Number | % | % |
|---|---|---|---|
| White | 2,337,489 | 84.7 | 79.8 |
| Black Caribbean | 123,253 | 4.5 | 4.4 |
| Black African | 57,671 | 2.1 | 2.4 |
| Black Other | 17,972 | 0.7 | 1.2 |
| Indian | 96,774 | 3.5 | 5.2 |
| Pakistani | 21,846 | 0.8 | 1.3 |
| Bangladeshi | 15,946 | 0.6 | 1.3 |
| Chinese | 18,802 | 0.7 | 0.8 |
| Other Asian | 35,988 | 1.3 | 1.7 |
| Other | 35,425 | 1.3 | 1.8 |
| Total | 2,761,166 | 100.0 | 100.0 |

*Source: 1991 Census, LRC Commissioned Table LRCT34*

Comparing the ethnic group of households and residents recorded in the Census shows that the proportion of White households in London was higher than of White residents (85 per cent compared with 80 per cent). The proportion of Black Caribbean households was also marginally higher (4.5 per cent compared with 4.4 per cent of residents), whereas for all other ethnic groups the proportion of households was smaller than the proportion of residents. This is largely because of differences in household size illustrated in Figure 4.1. However, it is also partly due to the way in which the household's ethnic group is determined for Census data. Not all residents in a household are necessarily of the same ethnic group as the head of household. For example, more than half of London's residents in the Black Other group lived in a household headed by someone from another ethnic group – mainly Black Caribbean or White. Similarly, around 40 per cent of household residents classified in the Other category lived in a household with a head from another group – mainly White. For all other ethnic groups, the proportion living in a household headed by someone from the same ethnic group was close to 90 per cent or higher – up to more than 99 per cent of Bangladeshis.

## Household size

Figure 4.1 shows clearly that there were substantial differences in the size of households according to their ethnic group. There were more White households with just one or two residents than for any other group. The contrast with the sizes of South Asian households is especially marked – particularly for Bangladeshi households. Nearly 30 per cent of Bangladeshi households had seven or more residents. Around three in four of all South Asian households had at least three residents, compared with one in three White households. Indian households were most likely to have four residents, whereas there were roughly comparable numbers of Pakistani households at each size. Black, Chinese and Other households fell between the two extremes of White and South Asian households in terms of size.

**Figure 4.1 Household size**

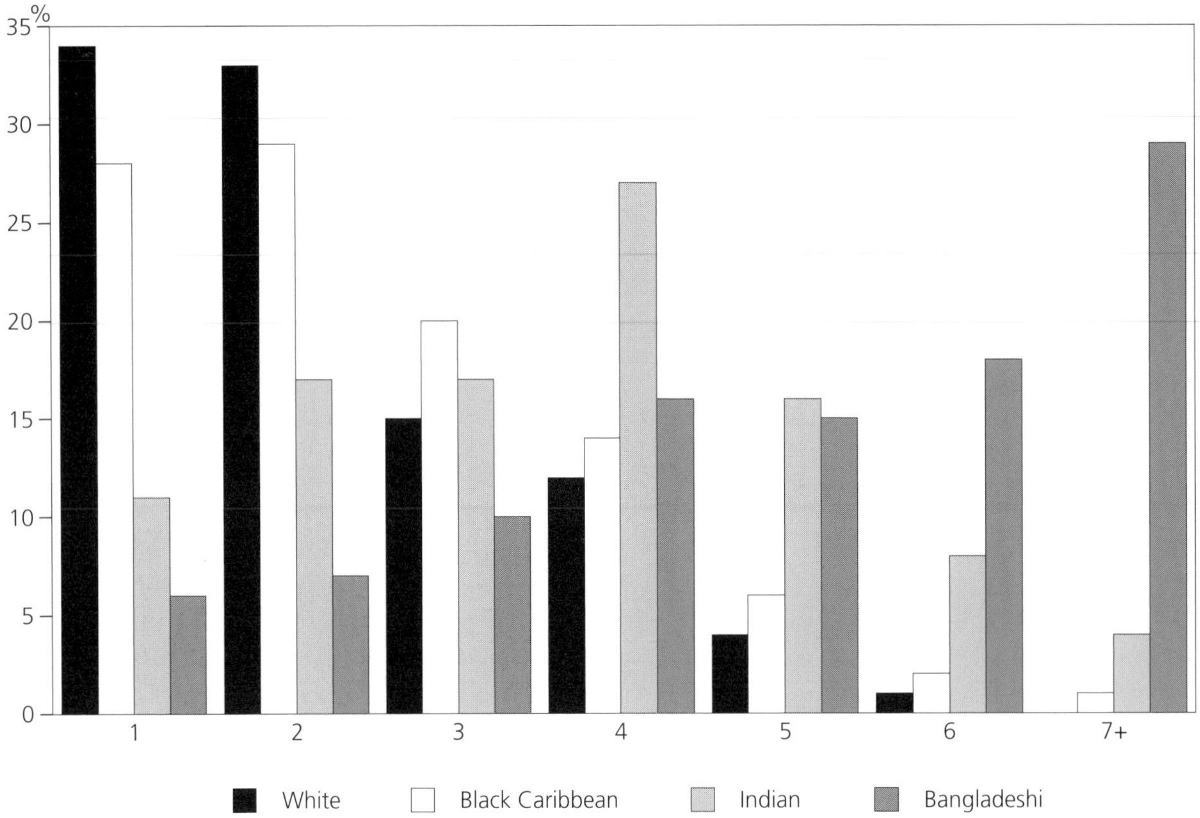

*Source: 1991 Census, LRC Commissioned Table LRCT11*

## Household Composition

While information on household size provides an outline perspective, the composition of households in terms of the number, age and sex of adults and the number of dependent children gives a more detailed description. This information, available for all households in London enumerated in the 1991 Census, enables us to gain a much fuller picture of the living arrangements of ethnic groups. This extra detail is undoubtedly useful, but must be interpreted with a degree of caution as there is no information on relationships in this data.

This makes it is impossible to say, for example, how many of the households with one female and one male adult are 'couple' households, although other information shows us that it is clearly the vast majority, since a woman living with her father or her 19 year old

son or a male lodger would also be included in this category. Conversely, a 'couple' where one partner works and lives away from home may be included in the Census as a household with one adult. Similarly, a household with one adult and one or more children is sometimes referred to as a 'lone parent' household and the adult as the lone mother or lone father. However, in some cases the adult may be, for example, an older brother or sister, grandparent, aunt or even an unrelated adult.

Figure 4.2 gives a general summary of the data on household composition for London. The three Black groups have broadly similar household compositions, as do the three South Asian groups. There are some significant differences within these groups and within the household types illustrated, however.

**Figure 4.2 Household composition in London by broad ethnic group**

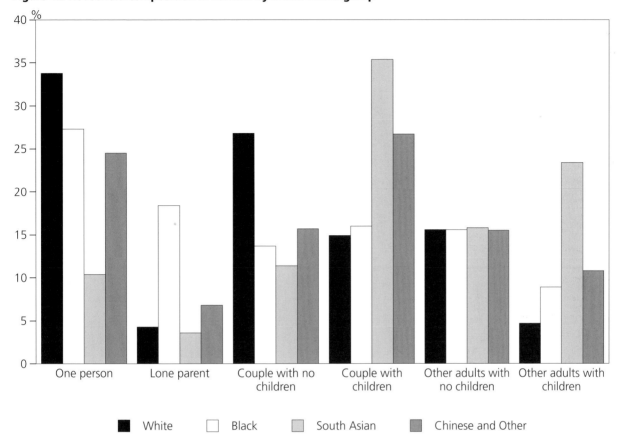

White   Black   South Asian   Chinese and Other

*Source: 1991 Census, Local Base Statistics Table 43*

Table 4.2 gives a detailed breakdown of household composition for all households in London. The household composition varies considerably between ethnic groups, as can be seen from Figure 4.1. Not surprisingly, the composition of White households is close to that of all households, since the vast majority of households (85 per cent) are White. The Other ethnic groups category also showed a very similar household composition profile to the overall picture for London, except that the proportion of men living alone was a little higher, while the proportion of women living alone was lower.

Some variation between ethnic groups in household composition is due to differences in age structures. For example, the proportions of White households consisting of pensioners living alone or of two adults, at least one of whom is of pensionable age, were higher than for ethnic minority groups. Almost half of all White one person households were pensioners, compared with just 14 per cent of ethnic minority one person households. This is partly because of the higher proportion of White pensioners, and partly because of other differences in household composition.

The lower proportion of women from the Other ethnic groups living alone is entirely due to the low proportion of pensioners – the proportion of women under retirement age from this group living alone was higher than average. With the exception of the Other ethnic groups category, Black residents under pensionable age, particularly men, were more likely to live alone than residents from other groups, whereas relatively few South Asians of any age lived alone.

## Table 4.2  Household composition in London

| Adults | | Dependent children | |
|---|---|---|---|
| None | | 1+ | 1,476 |
| 1 male | | | 376,425 |
| | Aged 65+ | 0 | 89,111 |
| | Aged under 65 | 0 | 277,018 |
| | Any age | 1 | 6,049 |
| | Any age | 2+ | 4,247 |
| 1 female | | | 651,630 |
| | Aged 60+ | 0 | 308,239 |
| | Aged under 60 | 0 | 206,158 |
| | Any age | 1 | 68,808 |
| | Any age | 2+ | 68,425 |
| total 1 male + 1 female | | | 1,134,885 |
| | Both under pensionable age | 0 | 398,428 |
| | 1 or both of pensionable age | 0 | 285,250 |
| | Any age | 1 | 157,810 |
| | Any age | 2 | 197,449 |
| | Any age | 3+ | 95,948 |
| total 2, same sex | | | 137,059 |
| | Both under pensionable age | 0 | 83,097 |
| | 1 or both of pensionable age | 0 | 35,199 |
| | Any age | 1+ | 18,763 |
| total 3+, male(s) + female(s) | | | 433,299 |
| | Any age | 0 | 286,447 |
| | Any age | 1 or 2 | 124,562 |
| | Any age | 3+ | 22,290 |
| total 3+, same sex | | | 28,392 |
| | Any age | 0 | 25,259 |
| | Any age | 1+ | 3,133 |
| Any | | 1+ | 768,960 |
| All households | | | 2,763,166 |

Source: 1991 Census, LRC Commissioned Table LRCT34

Higher proportions of Black Other households had just one resident than of Black Caribbean or Black African households.

Black households were also more likely to consist of one adult together with one or more dependent children, but again there were differences within this group. Although still a small proportion, Black African men were more likely to live with dependent children but with no other adults than others – almost 1.5 per cent of all Black African households were lone fathers compared with less than half of one per cent of all households in London. In contrast, the proportion of lone mothers was much higher among Black Others – nearly a quarter of all Black Other households consisted of one woman with one or more dependent children. The two other Black groups also had high proportions of 'lone mothers'.

There were more Black Caribbean and Black Other households recorded in the Census with one resident woman (with or without dependent children) than with one man and one woman (with or without dependent children).

As Table 4.2 shows, households with one male and one female adult were the most widespread type of household in London, forming over 40 per cent of the total. The percentage of Black African households of this type was also much lower than average (32 per cent) and again the proportion with one resident woman was higher than average.

Overall, only around 30 per cent of Black households contained one male and one female adult (with or without dependent children). This difference is only partly due to the higher proportion of Black men living alone. The proportion of Black Caribbean households containing three or more adults with no dependent children was also above average, whereas this proportion was lower among Black Other households than for any other group. This relatively small number of such households headed by someone in the Black

**Figure 4.3 Household composition in Black households**

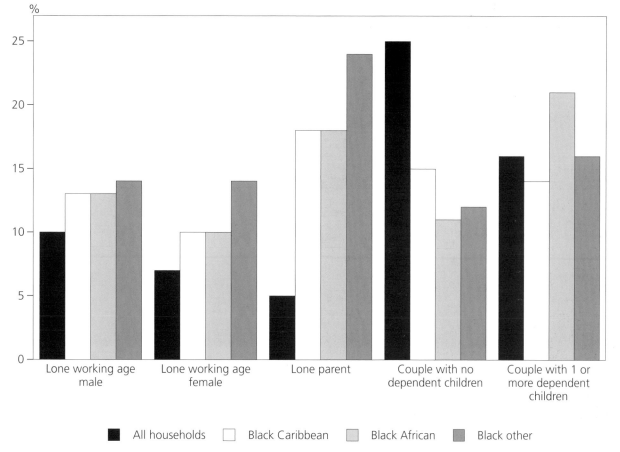

Source: 1991 Census, LRC Commissioned Table LRCT34

Other category is likely to be at least partly due to the very young age structure of this group. Black African households were the most likely to have two adults of the same sex, with or without dependent children.

Nearly half of South Asian households contained one male and one female adult – mostly with dependent children – a quarter of all Indian households consisted of one man, one woman and two or more dependent children. Among Pakistani households this figure was 30 per cent, while for Bangladeshi households, the proportion was even higher at 38 per cent. For each of these three groups over a third of households contained at least three adults. Over a fifth of Bangladeshi households had three or more adults, including at least one man and one woman, together with three or more dependent children.

Among Chinese households, the household composition figures were generally closer to those for all households in London. The proportion of Chinese households with a woman over retirement age living alone was much lower than average, mainly due to the small number of Chinese women in this age group, whereas the number of Chinese women aged under 60 living alone was higher than might be expected. Similarly, the age profile of the Chinese population accounts for the relatively low proportion of households consisting of one man and one woman, at least one of which is over retirement age. The higher than average proportions of Chinese households with one male and one female adult together with one or more dependent children mean that the overall proportion of Chinese households with one man and one woman was very close to average for London. The proportion of

**Figure 4.4 Household composition in South Asian households**

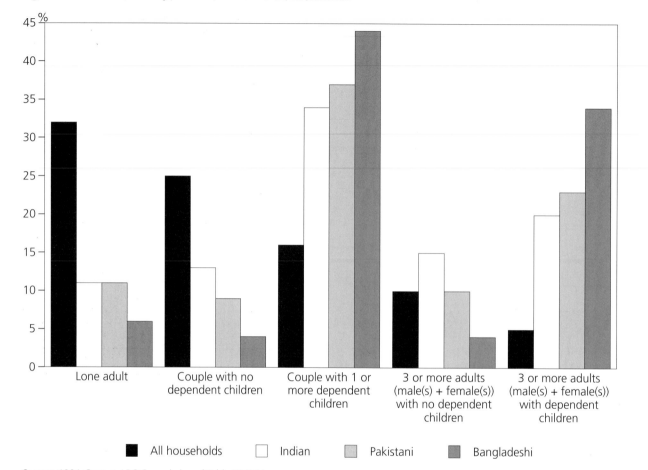

Source: 1991 Census, LRC Commissioned Table LRCT34

Chinese households with three or more adults, together with dependent children was also higher than average.

The household composition profile for households in the Other Asian category was similar to that for the Chinese group, except that a smaller proportion of Other Asian men lived alone, whereas the proportions of households consisting of one man and one woman together with one or two dependent children was higher. The only other notable difference between the composition of Chinese and Other Asian households was the higher than average proportion of Chinese households consisting of two adults of the same sex, while for Other Asian households this proportion was the same as that for all households in London.

The household composition patterns noted for an ethnic group across London as a whole were also generally apparent for the same ethnic group in each borough, although there were some differences. Overall, such differences tended to be reflected across all the ethnic groups within a given borough, so that, for example Inner London boroughs tended to have more households of one person and fewer households with one man and one woman (with or without dependent children). It is noticeable, however, that differences tended to be greatest for the South Asian groups.

**Economic Position of lone parents**

One issue related to household composition which is a frequent area of concern is the economic position of lone parent households. Information on the economic position of adults in households of just one adult with one or more children aged under 16 is given in Table

**Table 4.3  Economic position of lone parents\* by ethnic group and gender**

| | Male lone parent* | | | | | Female lone parent* | | | | |
|---|---|---|---|---|---|---|---|---|---|---|
| | Total | Employed | | Gov't Scheme | Unemp/ econ inactive | Total | Employed | | Gov't Scheme | Unemp/ econ inactive |
| | | F/t or s/e | P/t | | | | F/t or s/e | P/t | | |
| | Number | % | % | % | % | Number | % | % | % | % |
| White | 5,847 | 51 | 2 | 13 | 34 | 84,355 | 18 | 10 | 7 | 65 |
| Black Caribbean | 893 | 41 | 3 | 24 | 31 | 19,604 | 33 | 8 | 14 | 45 |
| Black African | 616 | 41 | 5 | 24 | 29 | 8,388 | 25 | 10 | 20 | 45 |
| Black Other | 138 | 38 | 3 | 22 | 37 | 3,973 | 26 | 7 | 16 | 51 |
| Indian | 217 | 55 | 2 | 14 | 29 | 2,238 | 29 | 9 | 11 | 51 |
| Pakistani | 55 | 49 | 0 | 27 | 24 | 800 | 10 | 4 | 15 | 71 |
| Bangladeshi | 64 | 23 | 5 | 27 | 45 | 437 | 7 | 4 | 11 | 78 |
| Chinese | 86 | 51 | 2 | 19 | 28 | 603 | 27 | 11 | 7 | 56 |
| Other Asian | 129 | 48 | 6 | 17 | 29 | 1,602 | 31 | 11 | 14 | 45 |
| Other | 188 | 43 | 3 | 26 | 29 | 2,589 | 23 | 8 | 13 | 56 |
| Total | 8,233 | 49 | 3 | 16 | 33 | 124,589 | 22 | 10 | 9 | 59 |

Source: 1991 Census, LRC Commissioned Table LRCT84
\* in household with one person aged 16 or over and one or more aged under 16
F/t is full-time employee, p/t is part-time employee and s/e is self-employed

4.3. This shows that there are clear differences between ethnic groups and between men and women in this type of household for every ethnic group.

Around half of all lone fathers were in full-time employment or self-employed, and for every ethnic group except Bangladeshis, this was the most common economic position. Bangladeshi lone fathers were more likely to be economically inactive. The only other ethnic group with fewer than 40 per cent of lone fathers in full-time employment or self-employed was Black Other. Lone fathers from all ethnic groups were much more likely to be unemployed than to be working part time, but less likely to be unemployed than to be economically inactive. The only exception was Pakistani lone fathers, although the number in this group was extremely small.

In contrast, 60 per cent of lone mothers in London were economically inactive. This was the largest economic category for lone mothers from all ethnic groups, ranging from 45 per cent of Black Caribbeans, Black Africans and Other Asians to 78 per cent of Bangladeshis. Of those lone mothers who were economically active, most worked full-time or were self-employed. This holds for all ethnic groups except Pakistanis and Bangladeshis, who were most likely to be unemployed. Only White and Chinese lone mothers were more likely to be working part-time than to be unemployed.

It is also clear from the data that the economic position of lone parents varied according to the age of the youngest child. Where the youngest child was of school age, the lone parent was much more likely to be employed full-time than where there were younger children in the household. This was true for every ethnic group and for both men and women.

**Table 4.4  Ethnic group of male and female partners in couples**

| Man's ethnic group | Woman's ethnic group | | | | |
| --- | --- | --- | --- | --- | --- |
| | Same | Other Black | Other S Asian | White | Other |
| White | 98 | | | | 2 |
| Black Caribbean | 78 | 3 | | 17 | 2 |
| Black African | 79 | 8 | | 11 | 3 |
| Black Other | 49 | 12 | | 33 | 6 |
| Indian | 93 | | 1 | 5 | 1 |
| Pakistani | 88 | | 3 | 7 | 2 |
| Bangladeshi | 96 | | 1 | 2 | 1 |
| Chinese | 85 | | | 12 | 3 |
| Other Asian | 86 | | | 10 | 4 |
| Other | 53 | | | 40 | 6 |
| | | | | | |
| All ethnic groups | | | | 84 | 16 |

| Woman's ethnic group | Man's ethnic group | | | | |
| --- | --- | --- | --- | --- | --- |
| | Same | Other Black | Other S Asian | White | Other |
| White | 98 | | | | 2 |
| Black Caribbean | 87 | 4 | | 8 | 1 |
| Black African | 87 | 4 | | 8 | 1 |
| Black Other | 46 | 24 | | 27 | 3 |
| Indian | 94 | | 1 | 4 | 1 |
| Pakistani | 93 | | 4 | 2 | 2 |
| Bangladeshi | 98 | | 1 | 1 | 1 |
| Chinese | 75 | | | 20 | 5 |
| Other Asian | 76 | | | 18 | 6 |
| Other | 61 | | | 31 | 8 |
| | | | | | |
| All ethnic groups | | | | 83 | 17 |

*Source: 1991 Census, LRC Commissioned Table LRCT60*

## Families

Families in the 1991 Census are defined as couples with or without children or lone parents with children. The couples may be married or cohabiting and the children may be dependent or not. The Census does not classify same sex couples as families. Families are determined from information given on the relationship of each household member to the head of household and therefore may be contained within larger households.

Since this information is complicated to derive, the data was based on a ten per cent sample of returned 1991 Census forms. The ethnic group of a family is given as that of the family head. This may be either partner in a couple or the lone parent. However, the ethnic group of every member is not always the same as that of the family head. The following section therefore looks at the ethnic group of people in couples.

## Couples

In the vast majority of couples in London (over 95 per cent), the partners were from the same ethnic group as each other. In over 80 per cent of all couples both partners were White. Over 98 per cent of White men in couples were with a White woman, while for White women, the figure was just below 98 per cent. White women were therefore slightly more likely than White men to be in a couple with someone from an ethnic minority group.

As Table 4.4 shows, the proportions of South Asians in couples with someone from the same ethnic group were also very high, particularly for Bangladeshis. The lowest proportion was for Pakistani men, of whom 88 per cent of those in couples had a Pakistani partner. For Black Caribbean and Black African men and women, the proportions with a partner from the same ethnic groups were also quite high, but noticeably higher for women than for men (around 87 per cent of women, compared with around 78 per cent of men). For Chinese men and women, the picture was reversed, with Chinese men being more likely to have a Chinese partner than Chinese women.

For all ethnic minority groups, those in a couple with someone from a different ethnic group were most likely to have a White partner – this was true of both men and women.

For those in a couple with a partner from neither their own group or White, there was a tendency for both men and women to form a couple with someone from within the same broad ethnic group. For example, Black Caribbeans and Black Africans were more likely to be with someone from one of the other Black groups than from an Asian or other group, while Pakistanis were more likely to be with an Indian or Bangladeshi partner.

The Black Other, Other Asian and Other categories are less easy to interpret, since the composition of these groups is varied. Each of these classifications includes a variety of ethnic groups. For example, the Other Asian group includes residents who are Japanese, Filipino, Sri Lankan and some people of mixed parentage, among others. While the proportion of Other Asian men in a couple with a partner who was also in the Other Asian category is high, it is not possible to say what proportion were from the same ethnic group.

Less than half of both men and women in the Black Other group, which includes Black British and mixed Black/White, among others, were in a couple with a partner who was also in the Black Other group. Nearly a third of Black Other men in a couple had a White partner, compared with 27 per cent of Black Other women. The proportions with a partner who was either Black Caribbean or Black African were also quite high - 24 per cent of women had a partner from one of the other Black groups, compared with 12 per cent of men.

The proportions of those in Other ethnic groups in a couple with a partner who was also in this category were also quite low (53 per cent of men and 61 per cent of women), with a high proportion having a White partner (40 per cent of men and 31 per cent of women). The proportion with a partner from one of

**Figure 4.5 Family types in London by ethnic group**

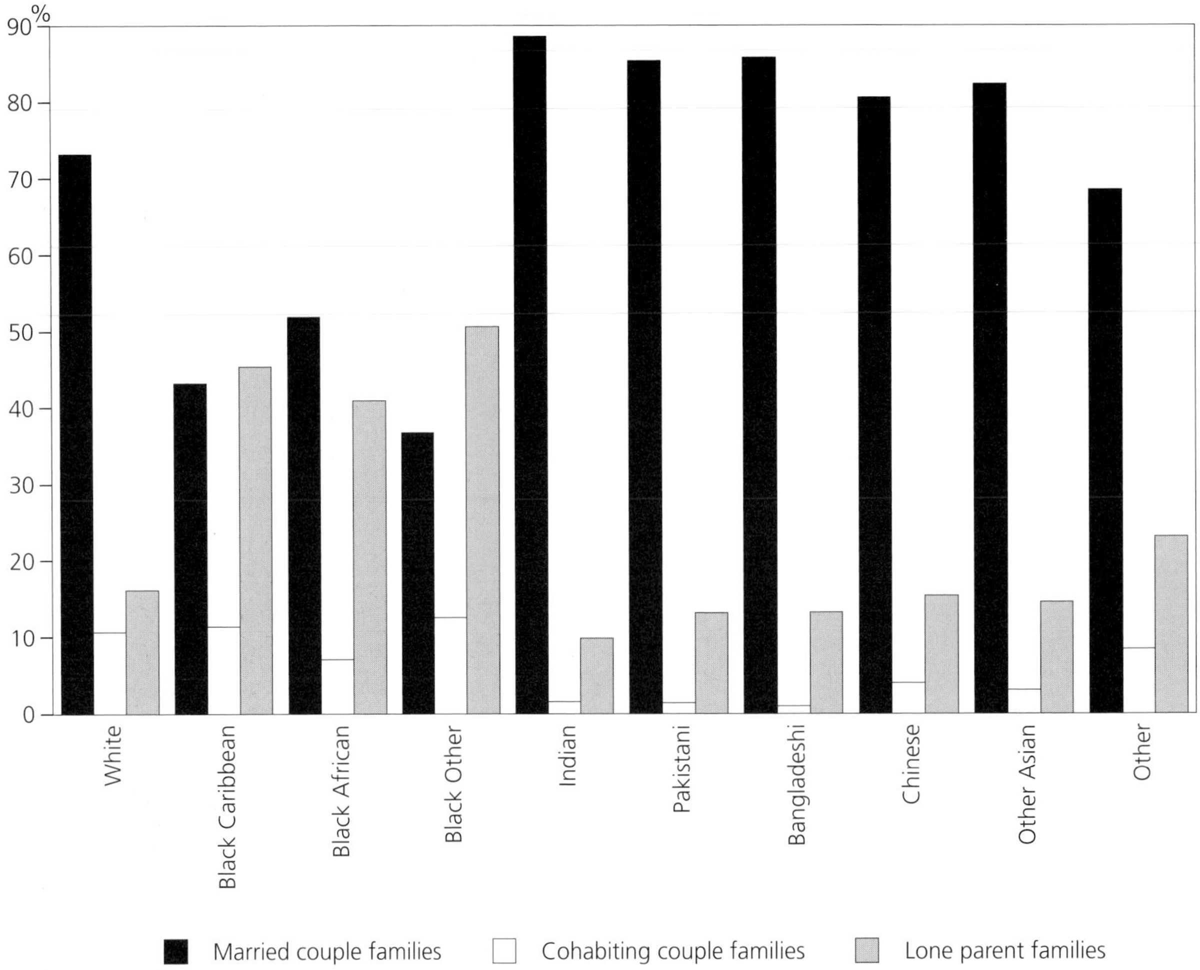

Married couple families     Cohabiting couple families     Lone parent families

*Source: 1991 Census, LRC Commissioned Table LRCT60 and LRCT61*

the other ethnic minority groups was higher than for any other group, although the proportion of Black Other men was only a little lower.

**Family types**

The report *London's Ethnic Minorities: One City Many Communities* gave information for families by ethnic group in the whole of Great Britain. Data is now available for London, and this shows that although the patterns of family types are broadly comparable to the national picture, there are some differences for families living in the capital.

**Married Couples**

The national data showed that married couple families were most widespread among the three South Asian groups and least common among the Black groups, which is consistent with the information given above for households. What is evident, however, is that the proportion of families with married couples was a little lower for most ethnic groups in London than nationally.

The national differences between ethnic groups regarding whether or not the married couples had children living with them are also reflected for London.

## Figure 4.6 Married couple family types

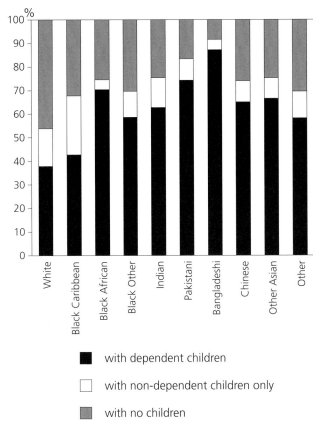

with dependent children

with non-dependent children only

with no children

*Source: 1991 Census, LRC Commissioned Table LRCT60*

Many married couples live with dependent children, but this does vary considerably between ethnic groups, as shown in Figure 4.6. Nearly 90 per cent of Bangladeshi married couple families included dependent children, while at the other end of the spectrum, less than 40 per cent of White married couple families and only slightly more Black Caribbean married couple families did so. While this is again related to the age structures of the populations to some extent, there are also other factors.

A quarter of Black Caribbean married couples lived with what the Census terms non-dependent children – the child or children of one or both of the couple who were no longer dependent. This proportion was higher than for married couples from other ethnic groups, while White married couples were most likely to be living with no children at all (46 per cent).

## Cohabiting couples

Given the proportions of married couple families among the South Asian groups, it is not surprising that there were very small proportions of cohabiting couple families in each of these groups. The London picture again reflects the national one to a large extent, with cohabiting couples being most widespread among Black Other and Black Caribbean families. The proportion of White families with a cohabiting couple was higher for London than nationally.

Whether or not there were children living with the cohabiting couple again varied between ethnic groups, as shown in Figure 4.5. Almost half of Black African and Black Caribbean cohabiting couples lived with dependent children, as did a quarter of White cohabiting couples. This suggests that Black Caribbean cohabiting couples were more likely to have dependent children than married couples, although there were

## Figure 4.7 Cohabiting couple family types

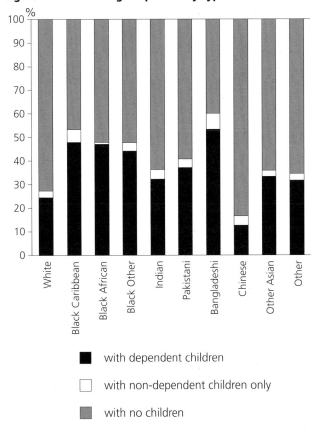

with dependent children

with non-dependent children only

with no children

*Source: 1991 Census, LRC Commissioned Table LRCT60*

## Figure 4.8 Lone parent family types

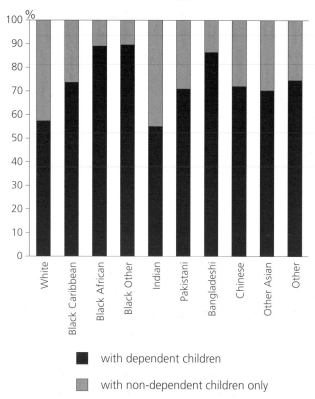

- ■ with dependent children
- ▨ with non-dependent children only

*Source: 1991 Census, LRC Commissioned Table LRCT60*

there were nearly 280,000 lone mothers, compared with under 40,000 lone fathers, a ratio of around seven women to one man. This varied considerably between ethnic groups, being lowest among Pakistani lone parent families where the ratio was around five women to one man, although the numbers in this group were quite small. The highest ratios were among Black Caribbean and Black Other lone parent families where there were nearly thirteen lone mothers for every Black Caribbean lone father and over sixteen Black Other lone mothers for every lone father.

Almost 60 per cent of lone fathers lived with non-dependent children only, compared with 35 per cent of lone mothers, but again this varied between ethnic groups, making the pattern of lone mothers and lone fathers with dependent children very different to that for all lone parent families. These differences can be seen from Figure 4.8.

The ratios of Black Caribbean and Black Other lone mothers to lone fathers with dependent children were much lower than for all lone parent families from these ethnic groups, whereas among South Asian lone parent families with dependent children, the proportions who were lone mothers were much higher. Over 70 per cent of all lone mothers had dependent children in all ethnic groups except Indian and White. The proportion was over 90 per cent for Black African and Black Other lone mothers. For these two groups, the proportions of lone fathers with dependent children were also high, at over 70 per cent.

For other minority groups, the proportions of lone fathers with dependent children were lower, ranging down to 50 per cent, but these proportions need to be treated with caution because of the small numbers involved. Just 35 per cent of White lone fathers had dependent children. For all ethnic groups except Indian, the figures show that lone mothers were more likely to have dependent children than lone fathers. For Indians, the proportions were about the same.

nearly four times as many married couple families. The numbers of cohabiting couple families for most other ethnic groups were small and so the figures should be treated with caution.

## Lone parents

Lone parent families, as with the other types of family with children, include a multitude of circumstances. Lone parent families may have one or more dependent children only, dependent children together with non-dependent children or non-dependent children only. The latter group is also diverse, since, for example, a lone parent with a child aged 19 (still in full-time education) would be in this category, as would a woman aged 70 who lived with her never married daughter aged 45.

In the vast majority of lone parent families from all ethnic groups, the lone parent was a woman. In all,

Another distinction between male and female lone parents and between ethnic groups is in their marital status. White and Indian lone fathers with non-dependent children only were most likely to be widowed, whereas those from other groups were most likely to be married, but recorded without a resident spouse or, for Black Caribbeans, divorced. In contrast, lone mothers with non-dependent children only from all except the Black groups were most likely to be widowed, while those from Black groups were most likely to be divorced or, in the case of Black Africans divorced or single.

The picture for lone parents with dependent children was very different. Both lone mothers and fathers who were Black Caribbean or Black Other were most likely to be single (never married). Black African lone mothers were also most likely to be single, whereas Black African lone fathers were most likely to be married. White lone mothers were also most likely to be single, but nearly as many were divorced, whereas White lone fathers were most likely to be divorced. The numbers of both lone mothers and lone fathers in the White category who were still married were quite high.

Asian lone parents were most likely to be married, with the exception of Bangladeshi lone mothers, the highest proportion of whom were widowed. It is important to remember the small numbers in each group, particularly of lone fathers, when interpreting these findings. Lone mothers from other ethnic groups were also most likely to be single.

## Ratios of family types

Another way of looking at differences in family types is provided by the figures in Table 4.5, which compare the proportion of families of each type for each ethnic minority group with the proportion of that type for the majority group – the White population. If the proportion of a family type in an ethnic group was the same as the White group, then the figure would be 1.0 for that ethnic group. Figures greater than one show a larger proportion of this type of family.

Table 4.5 shows that the proportions of families in all the ethnic minority groups consisting of just a married couple (with no children) were much smaller than for the White group. Similarly, a higher proportion of White families consisted of a married couple with non-

**Table 4.5  Ratio of family type by ethnic group to White**

| Ethnic group of lone parent or male partner | All families | Married couple families | | | Cohabiting couple families | | | Lone parent families | |
|---|---|---|---|---|---|---|---|---|---|
| | | no children | non-dependent children only | dependent children | no children | non-dependent children only | dependent children | non-dependent children only | dependent children |
| White | 135,580 | 1.0 | 1.0 | 1.0 | 1.0 | 1.0 | 1.0 | 1.0 | 1.0 |
| Black Caribbean | 8,212 | 0.4 | 0.9 | 0.7 | 0.7 | 2.0 | 2.1 | 1.7 | 3.6 |
| Black African | 3,386 | 0.4 | 0.2 | 1.3 | 0.5 | 0.2 | 1.3 | 0.6 | 3.9 |
| Black Other | 1,076 | 0.3 | 0.3 | 0.8 | 0.9 | 1.6 | 2.1 | 0.8 | 4.9 |
| Indian | 8,867 | 0.6 | 1.0 | 2.0 | 0.1 | 0.2 | 0.2 | 0.6 | 0.6 |
| Pakistani | 1,903 | 0.4 | 0.7 | 2.3 | 0.1 | 0.2 | 0.2 | 0.6 | 1.0 |
| Bangladeshi | 1,538 | 0.2 | 0.3 | 2.7 | 0.1 | 0.2 | 0.2 | 0.3 | 1.2 |
| Chinese | 1,209 | 0.6 | 0.6 | 1.9 | 0.4 | 0.6 | 0.2 | 0.6 | 1.2 |
| Other Asian | 2,581 | 0.6 | 0.6 | 2.0 | 0.3 | 0.3 | 0.4 | 0.6 | 1.1 |
| Other | 2,188 | 0.6 | 0.7 | 1.4 | 0.7 | 0.8 | 1.0 | 0.9 | 1.9 |

*Source: 1991 Census, LRC Commissioned Tables LRCT60 and LRCT61*

dependent children only, than of families from most ethnic minority groups. The only exception was Indian families, which had a similar proportion. The proportions of Black African, Black Other and Bangladeshi families in this category were particularly low, but this was at least partially due to the age structures of these populations.

Families from all Asian groups were around twice as likely as White families to consist of a married couple with dependent children. For Bangladeshi families, the ratio was even higher, at nearly three times the proportion of White families in this category.

The proportion of White families of a cohabiting couple without children was also higher than for any ethnic minority group. White families were ten times as likely as South Asian families to be of this type, but the differences for other groups were smaller, with only a slightly smaller proportion of Black Other families of this type. Black Other and Black Caribbean families were more likely than White families to be cohabiting couples with non-dependent children only or with dependent children. Black African families were also more likely than White families to be of the latter type. Again the proportions of South Asian families in these categories were much lower.

Only Black Caribbean families were more likely than

White families to consist of lone parents with non-dependent children only. All other ethnic minority groups had lower proportions of families of this type. In contrast only Indian families were less likely than White families to be lone parents with dependent children. The proportions of lone parent families with dependent children for all three Black groups were more than three times that of White families, up to almost five times the proportion among Black Other families.

## Household structure – number and type of family units

While the majority of households contain a single family with no other residents, some households do not contain families, such as one person households and households of unrelated adults. Other households contain two or more families. Some households with families may also contain non-family members, even though such people may be related, such as a grandparent. The relationship between families and households is therefore not a straightforward one and varies across family types and across ethnic groups.

Just over 90 per cent of all married couple families in London formed a household with no other residents, but this varied substantially for different ethnic groups. The data are only available by broad ethnic group, but show that over 93 per cent of White married couple

**Table 4.6  Household structure**

| Ethnic group of household head | Households with one family unit | | | | Households with 2 or more family units | Total |
| | Married couple | Cohabiting couple | Lone parent | Non family person | | |
|---|---|---|---|---|---|---|
| White | 92,794 | 13,343 | 18,991 | 73,516 | 23,657 | 222,301 |
| Black | 4,841 | 1,072 | 4,701 | 4,850 | 2,880 | 18,344 |
| South Asian | 7,435 | 144 | 915 | 1,273 | 3,015 | 12,782 |
| Chinese and other | 3,739 | 286 | 870 | 2,064 | 1,572 | 8,531 |
| Total | 108,809 | 14,845 | 25,477 | 81,703 | 31,124 | 261,958 |

*Source: 1991 Census, LRC Commissioned Table LRCT63*

**Figure 4.9 Number of family units in households**

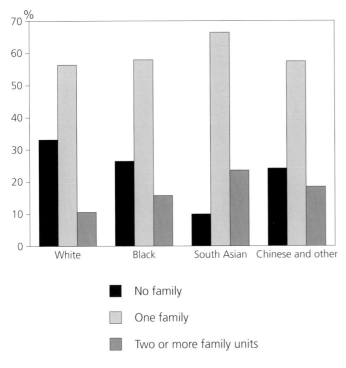

Source: *1991 Census, LRC Commissioned Table LRCT63*

families made up the entire household, whereas less than 70 per cent of South Asian married couple families did so. The comparable figures for Black and for Chinese and other married couple families were 85 and 81 per cent respectively.

The proportion of cohabiting couple families in households with no other residents was slightly higher overall, at just over 91 per cent. This was not the case for all ethnic groups, however. While the proportions of South Asian and Chinese and Other cohabiting couple families living alone were much higher than for married couple families from these ethnic groups, at 77 and 92 per cent respectively, the proportions were slightly lower than for married couple families for White and Black cohabiting couple families, at 92 and 81 per cent respectively. The numbers of Chinese and other cohabiting couple families and particularly of South Asian cohabiting couple families were quite small, however, as shown in Table 4.6.

Lone parent families were the least likely to live with no other residents. Just 85 per cent of lone parent families (including lone parents with non-dependent children) did so. Again, the figures differed considerably by ethnic group, ranging from under 70 per cent of South Asian lone parent families up to 87 per cent of White lone parent families. The proportions of Black and of Chinese and other lone parent families living alone were close to those for married couple families from these ethnic groups, at 83 and 81 per cent respectively.

These figures show that South Asian families of all types were most likely to live in households with other residents and White families of all types were least likely to do so. When considered from the perspective of households, rather than families, it is apparent that South Asian households were the most likely to contain a single family, as illustrated in Figure 4.9. This is because of the large proportion of White single person households (nearly a third) and the small proportion of South Asian single person households (10 per cent). Two thirds of all South Asian households consisted of a single family, whereas this was true of just 56 per cent of White households, 57 per cent of Chinese and other households and 58 per cent of Black households.

Just over 10 per cent of White households consisted of two or more family units. A family unit in this context means either a family, as defined above or a non-family member. Therefore two unrelated adults sharing a house or flat would be two family units, as would, for example, a family living with a related non-family member, such as a grandparent or two families living together. Nearly a quarter of all South Asian house-holds contained two or more family units. Again the proportions of Black and of Chinese and other households with two or more family units fell between these two extremes, at 16 and 18 per cent respectively.

# Chapter 5
# Housing

# Housing

## Introduction

In this chapter we look at a number of issues connected with housing in London, and the differences between ethnic groups in different tenures which become apparent when looking in detail at the 1991 Census commissioned tables. The major topics covered are tenure, possession of amenities and central heating, overcrowding, dwelling type and economic activity, unemployment and social class as they relate to tenure.

The overall picture is one of enormous differences across London, which we would expect, alongside huge differences between ethnic groups not explained by the parts of London in which they live. Further detail on these issues is included in the report *Dwelling on Difference* by Eileen Howes and David Mullins published by the London Research Centre in March 1999.

## Tenure

More than half of all households in London were owner occupiers (57 per cent) with nearly a quarter in local authority accommodation, 12 per cent renting privately, 6 per cent housed by housing associations and 2 per cent renting with a job. This is illustrated in Figure 5.1.

The overall London figures disguise the differences between different parts of London as well as between different ethnic groups. There were also considerable differences between ethnic minority groups in London and elsewhere.

The overall level of owner occupation was low in London compared with the level in the rest of Great Britain, where two thirds of all households were owner occupiers. The proportion of households in local authority accommodation was slightly higher in London than in Great Britain while higher proportions of households in London rented from both housing associations and private landlords. The level of renting with a job was low, at two per cent, in both London and Great Britain as a whole.

**Figure 5.1   Tenure of households in Greater London, 1991**

*Source: 1991 Census, LRC Commissioned Table LRCT11*

London figures as a whole, though, mask the enormous differences within London, and particularly the differences between Inner and Outer London. The level of owner occupation in Outer London was higher than that in Great Britain, at 69 per cent, while in Inner London the corresponding figure was only 39 per cent. All forms of renting featured more prominently in Inner than Outer London and Great Britain.

## Different ethnic groups in London

The overall tenure pattern in London reflected that of White households because White was by far the largest group. Overall patterns, therefore, disguised the differences between ethnic groups in London. The ethnic groups with the highest proportions of owner occupiers were Indian, with almost 80 per cent, and Pakistani, with almost 70 per cent, illustrated in Figure 5.2. These were the only two ethnic groups that were more likely than the White group to be owner occupiers.

At the other end of the scale only around a quarter of Black African and Bangladeshi households were owner occupiers. The likelihood of Black African and Bangladeshi households being in owner occupation was less than half of that for White households. Table 5.1 shows the distributions.

**Figure 5.2  Percentage of households in owner occupation, Greater London 1991**

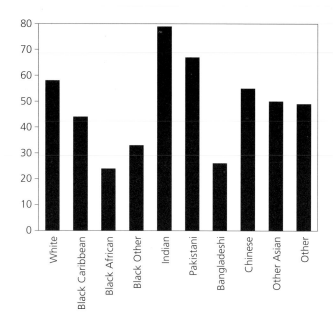

Source: 1991 Census, LRC Commissioned Table LRCT11

**Figure 5.3  Percentage of households in local authority accommodation, Greater London 1991**

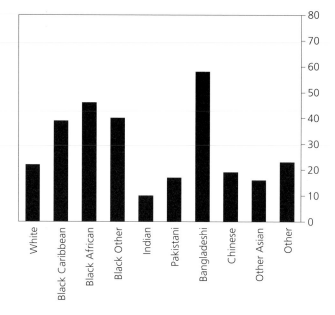

Source: 1991 Census, LRC Commissioned Table LRCT11

**Figure 5.4  Percentage of households housed by housing associations, Greater London 1991**

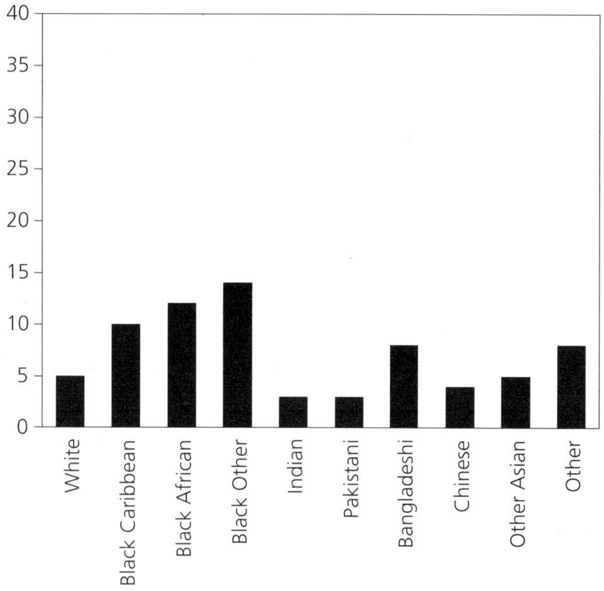

Source: 1991 Census, LRC Commissioned Table LRCT11

**Figure 5.5  Percentage of households renting privately, Greater London 1991**

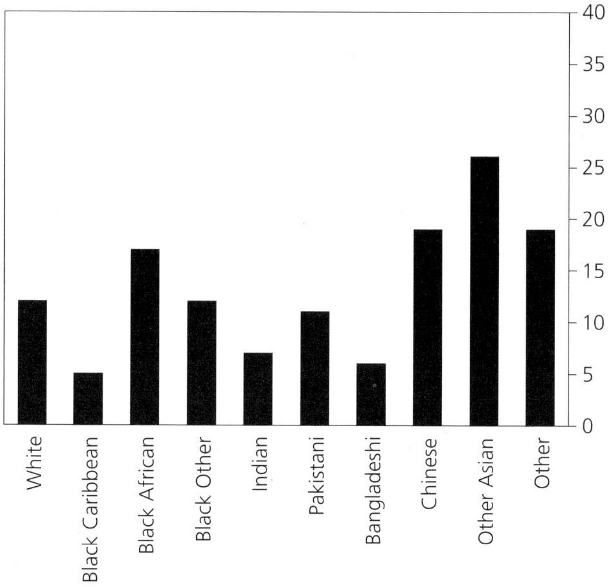

Source: 1991 Census, LRC Commissioned Table LRCT11

**Table 5.1 Tenure of households by ethnic group of head of household, Greater London, 1991**

| Ethnic group of head of household | Number of households | Total % | Owner occupiers | Local authority | Housing association | Private renters | Rent with a job |
|---|---|---|---|---|---|---|---|
| All groups | 2,763,166 | 100 | 57 | 23 | 6 | 12 | 2 |
| White | 2,337,489 | 100 | 58 | 22 | 5 | 12 | 2 |
| Black Caribbean | 125,253 | 100 | 44 | 39 | 10 | 5 | 1 |
| Black African | 57,671 | 100 | 24 | 46 | 12 | 17 | 2 |
| Black Other | 17,972 | 100 | 33 | 40 | 14 | 12 | 1 |
| Indian | 96,774 | 100 | 79 | 10 | 3 | 7 | 2 |
| Pakistani | 21,846 | 100 | 67 | 17 | 3 | 11 | 1 |
| Bangladeshi | 15,946 | 100 | 26 | 58 | 8 | 6 | 2 |
| Chinese | 18,802 | 100 | 55 | 19 | 4 | 19 | 3 |
| Other Asian | 35,988 | 100 | 50 | 16 | 5 | 26 | 3 |
| Other | 35,425 | 100 | 49 | 23 | 8 | 19 | 1 |

Source: 1991 Census, LRC Commissioned Table LRCT11

Local authority was the most important tenure for Bangladeshi and Black African households, and also accounted for high proportions of Black Caribbean and Black Other households, as shown in Figure 5.3. Bangladeshi households were more than two and a half times as likely as White households to be in local authority accommodation and Black African households more than twice as likely. The proportion of Indian households in local authority accommodation was very low, at only 10 per cent, and was also lower than average for Other Asian, Pakistani and Chinese households.

A larger than average proportion of all Black groups and Bangladeshis were in housing association accommodation compared with smaller proportions of Indian, Pakistani and Chinese groups. Black households were more than twice as likely as White households to be in housing association accommodation, as shown in Figure 5.4.

The groups with the highest proportions in privately rented accommodation were Other Asian, Other, Chinese and Black African. More than a quarter of Other Asians in London rented privately and the ratio to the White proportion is more than 2. Relatively few Black Caribbean, Bangladeshi and Indian households rented privately, as shown in Figure 5.5.

**Possession of amenities**

In 1991 the majority of households of all ethnic groups and tenures had basic amenities. Only one per cent of households in Great Britain lacked or shared basic amenities, with the figure rising to two per cent in Greater London. There were, nevertheless, differences between London and elsewhere and between ethnic groups in different tenures. These are discussed below.

There were significant differences between tenures within London – for example only one per cent or less of all owner occupiers lacked or shared basic amenities. Slightly more local authority tenants lacked or shared

**Table 5.2  Percentage of households lacking or sharing amenities by ethnic group of head of household and tenure, Greater London 1991**

| Ethnic group of head of household | All tenures | Owner occupiers | Local authority | Housing association | Private renters | Rent with a job |
|---|---|---|---|---|---|---|
| All groups | 2 | 1 | 1 | 3 | 12 | 3 |
| White | 2 | 1 | 1 | 3 | 12 | 3 |
| Black Caribbean | 2 | 1 | 1 | 2 | 13 | 2 |
| Black African | 5 | 1 | 2 | 6 | 19 | 4 |
| Black Other | 3 | 1 | 1 | 3 | 13 | 5 |
| Indian | 1 | 1 | 2 | 2 | 9 | 3 |
| Pakistani | 3 | 1 | 2 | 4 | 14 | 5 |
| Bangladeshi | 2 | 1 | 2 | 2 | 9 | 6 |
| Chinese | 4 | 0 | 2 | 5 | 14 | 6 |
| Other Asian | 4 | 1 | 2 | 4 | 11 | 4 |
| Other | 4 | 1 | 2 | 4 | 15 | 6 |

*Source: 1991 Census, LRC Commissioned Table LRCT11*

amenities but the proportion was very low – just over one per cent. Housing association tenants were more likely to lack or share amenities, three per cent, but the most significant levels of lacking or sharing amenities were amongst households renting privately, where one in eight households lacked or shared basic amenities.

### Ethnic groups lacking or sharing amenities in London

Indian households in London were the least likely to lack or share basic amenities – with only one per cent – followed by White, Black Caribbean and Bangladeshi households with two per cent. Those most likely to lack or share basic amenities were Black Africans, Chinese, Other Asian and Other ethnic groups who were all relatively concentrated in the private rented sector and therefore more likely to share amenities.

There were consistent differences in the proportions of households lacking or sharing amenities between ethnic groups within some tenures. Owner occupiers of all

ethnic groups had low levels of lacking or sharing amenities – one per cent or less for all groups. Local authority tenants also tended to have exclusive use of basic amenities, although the proportions lacking or sharing were slightly higher than for owner occupiers – two per cent or less for all ethnic groups.

The picture for housing association tenants was slightly different, showing more differences between ethnic groups and overall higher levels of lacking or sharing amenities. The lowest levels of lacking or sharing amenities was for Black Caribbean, Indian and Bangladeshi housing association tenants, with only two per cent, compared with six per cent of Black African housing association tenants.

Households renting privately had the highest levels of lacking or sharing amenities, 12 per cent in total, but varying from 9 per cent of Indian to 19 per cent of Black African private renters.

## Lacking or sharing amenities outside London

The proportion of households sharing amenities in London was higher than sharing outside London, mainly but not entirely because of the higher levels of private renting in London. For owner occupiers and local authority tenants the proportions of households lacking or sharing amenities were equally low in London and outside, at around one per cent. Outside London only one per cent of housing association tenants lacked or shared amenities, a third of the proportion in London, while the proportion of private renters lacking or sharing amenities outside London was only two thirds of the corresponding proportion in London – eight per cent. Those renting with a job were also more likely to lack or share amenities in London than elsewhere.

There were some differences between ethnic groups in specific tenures outside London, as well as within London. Most ethnic groups had lower proportions lacking or sharing amenities outside London, the exceptions being Indian and Bangladeshi households with only one and two per cent respectively lacking or sharing amenities in London and outside London.

Outside London only one per cent of White households lacked or shared amenities compared with two per cent in London, which explains the overall difference.

As in London, Black African households were the most likely to lack or share amenities but the proportion was slightly lower outside London. Around three per cent of Chinese households outside London lacked or shared amenities compared with four per cent in London.

Owner occupiers outside London had very low levels of lacking or sharing amenities, as they did within London. One per cent or less of households of all ethnic groups in London and elsewhere in Great Britain lacked or shared amenities.

Local authority tenants outside London also had low

levels of lacking or sharing amenities, although for a number of ethnic groups, local authority tenants in London were more likely to lack or share amenities than local authority tenants outside London.

For most ethnic groups the proportion of housing association tenants outside London lacking or sharing amenities was less than half the corresponding proportion in London, and for all ethnic groups the proportion was lower outside London.

Similarly, all ethnic groups renting privately were less likely to lack or share amenities outside London than in London. The largest difference for any ethnic group between those living in London and outside London was for Other Asians – five per cent of Other Asians renting privately outside London lacked or shared amenities compared with 11 per cent of Other Asians renting privately in London.

## Central heating

Central heating is one of the few measures in the 1991 Census that can give some indication of housing conditions, although it is not an ideal measure for this purpose. Nevertheless, there are some implications to be drawn from the data on lack of central heating by tenure and ethnic group and what this tells us about differential access to housing.

Nationally and in Greater London almost one in five households did not have central heating. The following sections look at the differences in possession of central heating between households in various tenures and in different ethnic groups.

It is not surprising that owner occupiers were the most likely to have central heating, with only around one in eight households in owner occupation having no central heating. Just over one in five local authority tenants and those renting with a job had no central heating while those in housing association property and private renters were the least likely to have central heating. Just under 40 per cent of those renting privately did not

**Table 5.3 Percentage of households with no central heating by ethnic group of head of household and tenure, Greater London, 1991**

| Ethnic group of head of household | All tenures | Owner occupiers | Local authority | Housing association | Private renters | Rent with a job |
|---|---|---|---|---|---|---|
| All groups | 19 | 12 | 22 | 31 | 39 | 21 |
| White | 20 | 13 | 23 | 32 | 41 | 20 |
| Black Caribbean | 15 | 10 | 14 | 30 | 30 | 17 |
| Black African | 15 | 9 | 13 | 26 | 20 | 14 |
| Black Other | 18 | 10 | 16 | 31 | 29 | 23 |
| Indian | 8 | 4 | 16 | 25 | 20 | 29 |
| Pakistani | 13 | 10 | 18 | 23 | 24 | 32 |
| Bangladeshi | 12 | 10 | 10 | 14 | 31 | 44 |
| Chinese | 13 | 6 | 15 | 27 | 24 | 39 |
| Other Asian | 11 | 6 | 15 | 28 | 15 | 11 |
| Other | 15 | 7 | 16 | 31 | 25 | 16 |

*Source: 1991 Census, LRC Commissioned Table LRCT11*

have central heating.

**Ethnic groups lacking central heating in London**
In London one in five White households had no central heating, the largest proportion of any ethnic group. This compares with only eight per cent of Indian households, the ethnic group most likely to have central heating. In between these two extremes 18 per cent of Black Others lacked central heating, as did 15 per cent of Black Caribbean, Black African and Other households. Between 11 and 13 per cent of Pakistani, Bangladeshi and Other Asian households had no central heating. These differences are, to some extent, a reflection of the different tenure distributions of these ethnic groups but not entirely.

As stated above, owner occupiers were more likely to have central heating than households in other tenures. While this is true, differences remain between owner occupiers of different ethnic groups. For example only four per cent of Indian owner occupiers in London

lacked central heating compared with 13 per cent of White owner occupiers. There could be many reasons for this, including the parts of London that different ethnic groups tend to live in, the types of housing, economic factors, household composition and age.

Chinese, Other Asian and Other ethnic groups in London also had low levels of lacking central heating, between six and seven per cent. Between nine and ten per cent of Black Caribbean, Black African, Black Other, Pakistani and Bangladeshi households had no central heating.

The proportion of local authority tenants with no central heating, shown in Figure 5.6, ranged from ten per cent of Bangladeshi to 23 per cent of White. This is probably a result of the concentration of the Bangladeshi population in Tower Hamlets and in purpose built flats, while White households may tend to be older and have been in their properties the longest.

**Figure 5.6 Percentage of local authority tenants with no central heating by ethnic group, Greater London 1991**

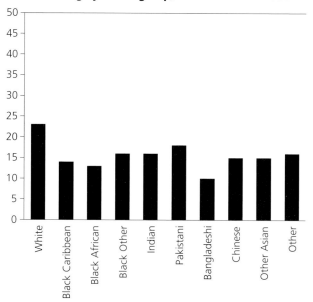

Source: 1991 Census, LRC Commissioned Table LRCT11

**Figure 5.7 Percentage of private renters with no central heating by ethnic group, Greater London 1991**

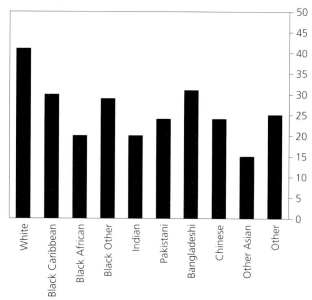

Source: 1991 Census, LRC Commissioned Table LRCT11

Black Caribbean and Black African local authority tenants were much more likely to have central heating than White local authority tenants, again probably because of the type of property they tend to occupy. Local authority tenants of all other ethnic groups had 18 per cent or less with no central heating.

Bangladeshi housing association tenants were the most likely to have central heating, although they were few in number. Less than 30 per cent of Pakistani, Indian, Black African, Chinese and Other Asian housing association tenants lacked central heating while 30 to 31 per cent of Black Caribbean, Black Other and Other housing association tenants also had no central heating. The highest rate was for White tenants, of whom 32 per cent lacked central heating.

White households renting privately were the most likely to lack central heating – 41 per cent. All ethnic minority groups renting privately were far more likely than White households to have central heating, as shown in Figure 5.7. Bangladeshis had the second highest proportion without central heating – 31 per

cent, followed by Black Caribbean and Black Other households – 30 to 31 per cent. The lowest proportions renting privately without central heating were Other Asians with only 15 per cent.

Households renting with a job had the widest range, from 44 per cent of Bangladeshis to 11 per cent of Other Asians lacking central heating.

**Central heating outside London**

The overall proportion of households without central heating was the same in London as outside London, 19 per cent. Owner occupiers outside London were slightly more likely to lack central heating while local authority tenants outside London were slightly more likely to have central heating. The difference between housing association tenants in London and outside was greater – with 31 per cent in London and only 16 per cent outside London lacking central heating. Almost half of households renting privately outside London had no central heating compared with 39 per cent in London.

In London the White group was the most likely to lack central heating (20 per cent). The corresponding proportion for White households outside London was similar at 19 per cent. The overall pattern outside London, though, was very different, with the White group among the least likely to have no central heating. The group most likely to lack central heating outside London was Bangladeshis, 40 per cent of whom had no central heating. Pakistanis outside London came a close second, with 36 per cent. All ethnic minority groups living in London were more likely than the same groups living outside London to have central heating. The differences between living in London and elsewhere were greatest for the Bangladeshi, Pakistani and Indian groups – the proportions with central heating were twice as high for Indians in London and around three times as high for Bangladeshis and Pakistanis in London.

Owner occupiers outside London were slightly more likely than those in London to lack central heating. This was true for all ethnic groups although the difference was small for the White group. Bangladeshi and Pakistani owner occupiers living outside Greater London were the most likely to have no central heating, and these two groups also had the largest differences between those living in London and outside London. There was also a large difference between Indian owner occupiers living in London and outside – four per cent of Indians in London and 14 per cent of Indians living outside London with no central heating. For many ethnic groups the proportion of owner occupiers outside London without central heating was around double that of owner occupiers of the same groups living in London. Only ten per cent of Other Asian owner occupiers living outside London had no central heating compared with six per cent in London.

Local authority tenants of all ethnic groups outside London were more likely to lack central heating than local authority tenants living in the capital. The difference between those living in London and elsewhere was smallest for the White group, 23 per cent in London compared with 25 per cent outside. The differences for all other ethnic groups were significant,

especially for Bangladeshis and Pakistanis. The local authority tenants most likely to have central heating outside London were Other Asian, 20 per cent of whom lacked central heating, and those least likely were Bangladeshis, 32 per cent of whom lacked central heating.

Housing association tenants living outside London were more likely to have central heating than housing association tenants living in London. Overall and for the White group, housing association tenants were twice as likely to have central heating if they lived outside London. All ethnic groups except Bangladeshi had a smaller percentage of housing association tenants with no central heating outside London than in London. For most ethnic minority groups the proportion of housing association tenants without central heating outside London was roughly two thirds the corresponding proportion in London. The exceptions were Pakistani housing association tenants – 23 per cent without central heating in London and 21 per cent outside London; and Bangladeshi housing association tenants – 14 per cent without central heating in London and 24 per cent outside London. Indian and White housing association tenants outside London were the most likely to have central heating, with only 16 per cent lacking.

Private renters from all ethnic groups living outside London were more likely to have no central heating than private renters living in London. The largest difference for any ethnic group between those living in London and outside was for the Pakistani group – 24 per cent of Pakistani private renters in London lacked central heating compared with 48 per cent of those living outside. Private renters living outside London most likely to have central heating were Other Asians – only 22 per cent of whom lacked central heating. Those least likely to have central heating were Bangladeshi and Pakistani groups – with 49 and 48 per cent lacking central heating. In comparison, 46 per cent of White private renters outside London had no central heating.

**Table 5.4  Percentage of households with more than one person per room, Greater London 1991**

| Ethnic group of head of household | All tenures | Owned outright | Buying with mortgage | Local authority | Housing assoc- iation | Private rented furn. | Private rented unfurn. | Rent with job |
|---|---|---|---|---|---|---|---|---|
| All groups | 4 | 1 | 3 | 7 | 5 | 7 | 3 | 5 |
| White | 3 | 0 | 2 | 4 | 4 | 6 | 2 | 3 |
| Black Caribbean | 6 | 2 | 4 | 8 | 6 | 8 | 7 | 4 |
| Black African | 17 | 10 | 11 | 20 | 16 | 17 | 15 | 16 |
| Black Other | 7 | 3 | 5 | 9 | 7 | 12 | 6 | 6 |
| Indian | 13 | 10 | 13 | 18 | 13 | 13 | 18 | 24 |
| Pakistani | 23 | 17 | 21 | 32 | 23 | 21 | 24 | 25 |
| Bangladeshi | 54 | 26 | 34 | 65 | 56 | 42 | 46 | 34 |
| Chinese | 11 | 4 | 6 | 24 | 19 | 11 | 14 | 17 |
| Other Asian | 12 | 6 | 11 | 20 | 16 | 10 | 20 | 8 |
| Other | 9 | 3 | 5 | 14 | 10 | 14 | 9 | 12 |

*Source: 1991 Census, LRC Commissioned Table LRCT11*

## Overcrowding

Overcrowding in this context is measured as a household living at a density of more than one person per room. As such it is directly linked to household size, which differs considerably by ethnic group (see Chapter 4). Overcrowding is also linked to a lack of suitable housing in an area and can be interpreted as indicating a degree of unmet housing need.

The level of overcrowding was higher in London than nationally, although only just over four per cent of households were overcrowded. This compares with two per cent nationally. Overcrowding was worse in Inner London and for households in all ethnic minority groups, both nationally and in London.

The following sections look in more detail at the differences between tenures and ethnic groups, and compare those living in London with national figures.

Owner occupiers were the least overcrowded, especially those who owned their properties outright. These households are likely to be older than average, hence smaller. Those renting privately in unfurnished property also had relatively low levels of overcrowding, and they are also likely to be older than average with smaller household sizes. Local authority tenants and households renting furnished property from a private landlord were the most overcrowded, around seven per cent. Housing association tenants and those renting with a job had slightly lower levels of overcrowding.

### Overcrowding by ethnic group in London

More than half of all Bangladeshi households in London were overcrowded, by far the highest proportion for any ethnic group, caused by the generally large household sizes for Bangladeshis. Almost a quarter of Pakistani households in London were overcrowded, followed by Black Africans with 17 per cent.

Indian, Chinese and Other Asian households all had

overcrowding levels of 11 to 13 per cent, while Black Caribbean and Black Other households had relatively low levels, between six and seven per cent. These compare with three per cent of White households. White households were the least overcrowded in all tenures, ranging from less than one per cent of White households owning outright to six per cent of White households renting furnished property from a private landlord. Black Caribbean households had similarly low levels of overcrowding, but generally double the proportions of White households. The pattern for overcrowding in Black Other households was similar again, but with levels slightly above those for Black Caribbean households. Black Africans were much more overcrowded than the other Black groups, especially in local authority accommodation where one in five households was overcrowded.

Indian households renting with a job had the highest levels of overcrowding (one in four) compared with 18 per cent of Indian local authority tenants and those renting privately unfurnished. Unusually, there was little difference between levels of overcrowding for Indian households buying with a mortgage, renting from a housing association or renting furnished property privately.

The highest levels of overcrowding in all tenures were among Bangladeshi and Pakistani households. Almost two thirds of Bangladeshi local authority tenants were overcrowded, and one in three Pakistani local authority tenants. This is lprobably because of a lack of suitable accommodation within the local authority sector.

More than 40 per cent of Bangladeshis renting their homes from private landlords were overcrowded, as well as 56 per cent of those renting from housing associations. Bangladeshis buying their homes or renting with a job were less likely to be overcrowded, but still one in three were overcrowded. Apart from local authority tenants, Pakistani households renting with a job, unfurnished from a private landlord or from a housing association were the most likely to be

overcrowded, around a quarter were living at over one person per room.

For Chinese, Other Asian and Other groups those renting from a local authority or housing association were most likely to be overcrowded. Other Asians renting unfurnished property privately also had relatively high levels of overcrowding.

**Overcrowding in Great Britain**
The proportion of households living at over one person per room in the whole of Great Britain was around half of that in London – two per cent in Great Britain compared to four per cent in London. The proportion was lower nationally for all tenures. The highest proportions nationally were five per cent for households renting furnished property privately and four per cent for local authority tenants. In London it was seven per cent for both. The data on overcrowding was provided by the Office for National Statistics in the form of percentages for London and Great Britain, so it is not possible to calculate the levels of overcrowding for ethnic minorities outside London. The comparison here, therefore, is with the national figures which include London. This must be remembered when looking at the differences between London and Great Britain, as there will be some understatement of the differences between those living in London and elsewhere for a number of ethnic groups.

All ethnic groups except Pakistani, Indian and Chinese were more overcrowded in London than nationally. Pakistani was the only ethnic group for which the proportion overcrowded was higher nationally than in London, 30 per cent in Great Britain compared with 23 per cent in London. There was no difference between London and Great Britain for the Indian and Chinese groups. The ranking of ethnic groups in this context was similar in Great Britain and London, with Bangladeshis the most likely to be overcrowded. The proportion of Bangladeshis living at over one person per room was just under half, compared with just over half of those who lived in London.

White and Black Caribbean households owning their properties outright showed no difference in the proportions overcrowded in London and Great Britain. Both were low – less than one per cent for White and two per cent for Black Caribbean households. A slightly larger proportion of Black African households owning outright and living in London were overcrowded than in Great Britain, ten per cent in London compared with nine per cent in Great Britain.

For all other ethnic groups the proportion of those owning outright who were overcrowded was higher in Great Britain as a whole than in London. In particular the proportion of overcrowded Pakistani households owning outright in Great Britain was double the proportion in London (34 and 17 per cent). The proportion of Chinese households in Great Britain overcrowded and owning outright was also double the corresponding proportion in London, although at a much smaller scale (eight and four per cent). The largest other difference was in the proportion of Bangladeshis owning outright overcrowded in Great Britain, 41 per cent, compared with 26 per cent in London.

Those buying with a mortgage were more likely to be overcrowded in London than in Great Britain but the levels of overcrowding were relatively low. The same applied for all ethnic groups except Pakistani, Bangladeshi and Chinese, all of whom were more likely to be overcrowded outside London. The largest difference between London and Great Britain was for Pakistani households (30 per cent overcrowded in Great Britain and 21 per cent in London) while the highest level of overcrowding in Great Britain was for Bangladeshis buying their property (38 per cent in Great Britain compared with 34 per cent in Greater London). The differences between London and Great Britain were relatively small for all other ethnic groups.

Local authority tenants were more likely to be overcrowded in London than in Great Britain for all ethnic groups except White, for whom the proportion

was the same. The largest differences between those living in London and Great Britain were for Chinese (24 and 19 per cent) and Bangladeshi households (65 and 61 per cent). Housing association tenants were also more likely to be overcrowded in London than elsewhere, with only Pakistani and Other Asian households at the same level of overcrowding.

Households renting furnished property privately were more likely to be overcrowded in London than in Great Britain, except for Pakistani and Other Asian households for whom the proportions overcrowded were the same. For those renting unfurnished property the proportions overcrowded were generally, and for most ethnic groups, higher in London than in Great Britain. The exceptions were Pakistani and Chinese households, who were more likely to be overcrowded outside London, and White households, for whom the rates were the same in London and Great Britain. People of all ethnic groups renting with a job were more likely to be overcrowded in London.

**Dwelling type**
The greatest contrast in the housing experiences of ethnic groups indicated by the 1991 Census were in the type of dwelling occupied (as defined by 'household space type'). The type of housing occupied depends, to a large extent, on the housing stock in an area and the tenure distribution of that stock. The types of dwelling occupied by different ethnic groups in each tenure will therefore be compared in London and the rest of Great Britain.

Just over half of White households in London lived in houses compared with almost 80 per cent in Great Britain as a whole. For some ethnic groups a minority of households lived in houses (all Black groups, Bangladeshis, Chinese and Other groups). However, Indian and Pakistani groups are even more likely to live in houses rather than flats than the White group. Although similar proportions of Other Asian and White households lived in houses, there were noticeable differences between the types of houses occupied.

**Table 5.5 Percentage of households in each dwelling type by ethnic group of head of household, Greater London 1991**

| Ethnic group of head of household | All types | Detached house | Semi-detached house | Terraced house | Purpose built flat | Converted flat | Not self-contained flat |
|---|---|---|---|---|---|---|---|
| All groups | 100 | 5 | 17 | 30 | 33 | 12 | 3 |
| White | 100 | 6 | 18 | 29 | 33 | 12 | 3 |
| Black Caribbean | 100 | 1 | 7 | 35 | 40 | 15 | 2 |
| Black African | 100 | 1 | 5 | 23 | 50 | 14 | 7 |
| Black Other | 100 | 1 | 6 | 24 | 46 | 19 | 4 |
| Indian | 100 | 6 | 25 | 43 | 19 | 6 | 1 |
| Pakistani | 100 | 4 | 16 | 48 | 22 | 7 | 3 |
| Bangladeshi | 100 | 1 | 6 | 27 | 58 | 7 | 1 |
| Chinese | 100 | 4 | 13 | 27 | 38 | 13 | 5 |
| Other Asian | 100 | 6 | 16 | 30 | 31 | 12 | 5 |
| Other | 100 | 3 | 12 | 24 | 38 | 17 | 5 |

*Source: 1991 Census, LRC Commissioned Table LRCT11*

Six per cent of White, Indian and Other Asian households lived in detached houses, compared with four per cent of Pakistani and Chinese households and three per cent of Other groups. Only one per cent of all Black groups and Bangladeshi households lived in detached houses. These figures compare unfavourably with the rest of Great Britain where 21 per cent of White households lived in detached houses, as well as 14 per cent of Chinese and 13 per cent of Indian and Other Asian households.

A quarter of all Indian households in London lived in semi-detached houses compared to 18 per cent of White and 16 per cent of Pakistani and Other Asian households. This reflects the fact that Indian households tend to live in Outer London where there are more semi-detached houses, as well as their relative economic superiority. The groups least likely to live in semi-detached houses were all Black groups and Bangladeshis.

Almost half of Pakistani households in London lived in terraced houses, as well as 43 per cent of Indian and 35 per cent of Black Caribbean households. Only 29 per cent of White households lived in terraced houses.

Bangladeshi households were largely concentrated in purpose built flats (58 per cent), as well as half of Black African and 46 per cent of Black Other households. A third of White households lived in purpose built flats. The ethnic groups least likely to live in purpose built flats were Indian (19 per cent) and Pakistani (22 per cent). These two groups were concentrated in houses rather than flats.

Black and Other groups, especially the Black Other group, were the most likely to lived in converted flats. The Indian, Pakistani and Bangladeshi groups were the least likely to live in converted or not self-contained flats. Black Africans were the group most likely to be

**Figure 5.8 Dwelling type for selected ethnic groups, Greater London 1991**

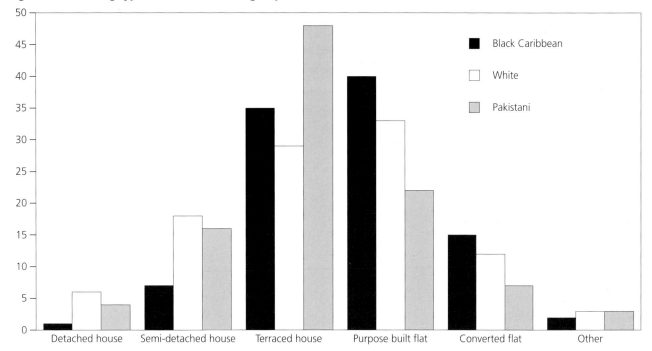

*Source: 1991 Census, LRC Commissioned Table LRCT11*

living in not self-contained flats. Figure 5.8 illustrates the differences between the types of housing occupied by White, Black Caribbean and Pakistani households.

There was a striking difference between ethnic groups within London and outside. In particular there were far higher proportions of most ethnic groups living in detached houses. The ethnic group with the largest proportion living in detached houses was Other Asian, followed by White and Chinese, all with more than one in five households living in detached houses. The smallest proportions living in detached houses outside London were of Black Caribbean, Bangladeshi and Pakistani households – all around six or seven per cent. One of the most significant differences is with Pakistani households. While only four per cent of London's Pakistani households lived in detached houses, this was one of the largest proportions, and not one of the smallest, as in the rest of Great Britain.

The proportion of households living in semi-detached houses was highest for White households outside London, followed by Indian. In London the position of these two groups was reversed. All Black groups and Bangladeshis were much more likely to live in semi-detached houses outside London, between 21 and 25 per cent for Black groups and 14 per cent for Bangladeshis. These proportions were more in line with other ethnic groups outside London, whereas in London, Black groups and Bangladeshis stood out as a very small proportion of them lived in semi-detached houses.

A similar proportion of White households, 29 per cent, lived in terraced houses both in and out of London. For other groups, though, there were some quite large differences. Most ethnic minority groups had larger proportions living in terraced houses outside London. The only exceptions to this were the Indian and Chinese groups both of which had slightly higher proportions living in terraced houses within London. The largest differences were for Pakistani and Bangladeshi households. Outside London 64 per cent of Pakistani and Bangladeshi households lived in terraced houses, as against 48 and 27 per cent in London.

Purpose built flats were much less common outside London. The Chinese group had the largest proportion living in them outside London, at 27 per cent. Just over 20 per cent of all Black groups outside London lived in purpose built flats, as well as 13 per cent of Bangladeshi households. This compares with a high of 58 per cent of Bangladeshi households in London living in purpose built flats.

Converted flats were far less common outside London. Only two per cent of households lived in them compared to 12 per cent in London. Not self-contained flats were also far less common outside London, but Black African households were still the most likely to live in them.

**Dwelling type by tenure**
Two thirds of local authority tenants in London lived in purpose built flats while one in five lived in terraced houses. The proportion of local authority tenants in any other type of dwelling was small. This partly explains the relatively large proportions of Bangladeshi and Black Caribbean households in London living in purpose built flats.

Owner occupiers were largely concentrated in houses, with terraced houses being the most common. Around 11 per cent of households owning outright lived in detached houses as well as seven per cent of households buying their property. Housing association tenants tended to live in flats, with 47 per cent in purpose built and 32 per cent in converted flats. Those renting privately also tended to live in purpose built flats (31 per cent), with a relatively large proportion in converted flats (26 per cent). A very high proportion of private renters lived in not self-contained flats (15 per cent) – far more than in any other tenure. Almost two thirds

of households renting with a job lived in flats, but a relatively high proportion, eight per cent, lived in detached houses.

For households living in the rest of Great Britain the dwelling distribution was very different. Almost two thirds of local authority tenants outside London lived in houses, while a third lived in purpose built flats. There were very few local authority tenants outside London living in converted or not self-contained flats.

More than 90 per cent of owner occupiers outside London lived in houses. For those owning outright, detached and semi-detached houses were the most common – 34 per cent each – with 24 per cent in terraced houses. Households buying with a mortgage were most likely to live in semi-detached houses outside London (35 per cent), with 29 and 28 per cent respectively buying terraced and detached houses.

Just over half of housing association tenants outside London lived in purpose built flats, with a further 42 per cent living in houses. Terraced houses were the most likely type of house for housing association tenants. While 32 per cent of housing association tenants in London lived in converted flats, the corresponding proportion for the rest of the country was only six per cent. Almost 60 per cent of private renters outside London rented houses, compared with 27 per cent in London. Correspondingly lower proportions of private renters outside London rented flats.

The position was similar for those renting with a job, with the largest proportions renting houses living outside London and flats within London. The most common type of property for households renting with a job outside London was a detached house (31 per cent), followed by a semi-detached house (26 per cent). In London the two most common types of dwelling for those renting with a job were purpose built flats (53 per cent) and terraced houses (17 per cent).

**Figure 5.9 Percentage of local authority tenants living in terraced houses, Greater London 1991**

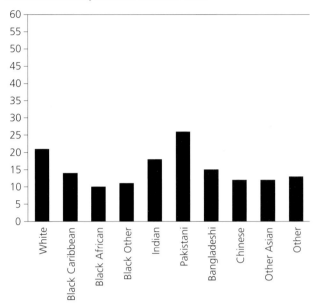

*Source: 1991 Census, LRC Commissioned Table LRCT11*

**Figure 5.10 Percentage of households buying with a mortgage living in terraced houses, Greater London 1991**

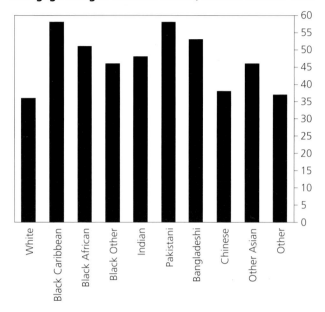

*Source: 1991 Census, LRC Commissioned Table LRCT11*

## Dwelling type by ethnic group and tenure in London

The relatively higher rates of home ownership for Indian and Pakistani groups (30 and 10 per cent more than for the White group) and the relatively low rates of home ownership for Black African and Bangladeshi groups (half or less than the corresponding rate for the White group) were explored earlier, as were the concentrations of some other ethnic minority groups in local authority and housing association property. These factors give some clues to the differences between ethnic groups within tenures.

There were relatively more Pakistani and Indian local authority tenants living in detached houses than there were White local authority tenants. The ratio of Pakistani to White tenants was 1.71 – the proportion of Pakistani local authority tenants in detached houses was 70 per cent more than White local authority tenants in detached houses. The ratios for all other ethnic groups were less than one, showing that they were relatively less likely to live in detached houses than White local authority tenants. The lowest ratio was for the Black

Other group, at 0.52. In Great Britain as a whole Pakistani local authority tenants were the only ethnic group to have a ratio above one, and the smallest ratio was 0.4 for all Black groups.

All ethnic minority local authority tenants were less likely than White local authority tenants to live in semi-detached houses, although the ratios for Pakistani and Indian local authority tenants were 0.93 and 0.80. The same was true in Great Britain, but the ratios for Pakistani and Indian local authority tenants were lower than in London. All ethnic minority groups except Pakistani had ratios of less than one for local authority tenants living in terraced houses, both in London and Great Britain. Figure 5.9 shows the percentage of local authority tenants living in terraced houses by ethnic group.

All ethnic minority groups except Pakistani had ratios of more than one for local authority tenants living in purpose built flats. In Great Britain all groups had ratios of one or more. All ethnic minority groups had ratios of more than one for local authority tenants living in converted and not self-contained flats, except for Bangladeshi local authority tenants in converted flats. The ratios for these dwelling types were all above one outside London, and were much larger outside London, indicating a much greater disparity between ethnic minority and White local authority tenants in the rest of Great Britain.

Indian, Pakistani and Other Asian housing association tenants were more likely to live in detached and semi-detached houses than White housing association tenants. However, all other ethnic minority groups were less likely to live in detached houses. Indian, Pakistani and Bangladeshi housing association tenants were more likely to live in terraced houses than White housing association tenants, while all other groups were less likely. Bangladeshi and Chinese were slightly more likely to live in purpose built flats than White housing association tenants, but most groups were less likely to. All groups except Pakistani, Bangladeshi and Chinese were more likely to live in converted flats than White housing association tenants. Black Caribbean and Black Others had the highest ratios, although they were not as high as in Great Britain as a whole, where Black and Other groups were three times more likely to live in converted flats than White housing association tenants.

Indian, Pakistani and Other Asian private renters were more likely to rent detached houses than White private renters. In particular the ratio for Other Asians was more than five. The same groups and Black African and Other private renters were more likely to rent semi-detached houses than White private renters. In Great Britain as a whole all ethnic minority groups were less likely to rent detached or semi-detached houses than White private renters. Most groups were more likely to rent terraced houses than White private renters, with the exception of the Black Other, Chinese, Other Asian and Other private renters.

Most ethnic minority groups in London were less likely to rent purpose built flats than White private renters, the exceptions being Bangladeshi, Chinese and Other

private renters. The opposite was true in Great Britain, where all ethnic minority groups were more likely to rent purpose built flats than White private renters. Black Caribbean and Black Other private renters were the only groups more likely than White to rent converted flats, although the ratios were only just above one. In Great Britain all Black private renters were two or three times as likely to rent converted flats as White private renters. All ethnic minority groups except Indian, Bangladeshi and Other Asian private renters were more likely to rent not self-contained flats than White private renters. In Great Britain as a whole all ethnic minority groups were more likely than White to rent not self-contained flats.

The picture for households owning outright was much more consistent. All ethnic minority groups were less likely to own detached or semi-detached houses than White households owning outright. All ethnic minority groups except Chinese were more likely to own terraced houses than White households owning outright. Black Caribbean, Indian and Pakistani households were less likely than White to own purpose built flats, while all other groups were more likely. All groups except Indian and Pakistani were more likely to own converted flats than White households owning outright.

There were similar patterns for those buying with a mortgage. All ethnic minority groups were less likely to have been buying a detached house, and most, except Indian, less likely to have been buying a semi-detached house. All ethnic minority groups were more likely to be buying a terraced house than White households, as shown in Figure 5.10.

**Economic factors**
Economic factors are a key determinant of housing tenure. The reasons for greater representation of certain ethnic minority groups are clearly related to their positions in the changing economy and labour market. Statistics from the 1991 Census allow an analysis of economic activity and inactivity by ethnic group and tenure, as well as of unemployment rates for those who

**Table 5.6 Percentage of residents economically active by tenure and ethnic group , Greater London, 1991**

| Ethnic group | All tenures | Owning outright | Owned buying | Local authority | Housing association | Private renters | Rent with a job |
|---|---|---|---|---|---|---|---|
| All groups | 64 | 42 | 79 | 49 | 54 | 69 | 76 |
| White | 63 | 40 | 80 | 47 | 51 | 70 | 77 |
| Black Caribbean | 74 | 63 | 83 | 65 | 68 | 76 | 78 |
| Black African | 66 | 55 | 76 | 62 | 65 | 64 | 70 |
| Black Other | 72 | 69 | 78 | 66 | 69 | 77 | 81 |
| Indian | 67 | 58 | 71 | 52 | 56 | 65 | 75 |
| Pakistani | 55 | 49 | 57 | 47 | 52 | 59 | 66 |
| Bangladeshi | 47 | 50 | 56 | 43 | 45 | 52 | 72 |
| Chinese | 63 | 53 | 73 | 51 | 56 | 57 | 75 |
| Other Asian | 67 | 58 | 76 | 60 | 63 | 57 | 66 |
| Other | 66 | 50 | 74 | 58 | 64 | 65 | 68 |

*Source: 1991 Census, Commissioned Table LRCT82*

were economically active. The following sections look at all these issues, and also examine the social class profiles of ethnic groups by tenure. A more detailed picture of economic issues is given in Chapter 7.

The tables which follow are based on residents and not on households, which has some implications for interpretation. Previous sections have talked about households in particular tenures and households lacking amenities or being overcrowded. The switch to residents in this section has the effect of measuring the extent of economic activity, inactivity and unemployment more accurately. It also has the effect of overstating the effect of unemployment at a household level in comparison with, for example, overcrowding. This is because larger households may have more than one person economically active, inactive, in work or unemployed, and particular ethnic minority groups tend to have larger households containing a number of adults.

**Economic activity**

Residents who were economically active in the 1991 Census were those aged 16 or over who were either in work or looking for work in the week before the Census. Those classed as economically inactive included those retired from paid work, students who were not working, and other people not in paid work because they were looking after a home or family or were permanently sick or disabled.

Just under two thirds of Greater London residents aged 16 and over were economically active, similar to the proportion in Great Britain, although the rate varied considerably by tenure and by ethnic group. Residents buying with a mortgage and renting privately, or with a job, had the highest economic activity rates while those owning outright had the lowest. Local authority and housing association tenants also had relatively low economic activity rates. Table 5.6 gives the details.

Some ethnic minority groups, especially Black Caribbean and Black Other, had higher economic activity rates than the White group. These two ethnic groups had the highest rates of economic activity in all tenures. The overall rates for Indian, Other Asian, Black African and Other groups were also higher than the rate for White residents, while Chinese had the same rate as White residents. The only ethnic minority groups with an economic activity rate lower than that of the White group were the Bangladeshi and Pakistani groups. Less than half of Bangladeshi residents aged 16 or over were economically active (47 per cent) and just over half (55 per cent) of Pakistani residents. These figures may reflect the low economic activity rates for Bangladeshi and Pakistani women and the younger age structure of these populations.

Only 40 per cent of White residents living in property that was owned outright were economically active, the lowest rate for any ethnic group. This is largely because of the much older age distribution of White residents in this tenure compared with other ethnic groups (see Chapter 7). The activity rates for Black Other and Black Caribbean residents owning outright were particularly high – 69 and 63 per cent. The rates were less than 50 per cent only for White and Pakistani residents owning outright.

Those buying with a mortgage were much more likely to be economically active, with the rates ranging from 83 per cent of Black Caribbean residents to 56 and 57 per cent of Bangladeshi and Pakistani residents buying their homes.

Economic activity rates for local authority tenants were low, with less than half economically active. Bangladeshi local authority tenants had the lowest economic activity rates – only 43 per cent were economically active. White and Pakistani local authority tenants had the next lowest rates, both had only 47 per cent economically active. Around two thirds of Black Other and Black Caribbean local authority tenants were economically active, the highest rates for any ethnic

group. The relative positions of ethnic groups were similar for housing association tenants, although the rates were slightly higher than those for local authority tenants.

These low economic activity rates among local authority and housing association tenants are at least partly related to the type of households given priority in accessing this housing. For example, lone parents, who have low economic activity rates (see Chapter 4), are more likely to live in this type of housing than most other household types.

The rates for Black Other and Black Caribbean private renters were 77 and 76 per cent, while the White group had an economic activity rate of 70 per cent. All other ethnic minority groups had lower economic activity rates, the lowest being for Bangladeshi private renters at 52 per cent. The economic activity rates for those renting with a job were, by definition, high and varied between 66 per cent of Pakistani and Other Asian residents and 81 per cent of Black Other residents renting with a job.

**Unemployment**

Economic activity is only part of the picture, because it only shows the proportion of people who were in work or looking for work. The very high unemployment rates for some ethnic minority groups show the very different labour market positions of some of these groups compared to the White group. There were also enormous differences unemployment levels between tenures.

The highest levels of unemployment were among local authority tenants, a quarter of whom were unemployed, followed by housing association tenants at 22 per cent. In comparison, owner occupiers and those renting with a job had very low unemployment rates, between six and nine per cent. The unemployment rates for White residents in these tenures were all slightly below these overall figures but maintaining the same relative positions. Table 5.7 gives the details.

**Table 5.7  Percentage of economically active residents unemployed by tenure and ethnic group , Greater London, 1991**

| Ethnic group | All tenures | Owning outright | Owned buying | Local authority | Housing association | Private renters | Rent with a job |
|---|---|---|---|---|---|---|---|
| All groups | 11 | 9 | 7 | 25 | 22 | 15 | 6 |
| White | 10 | 8 | 6 | 23 | 19 | 13 | 5 |
| Black Caribbean | 19 | 16 | 11 | 29 | 27 | 23 | 16 |
| Black African | 29 | 22 | 15 | 33 | 33 | 44 | 20 |
| Black Other | 24 | 19 | 14 | 35 | 30 | 25 | 12 |
| Indian | 12 | 12 | 10 | 27 | 23 | 19 | 5 |
| Pakistani | 24 | 21 | 18 | 41 | 29 | 39 | 11 |
| Bangladeshi | 35 | 17 | 20 | 46 | 42 | 31 | 8 |
| Chinese | 13 | 10 | 6 | 35 | 30 | 13 | 2 |
| Other Asian | 15 | 11 | 10 | 33 | 25 | 16 | 5 |
| Other | 19 | 14 | 11 | 34 | 29 | 27 | 12 |

*Source: 1991 Census, Commissioned Table LRCT82*

**Figure 5.11  Percentage of those buying with a mortgage unemployed, Greater London 1991**

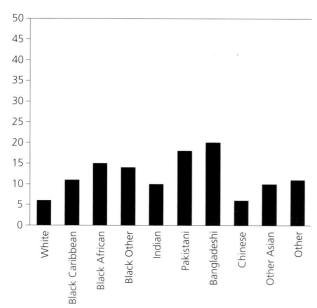

*Source: 1991 Census, LRC Commissioned Table LRCT82*

**Figure 5.12  Percentage of local authority tenants unemployed, Greater London 1991**

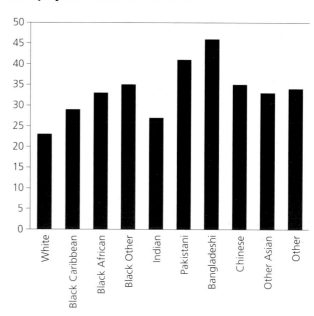

*Source: 1991 Census, LRC Commissioned Table LRCT82*

All ethnic minority groups had higher unemployment rates than White residents, although the rates for Indian, Chinese and Other Asian residents were not as high as those for other ethnic minority groups. Bangladeshi residents were the most likely to be unemployed, 35 per cent overall, and when considering the economic activity rate of 47 per cent this paints a very stark picture of the position for London's Bangladeshi population. Black African, Black Other and Pakistani residents also had very high unemployment rates, 24 to 29 per cent, compared with ten per cent of White residents.

Those renting with a job had the lowest unemployment rates, as might be expected, but 20 per cent of Black Africans in this tenure were unemployed, compared with only two per cent of Chinese residents. Owner occupiers also had relatively low unemployment rates, but still more than 20 per cent of Black Africans and Pakistanis owning outright, and Bangladeshis buying with a mortgage, were unemployed. Black African private renters had the highest unemployment rates, with 44 per cent out of work, followed by 39 per cent of Pakistani and 31 per cent of Bangladeshi residents renting privately.

Residents in social housing, local authority and housing association property, had by far the highest unemployment rates. Almost half of Bangladeshi local authority tenants were unemployed, 46 per cent, as well as 41 per cent of Pakistani local authority tenants. These figures compare with 23 per cent of White local authority tenants unemployed. Local authority tenants of all ethnic minority groups had higher unemployment rates than White local authority tenants. Indian residents had the lowest rates among ethnic minority groups, with 27 per cent of Indian local authority tenants unemployed. Bangladeshi and Black African housing association tenants had the highest rates, with 42 and 33 per cent unemployed, although these figures were slightly lower than those for local authority tenants in the same ethnic groups.

**Social class by ethnic group and tenure**

For all residents who either had a job or had been working in the last ten years, social class is determined by the person's occupation as well as their employment status. Social class I is defined as professional occupations; social class II is managerial and technical occupations; social class III(N) covers skilled non-manual occupations; social class III(M) is skilled manual occupations; social class IV is semi-skilled occupations and social class V is unskilled occupations. Members of the armed forces and those with inadequately described occupations are not allocated to a social class.

Social class varies considerably between different ethnic groups as detailed in Chapter 7. It also varies for ethnic groups in each tenure. Social class is probably also a factor which determines the tenure that people are in because it is directly linked with the income a person is likely to earn.

In general, owner occupiers and private renters had a much higher social profile than those in social housing, local authority and housing association accommodation. Some of the tenure and social class differences may also be affected by the different age distributions of ethnic minority groups.

White residents buying with a mortgage or renting privately had the highest social profile with large proportions in social classes I and II. The distributions for White residents in local authority and housing association housing were similar, with very low proportions in social class I and relatively high proportions in all manual social classes. For White residents renting with a job there were relatively large proportions in social classes II and IV.

The proportion of Black Caribbean residents in social class I was highest for those renting with a job (five per cent) and lowest, at less than 0.5 per cent, for local authority tenants. Social class III(M) contained the largest proportion of Black Caribbeans owning outright,

**Table 5.8 Percentage of residents in social class I by tenure and ethnic group , Greater London, 1991**

| Ethnic group | All tenures | Owning outright | Owned buying | Local authority | Housing association | Private renters | Rent with a job |
|---|---|---|---|---|---|---|---|
| All groups | 7 | 6 | 8 | 1 | 2 | 9 | 7 |
| White | 7 | 6 | 8 | 1 | 2 | 9 | 7 |
| Black Caribbean | 2 | 1 | 2 | 0 | 2 | 3 | 5 |
| Black African | 7 | 13 | 8 | 4 | 4 | 9 | 20 |
| Black Other | 3 | 2 | 4 | 1 | 2 | 7 | - |
| Indian | 9 | 8 | 9 | 3 | 6 | 10 | 7 |
| Pakistani | 7 | 8 | 8 | 2 | 2 | 8 | - |
| Bangladeshi | 4 | 7 | 8 | 1 | 3 | 4 | - |
| Chinese | 15 | 17 | 15 | 2 | 10 | 29 | 2 |
| Other Asian | 7 | 8 | 9 | 2 | 5 | 6 | 6 |
| Other | 9 | 11 | 10 | 2 | 5 | 10 | 32 |

*Source: 1991 Census, Commissioned Table LRCT83*

while social class II was the largest class for those buying with a mortgage. As with White residents, Black Caribbeans renting with a job were most likely to be in social classes II and IV.

Black African residents were much more likely than Black Caribbeans to be in social class I, particularly those renting with a job, 20 per cent of whom were in this social class. Black Others were unusual in that the pattern of social classes was the same for all tenures except private renters, although the proportions differed slightly. Black Others renting privately were most likely to be in social class II, unlike other tenures in which they were most likely to be in social class III(N). The numbers of Black Others renting with a job were small.

There were relatively large proportions of Indian owner occupiers and private renters in social class I, and for these tenures social classes II and III(N) were the most common. There was also a large proportion of Indian residents in local authority and housing association accommodation in social class IV. Almost half of Indian residents renting with a job were in social class II.
In most tenures social class III(N) accounted for the largest proportion of Pakistani residents, the exception was those buying with a mortgage who were most likely to be in social class II.

Bangladeshi residents were particularly concentrated in social class IV, especially Bangladeshi local authority tenants. Bangladeshis owning their property outright were most likely to be in social class II but this was not the case for those buying their property, who were concentrated in social classes II, III(N) and IV. Chinese residents, as Chapter 7 shows, had a relatively high social profile, with large proportions in social class I. This was especially true of Chinese private renters, 29 per cent of whom were in social class I. For owner occupiers social classes II, III(N) and I were the most common, but for Chinese local authority tenants, social class III(M) was most common.

**Table 5.9 Percentage of residents in social class IV by tenure and ethnic group , Greater London, 1991**

| Ethnic group | All tenures | Owning outright | Owned buying | Local authority | Housing association | Private renters | Rent with a job |
|---|---|---|---|---|---|---|---|
| All groups | 12 | 12 | 9 | 22 | 17 | 10 | 18 |
| White | 11 | 11 | 8 | 22 | 17 | 9 | 19 |
| Black Caribbean | 17 | 20 | 15 | 21 | 16 | 14 | 23 |
| Black African | 17 | 8 | 15 | 19 | 18 | 19 | 9 |
| Black Other | 12 | 14 | 11 | 16 | 8 | 11 | - |
| Indian | 16 | 15 | 15 | 23 | 20 | 13 | 8 |
| Pakistani | 16 | 16 | 15 | 23 | 13 | 14 | - |
| Bangladeshi | 30 | 16 | 19 | 43 | 28 | 22 | - |
| Chinese | 9 | 5 | 8 | 19 | 14 | 10 | 8 |
| Other Asian | 14 | 12 | 13 | 30 | 21 | 7 | 13 |
| Other | 10 | 9 | 8 | 17 | 15 | 10 | 7 |

*Source: 1991 Census, Commissioned Table LRCT83*

The social class distributions for Other Asian residents were similar to those of Indian residents in many respects, but the major differences were the larger proportion of Other Asian local authority tenants in social class IV and the very large proportion of Other Asian private renters in social class II. As for Indian residents, a large proportion of Other Asians renting with a job were in social class II.

Residents in Other groups were most like to be in social classes II and III(N), especially owner occupiers and private renters. Other groups in local authority accommodation had the usual low proportions in social classes I and II, and correspondingly larger proportions in social classes III(M), IV and V. Other groups in housing association property, though, were most likely to be in social class II, the only ethnic group for which this was the case. In addition, Other groups renting with a job were most likely to be in social class I, followed by II, a very unusual distribution. Figures 5.13 and 5.14 illustrate some of the different social class distributions.

**Figure 5.13  Social class of local authority tenants in selected ethnic groups, Greater London, 1991**

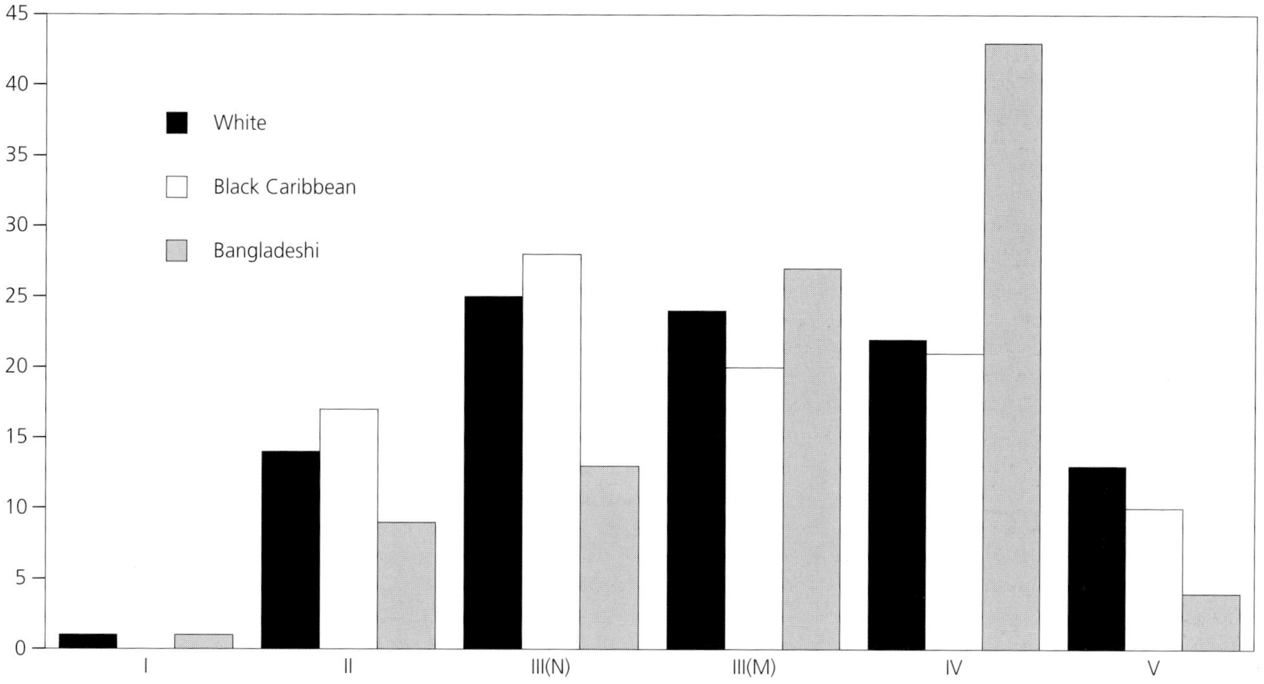

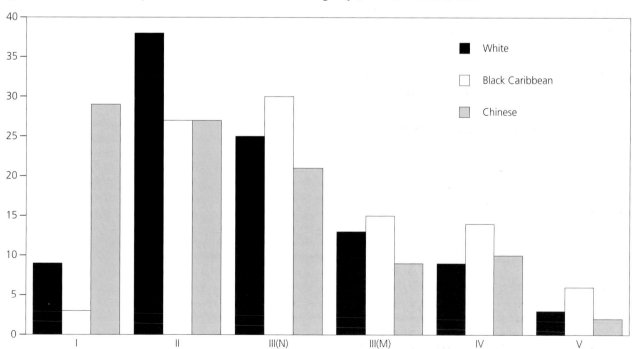

Source: 1991 Census, LRC Commissioned Table LRCT83

**Figure 5.14  Social class of private renters in selected ethnic groups, Greater London, 1991**

Source: 1991 Census, LRC Commissioned Table LRCT83

# Chapter 6
# Health

# Health

## Introduction

The 1991 Census included for the first time a question on limiting long-term illness. Respondents were asked whether they had any long-term illness, health problem or handicap which limited their daily activities or the work they could do. Those who answered yes to this question were described as having a limiting long-term illness in the Census output. Although this is a subjective question, and different people in the same state of health may have given different responses, it is still a useful indicator of people's perceptions of their situation and thus their need for a variety of services. Comparison with data from the OPCS Disability Surveys of 1985/86, suggests that this is a wider group than just those with a disability.

## Rates of limiting long term illness

A breakdown of the data on people with a limiting long-term illness by ethnic group is only available for residents in households, not for residents in communal establishments, who are a much smaller group of people, but who have much higher rates of limiting long-term illness. A total of 742,870 people in households were reported to have a limiting long-term

illness in London in 1991 – 11 per cent of the total household population. Table 6.1 shows the breakdown by ethnic group, with the rate giving the percentage of all residents in that group who had a limiting long-term illness.

This table shows that the White population had the highest proportion of residents with a limiting long-term illness and that overall more women than men had a limiting long-term illness. What this conceals is the variation by age, with small proportions below age 35 but much higher rates of limiting long-term illness among older age groups. It also hides the fact that generally rates were higher among men than among women of the same age, as shown in Figure 6.1.

As Chapter 2 indicates, most of the ethnic minority groups have a younger age structure than the White population, so it is not surprising that a higher proportion of White residents had a limiting long-term illness. In order to make comparisons, it is therefore necessary to look at the prevalence rates for each age group. This is done by comparing the proportion of residents in an age group with a limiting long-term

**Table 6.1 Total numbers and rates of people with limiting long-term illness in households in Greater London, by ethnic group**

|  | Total number | | | Overall rate as % | | |
|---|---|---|---|---|---|---|
|  | **Males** | **Females** | **Total** | **Males** | **Females** | **Total** |
| White | 279,694 | 355,331 | 635,025 | 11 | 13 | 12 |
| Black Caribbean | 13,965 | 17,235 | 31,200 | 11 | 11 | 11 |
| Black African | 3,915 | 4,602 | 8,517 | 5` | 6 | 5 |
| Black Other | 2,387 | 2,523 | 4,910 | 6 | 6 | 6 |
| Indian | 14,519 | 15,962 | 30,481 | 8 | 9 | 9 |
| Pakistani | 4,022 | 3,535 | 7,557 | 9 | 8 | 9 |
| Bangladeshi | 4,690 | 2,912 | 7,602 | 11 | 7 | 9 |
| Chinese | 1,192 | 1,268 | 2,460 | 4 | 4 | 4 |
| Other Asian | 2,921 | 3,370 | 6,291 | 5 | 6 | 6 |
| Other groups | 4,297 | 4,530 | 8,827 | 7 | 8 | 7 |
| All ethnic groups | 331,602 | 411,268 | 742,870 | 10 | 12 | 11 |

*Source: 1991 Census, LRC Commissioned Table LRCT1*

**Figure 6.1 Percentage of household residents with a limiting long-term illness by age and gender**

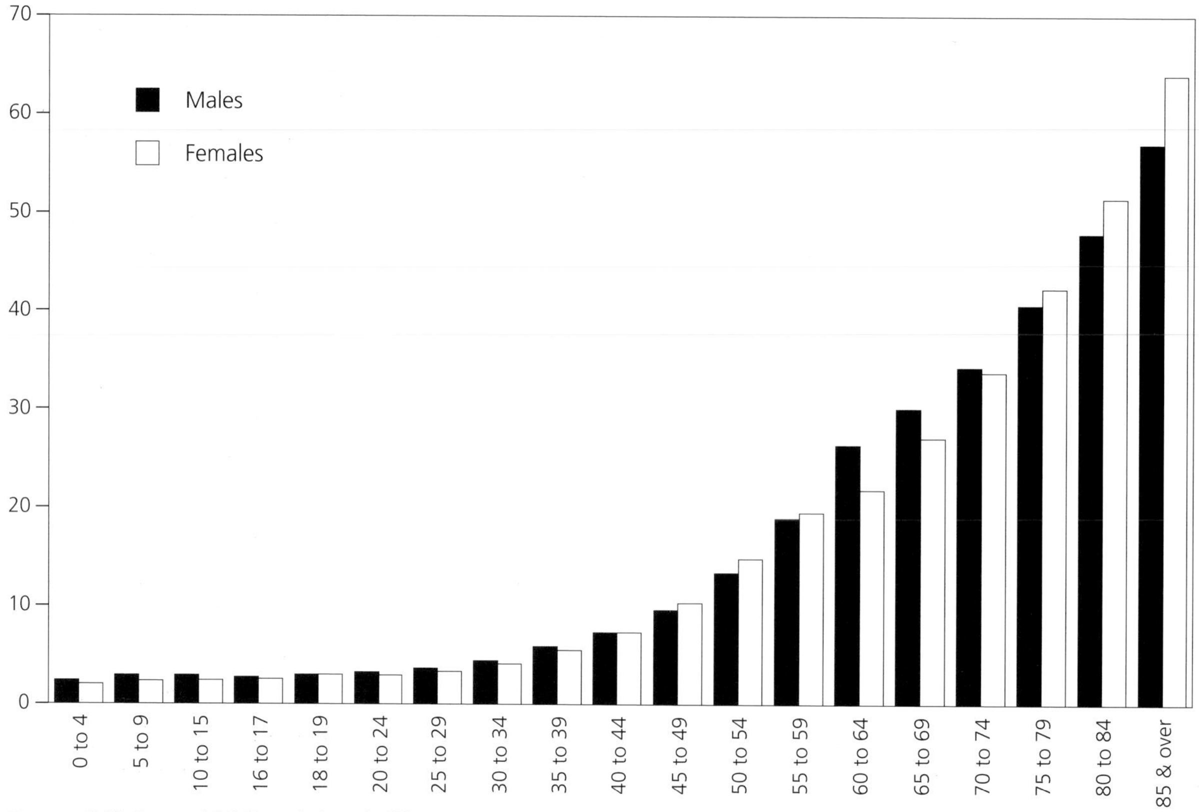

*Source: 1991 Census, LRC Commissioned Table LRCT1*

illness from each ethnic minority group to the proportion of White residents in the same age group with a limiting long-term illness. Thus a ratio of 1.0 shows the same rate of limiting long-term illness as among the White (majority) population, a ratio of less than 1.0 shows a lower rate of limiting long-term illness, while a ratio of more than 1.0 shows a higher rate than among White residents for that age group.

### Children and young people (aged under 18)

Table 6.2 gives the ratios of the prevalence rates of males and females under 18 for each ethnic group compared to the White group. This shows that there were some differences, but most ratios were fairly close to 1.0. The ratios were highest for Black Other males, who were 60 per cent more likely than White males to have a limiting long-term illness, and lowest among Chinese females who were 40 per cent less likely than White females to have a limiting long-term illness.

**Table 6.2 Ratio of rates of limiting long-term illness for ages 0-17**

|  | Male | Female | Both |
|---|---|---|---|
| White | 1.0 | 1.0 | 1.0 |
| Black Caribbean | 1.5 | 1.4 | 1.5 |
| Black African | 1.3 | 1.4 | 1.3 |
| Black other | 1.6 | 1.5 | 1.5 |
| Indian | 0.9 | 0.8 | 0.9 |
| Pakistani | 1.2 | 1.2 | 1.2 |
| Bangladeshi | 1.2 | 1.2 | 1.2 |
| Chinese | 0.7 | 0.6 | 0.6 |
| Other Asian | 1.0 | 0.8 | 0.9 |
| Other groups | 1.2 | 1.3 | 1.3 |
|  |  |  |  |
| All ethnic groups | 1.1 | 1.1 | 1.1 |

*Source: 1991 Census, LRC Commissioned Table LRCT1*

The figures in Table 6.2 show the higher rates among the Black groups, whereas Indians and particularly Chinese were less likely than White residents in this age range to have a limiting long-term illness. Within this broad age group these characteristics generally hold true for smaller age groups, although the extent varies. For example, among Chinese children aged under five the prevalence rates were only half those of the White group, whereas boys from the Black Caribbean and Black Other groups were 70 per cent more likely than White boys aged under five to have a limiting long-term illness.

The rates were fairly similar for each of the 5-9, 10-15 and 16-17 age groups within each ethnic group, and remained a very small proportion of the total. The highest proportions were among Black Other males aged 5-9 and 10-14, with just over four per cent of all those resident in households in London having a limiting long-term illness. For all these age groups and for all ethnic groups, the percentage of males with a limiting long-term illness was higher than the percentage of females except in the 16-17 age group, where Black Africans and Bangladeshis had higher rates among young women than men.

For those under the age of 16 the overall rates of limiting long-term illness were higher in London than in the rest of Great Britain. However, this was not consistent between age groups or between ethnic groups. Among the youngest age group (under five), White children in London were slightly more likely than those in the rest of Great Britain to have a limiting long-term illness, but the biggest differences were among Black Africans and Pakistanis. Black African boys and girls aged under five living in Great Britain outside London were more than three times as likely as those living in London to have a limiting long-term illness. The rates among Pakistanis of this age were a little higher outside London, whereas among Bangladeshi and Other Asian boys the rates were marginally higher in London.

Many of the differences between London and the rest of Great Britain among the under five age group were also apparent at older ages. For Black Africans in all age groups under 18 the proportions with a limiting long-term illness outside London were substantially higher than among those living in the capital. Other differences were relatively small, with slightly higher rates among both Pakistanis and Black Caribbeans from several age/gender groups outside London.

## Young adults (aged 18-29)

Broadly, the pattern of prevalence among the 18-29 age range was similar to the pattern among the younger age groups, with very low proportions among the Chinese group, at under half the White rates. The highest rates in this age range were for the Black Other group. Table 6.3 shows that the rates among Black Caribbeans were also well above those for the White group, while Black Africans, Bangladeshis and the Other category all had slightly higher prevalence rates than the White group. As for the younger age range, the rates among Indians and Other Asians were a little lower than among the White group.

**Table 6.3 Ratio of rates of limiting long-term illness for ages 18-29**

|  | Male | Female | Both |
| --- | --- | --- | --- |
| White | 1.0 | 1.0 | 1.0 |
| Black Caribbean | 1.6 | 1.5 | 1.5 |
| Black African | 1.2 | 1.3 | 1.2 |
| Black Other | 1.8 | 1.8 | 1.8 |
| Indian | 0.8 | 0.9 | 0.9 |
| Pakistani | 1.0 | 1.2 | 1.1 |
| Bangladeshi | 1.3 | 1.3 | 1.3 |
| Chinese | 0.4 | 0.5 | 0.5 |
| Other Asian | 0.7 | 0.8 | 0.8 |
| Other groups | 1.3 | 1.4 | 1.4 |
| | | | |
| All ethnic groups | 1.0 | 1.0 | 1.0 |

*Source: 1991 Census, LRC Commissioned Table LRCT1*

Again, there was some variation within this age group. Among 18-19 year olds, the highest rate of limiting long-term illness was among Black African men, while for the 20-24 and 25-29 age groups the highest rates were among the Black Other group. Both men and women in the Black Other category aged 25-29 were twice as likely to have a limiting long-term illness as White residents of the same age. In contrast, White men and women aged 18-19 were around three times as likely as Chinese household residents in London to have a limiting long-term illness. For most groups, the rates among men were higher than among women. The most significant exception was among Pakistanis in the 25-29 age group.

Comparisons of the rates for London with those for the rest of Great Britain show that for most age, gender and ethnic groups in the 18-29 age range the rates of limiting long-term illness were higher outside London. The only notable exceptions were for Bangladeshi women aged 20-24 and men aged 25-29 and for Black Other men and women aged 25-29. Again, these differences were small compared to the substantially higher rates among Black Africans in all these age groups outside London.

### Main working age adults (aged 30-49)

The pattern of prevalence rates among the 30-49 age range was somewhat different to that seen for the younger age groups. As Table 6.4 shows, Pakistanis and Bangladeshis had the highest rates of limiting long-term illness, while the lowest rates were still among the Chinese group, although the proportion of Black African men in this age range with a limiting long-term illness was only just above that among Chinese men.

Overall, the proportions of men and women in this age range with a limiting long-term illness were the same and were still fairly low, at under seven per cent. For most ethnic minority groups, however, the proportion was higher among women than men, whereas for the White group this position was reversed. Another difference from the younger age ranges is that in those

**Table 6.4 Ratio of rates of limiting long-term illness for ages 30-49**

|  | Male | Female | Both |
|---|---|---|---|
| White | 1.0 | 1.0 | 1.0 |
| Black Caribbean | 1.1 | 1.3 | 1.2 |
| Black African | 0.6 | 1.1 | 0.9 |
| Black other | 1.2 | 1.4 | 1.3 |
| Indian | 1.0 | 1.2 | 1.1 |
| Pakistani | 1.4 | 1.8 | 1.6 |
| Bangladeshi | 1.8 | 2.1 | 2.0 |
| Chinese | 0.5 | 0.5 | 0.5 |
| Other Asian | 0.7 | 0.8 | 0.7 |
| Other groups | 1.2 | 1.3 | 1.3 |
|  |  |  |  |
| All ethnic groups | 1.0 | 1.0 | 1.0 |

*Source: 1991 Census, LRC Commissioned Table LRCT1*

groups the rates were fairly static across the whole of the age range, whereas within the 30-49 age range, there is evidence of an increase with age.

The highest rate of limiting long-term illness in this age range was among Bangladeshi men aged 45-49, at more than one in five, although the rates among Bangladeshi and Pakistani women in this age group were also close to one in five. Whereas the rates among Bangladeshis were generally close to or just a little above White rates in the 18-29 age groups, from ages 30-49 the Bangladeshi rates were higher than for any other group, both for men and women. The rates were more than twice those of the White group for some ages – both men and women aged 35-39, women aged 40-44 and men and women aged 45-49. The rates among Pakistanis were also higher for these ages, up to twice the White rate among women aged 40-49. In this age range the rates among Indians also moved slightly higher than the White rates for the 40 - 49 age groups, whereas the rates among the Black Other group were decreasing in relation to White. Rates among Black Caribbeans were only a little above those for the White group, while rates of limiting long-term illness among

Black Africans were below those of the White group for men, but above for women. As for the younger age groups, the rates among the Other Asian group were generally a little lower than for the White group, whereas the rates among residents in the Other ethnic groups category were a little higher.

In comparing rates of limiting long-term illness in London with the rest of Great Britain, some similar patterns emerge to those for the younger age groups, The rates among Black Africans were consistently substantially higher outside London. The rates among Pakistanis were also a little higher outside London for nearly all age/gender groups. In contrast the rates among Bangladeshis were higher inside London for most age/gender groups. The pattern was also different to that seen for the younger age groups.In this age range, the proportions of Indians with a limiting long-term illness were a little higher outside London for many age/gender groups, but for those in the Other ethnic groups category, the rates were a little higher inside London.

## Older working age adults (aged 50-64)

In younger age groups, the proportions of residents with a limiting long-term illness were generally quite low, but in this age range there is the start of a dramatic increase in the rates of limiting long-term illness. Altogether, nearly one in five Londoners aged 50-64 had a limiting long-term illness. The pattern of rates in this age range builds on that seen for 30-49 age range. The highest rates among were among Bangladeshis and Pakistanis, the lowest among Chinese. However, the rate among the White group was only a little higher than among the Chinese, with all other ethnic minority groups having higher rates than the White group, as shown in Table 6.5. For most ethnic groups (all except White, Bangladeshi and Chinese) the rates were higher among women than men over this age range as a whole, although because the White group was much bigger than other groups, the proportion of men with a limiting long-term illness was higher than the proportion of women overall.

**Table 6.5 Ratio of rates of limiting long-term illness for ages 50-64**

|  | Male | Female | Both |
|---|---|---|---|
| White | 1.0 | 1.0 | 1.0 |
| Black Caribbean | 1.1 | 1.6 | 1.3 |
| Black African | 0.9 | 1.3 | 1.0 |
| Black Other | 1.4 | 1.7 | 1.5 |
| Indian | 1.3 | 1.8 | 1.5 |
| Pakistani | 1.5 | 2.0 | 1.7 |
| Bangladeshi | 2.2 | 1.8 | 2.1 |
| Chinese | 0.9 | 0.9 | 0.9 |
| Other Asian | 0.9 | 1.1 | 1.0 |
| Other groups | 1.1 | 1.4 | 1.2 |
|  |  |  |  |
| All ethnic groups | 1.0 | 1.1 | 1.1 |

*Source: 1991 Census, LRC Commissioned Table LRCT1*

The patterns for ethnic groups within this age range were similar to those seen for the age range as a whole. All ethnic groups showed a significant increase in the rates of limiting long-term illness in both men and women across the three five-year age bands making up this range. The proportion of men with a limiting long-term illness was more than twice as high in the 60-64 age group as in the 50-54 age group. Nearly half of Bangladeshi and Pakistani men aged 60-64 and 40 per cent of Pakistani women in this age group had a limiting long-term illness. The rates among the White group increased faster than among the Bangladeshi group so that while the Bangladeshi rates were over twice those of the White group in the 50-54 age group, only Pakistani women had a rate double White women in the 60-64 age group. The highest rate of increase was among the Chinese group, so that by the 60-64 age group, the rates were almost as high as among the White group.

In the 50-64 age range, the rates of limiting long-term illness for each ethnic group in London were nearly always lower than for the same group in the rest of Great Britain. Again Black African prevalence rates showed the greatest difference, for example 17 per cent of Black African men aged 50-54 in London reported a limiting long-term illness, compared with 27 per cent of those living elsewhere in Britain. There were also substantial differences for some other groups. White men and women in all age groups 50-64 had higher rates of limiting long-term illness outside London. There were only a few groups for which the rates were higher in London than outside.

## Older people (aged 65 and over)

As Figure 6.1 shows, the rates for this age group are much higher than for younger age groups and there is a clear increase with age across this range. This is not surprising, as the Census question said to include problems due to old age. Nearly a third of Londoners in the 65-74 age range had a limiting long-term illness, rising to just over half of those aged 85 and over. These proportions were marginally lower than the proportions among these age groups in the rest of Great Britain. In age bands at the younger end of this range, that is the 65-69 and 70-74 age groups, the proportion of men with a limiting long-term illness was higher than the proportion of women. For the older age groups, this was reversed. This is probably because of the shorter life expectancy of men, so that in each five year age band there were far more women than men at the older end of each group.

Taken across this age range as a whole, all ethnic minority groups had similar proportions of residents with a limiting long-term illness to the White group. However, when looking at narrower age bands, some differences are apparent. As for the 50-64 age range, Bangladeshis and Pakistanis were most likely to have a limiting long-term illness in the 65-74 age group, although the differences were less marked than for the younger age group. Figures for this age range need to be treated with caution because the numbers of people aged 65 and over were quite small for all ethnic minority groups, and for the older age groups for some

**Table 6.6 Ratio of rates of limiting long-term illness for ages 65 and over**

|  | Male | Female | Both |
|---|---|---|---|
| White | 1.0 | 1.0 | 1.0 |
| Black Caribbean | 1.0 | 1.2 | 1.1 |
| Black African | 0.9 | 1.0 | 0.9 |
| Black other | 1.0 | 1.1 | 1.0 |
| Indian | 1.1 | 1.2 | 1.2 |
| Pakistani | 1.2 | 1.3 | 1.2 |
| Bangladeshi | 1.2 | 0.9 | 1.0 |
| Chinese | 0.8 | 0.9 | 0.8 |
| Other Asian | 1.0 | 1.0 | 1.0 |
| Other groups | 1.0 | 1.1 | 1.1 |
|  |  |  |  |
| All ethnic groups | 1.0 | 1.0 | 1.0 |

Source: 1991 Census, LRC Commissioned Table LRCT1

ethnic groups were extremely small. The younger age structure of ethnic minority groups within each of the older age bands also leads to lower rates of limiting long-term illness for each five year age group. The proportions of residents aged 85 and over with a limiting long-term illness were smaller for all ethnic minority groups than for the White group, although for some groups, such as Chinese women, the proportions were very close.

Throughout this age range, as for the younger age groups, Black Africans living outside London had higher rates of limiting long-term illness than those living in the capital, although the differences for women at some ages were small. Generally the proportions with a limiting long-term illness were quite similar inside and outside London within this age range. It is interesting to note that there were more groups with higher rates inside London among the 85 and over age group than for younger age groups, although the actual numbers involved in most cases were small.

# Chapter 7
## Employment

# Employment

## Introduction

There are huge differences in the employment patterns of people from different ethnic groups in London. The numbers in full and part-time employment, the proportion who are unemployed, the age at which people leave full-time education, the age at which they retire, the proportions who are unable to work due to disability or illness and the numbers who are looking after the home or family, all show widely varying patterns between ethnic groups. However, this is still only part of the picture. The levels of qualifications, the occupations followed, the social class and the industries in which they work also reveal marked differences between London's ethnic groups.

This chapter explores some of these differences through the 1991 Census, which provides a wealth of information on employment issues by taking a snapshot of information on all London's residents. This allows comparisons between ethnic groups for all residents aged 16 and over.

**Figure 7.1 Economic activity rates for men and women by ethnic group**

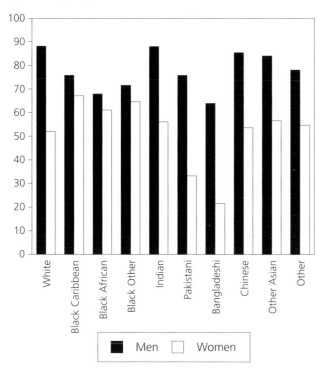

Source: 1991 Census, LRC Commissioned Table LRCT15

## Economically active

The primary distinction for economic position of people is whether they are economically active or economically inactive. Economically active means people are either in employment or unemployed and looking for work. The economically inactive group includes many, but not all, students, people who are retired from paid work or permanently sick and other inactive residents. This last category is mainly made up of people looking after a home or family, but also includes people of independent means.

Altogether, just under two thirds of Londoners aged 16 and over were economically active in 1991. Not surprisingly, the proportions were different for men and women, with three quarters of men either working or looking for work, compared to just over half of women. These proportions varied across ethnic groups, but were consistently higher for men than for women. The variation between ethnic groups was much greater for women than for men, ranging from less than a quarter of Bangladeshi women and a third of Pakistani women to over two thirds of Black Caribbean women. Among men the range was from just over 70 per cent of Black African and Bangladeshi men to just over 80 per cent of Black Caribbean and Black Other men. Such differences between the patterns for men and women are apparent in all aspects of employment, so throughout this chapter they are considered separately.

Another key factor in economic position is age. Well over 90 per cent of men in all age groups between 25 and 49 were economically active. For women there were two peaks in economic activity, reaching over 70 per cent for the 20-29 and 40-49 age groups. The substantial differences between ethnic groups are explored in more detail later in this chapter.

## Economically inactive

As Figures 7.2 and 7.3 illustrate, the extent to which people are classified in each of the economically inactive categories varies considerably with age. As expected, many younger adults were economically inactive

**Figure 7.2 Economically inactive men by age**

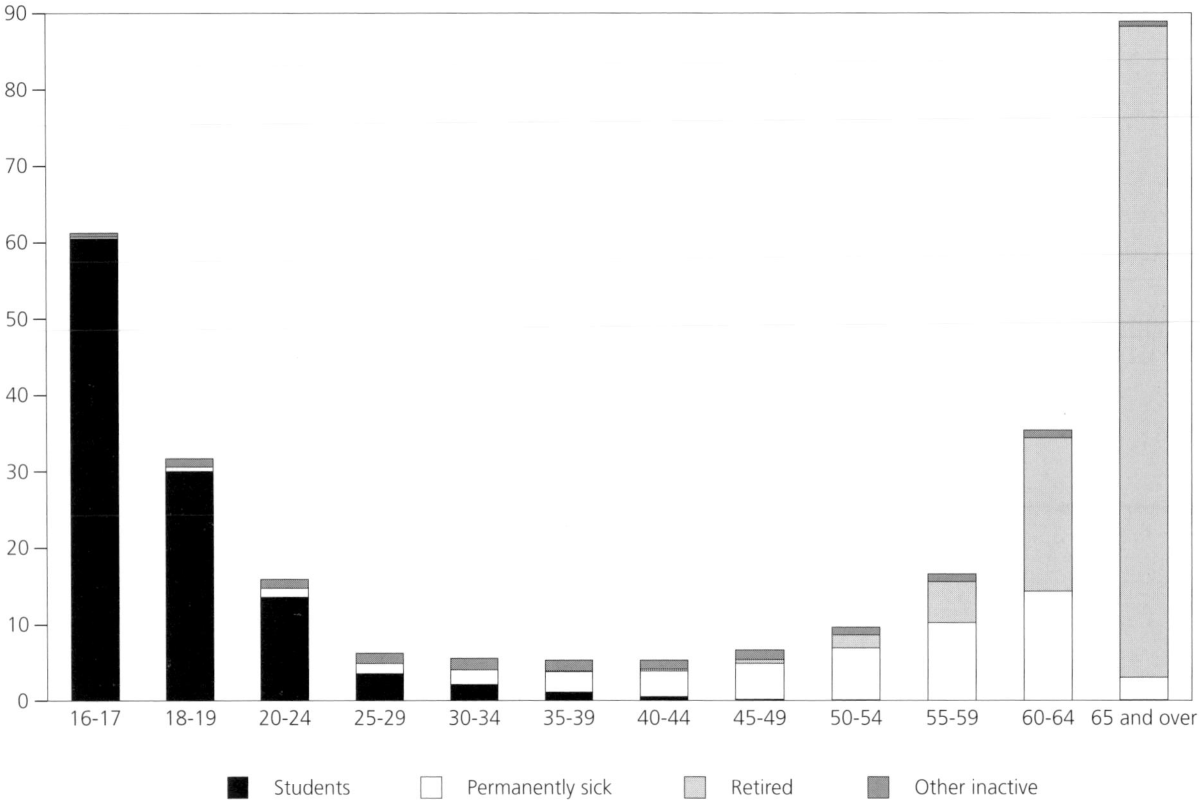

Source: 1991 Census, LRC Commissioned Table LRCT15

students, but by the age of 30 these proportions were very small. What these figures do show is that more young women stay on in education up to age 18 than young men, whereas the proportion of young women in full-time education after age 20 was lower.

At the other end of the age spectrum, the retired category was, of course, the most significant. Many women aged 60 and over were, however, included in the 'other economically inactive' category, probably as they had spent relatively little of their adult lives in employment and therefore were not retired from paid work. Nearly a third of women aged 30-34 were included in this category.

*White, Black Caribbean and Black Other*
Among the most notable features of each of these three ethnic categories were the high economic activity rates for both men and women, particularly among Black

Caribbean women. These high rates were especially apparent for the younger age groups, as the numbers of economically inactive students were lower than among other ethnic groups. Even with the relatively high proportions of young White students working part-time, White Londoners aged under 20 were less likely to be in full-time education than any other ethnic group. In the 20-24 age group, the proportion of full-time students was lowest among Black Caribbeans.

Retirement rates were also high for these three ethnic groups because of the large numbers who had been in work at younger ages, but it is quite clear that early retirement was most common among White men.

*Black African, Indian, Chinese and Other Asian*
High proportions of both male and female economically inactive students were a feature of each of these ethnic groups. All had high rates up to age 24, but

**Figure 7.3 Economically inactive women by age**

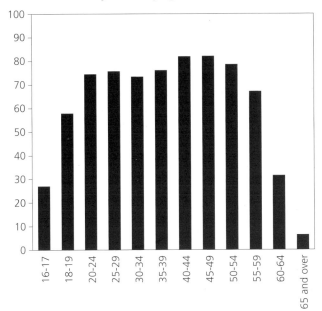

Source: 1991 Census, LRC Commissioned Table LRCT15

**Figure 7.4 Percentage of Black Caribbean women who were economically active by age**

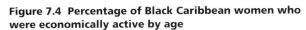

Source: 1991 Census, LRC Commissioned Table LRCT15

for Chinese people and particularly for the Black African, these high rates continued to older age groups, with around one in five Black African men aged 25-34 in this economic category.

A relatively high percentage of Black African men, particularly under age 44 were also in the other economically inactive category, although this was still lower than for women in this category from any ethnic group. This lead to low economic activity rates for Black African men. In contrast, Indian, Chinese and Other Asian men had high economic activity rates between finishing education and retiring, at well over 90 per cent for most ages. Economic activity rates among Indian women were also high up to age 44, whereas in the 45 and over age range a large proportion were looking after the home and family. The difference in economic activity rates of Indian women aged under 45 and over 45 may be related to the lifestage at which

**Figure 7.5 Percentage of Black African men who were economically inactive students by age**

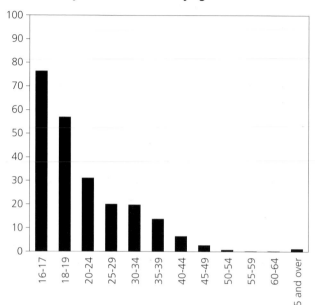

*Source: 1991 Census, LRC Commissioned Table LRCT15*

these women came to Britain. Many women aged 45 and over would have come to Britain in their late teenage years or early twenties and so the culture in which they grew up was one which did not expect women to have a job, whereas many of the younger women would have spent at least part of their youth in

Britain and so their expectations of life and work would have been different.

In contrast to Indian women, high economic activity rates among Indian men continued up to state retirement age, while early retirement was relatively common among Chinese men and women, but few Other Asians were retired even after state retirement age.

*Pakistani and Bangladeshi*

One of the most distinctive features in the economic profiles of these communities is the large number of women in the other economically inactive category, leading to very low economic activity rates among women from both ethnic groups. Fewer than one in five Bangladeshi women in most of the 25-59 age range were economically active. The proportions of Bangladeshi men in the other economically inactive category were also high compared to other ethnic groups, but at under five per cent remained well below those for women from any ethnic group.

Both the Pakistani and Bangladeshi ethnic groups had

**Figure 7.6 Percentage of Indian men who were economically active by age**

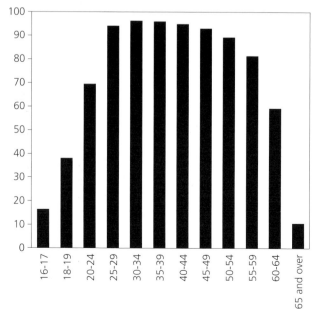

*Source: 1991 Census, LRC Commissioned Table LRCT15*

**Figure 7.7 Percentage of Bangladeshi women in the other economically inactive category by age**

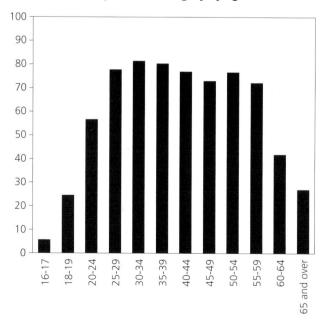

*Source: 1991 Census, LRC Commissioned Table LRCT15*

**Figure 7.8 Percentage of Pakistani men who were permanently sick by age**

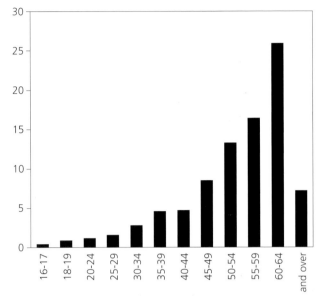

*Source: 1991 Census, LRC Commissioned Table LRCT15*

high proportions in the permanently sick category, particularly for men, ranging up to almost 30 per cent of Bangladeshi men aged 55-64. One distinction between these ethnic groups was in the proportion of economically inactive students. The proportion of young Pakistanis still in full-time education was quite high – only a little below the rates among Indian Londoners, whereas the proportions among young Bangladeshis were much lower, but still higher than among White, Black Caribbean and Black Other residents.

**Unemployment**

There were clear differences in the proportions of ethnic groups who were unemployed at the time of the 1991 Census. Overall, London's White residents were least likely to be unemployed (one in ten economically active residents). The highest rates of unemployment were among the Bangladeshis (35 per cent overall). Again, there were marked differences by age and gender.

For most ethnic groups, unemployment was highest among 16-17 year olds and then decreased with age, reaching the lowest levels for the 40-49 age group. Unemployment rates were slightly higher for older age

groups up to state retirement age. These patterns were apparent for both men and women, although the rates tended to be lower among women.

Generally, high unemployment rates among economically active residents coincided with high proportions of economically inactive residents. At the same time, groups with high economic activity rates tended to have lower unemployment rates. For example, the group with the lowest unemployment rates in the 25-44 age groups was Indian men, which also had some of the highest economic activity rates. In fact, Indian women, as well as men were among those least likely to be unemployed at all ages. For most other age/gender groups, the lowest unemployment rates were among White residents.

At the opposite end of the scale were Bangladeshis, whose economic activity rates were low, while unemployment rates were exceptionally high - more than one in three economically active Bangladeshis in most age groups were unemployed. This rose to more than half of some age groups. Just 30 per cent of

**Figure 7.9 Percentage of 20-24 year olds unemployed by ethnic group and gender**

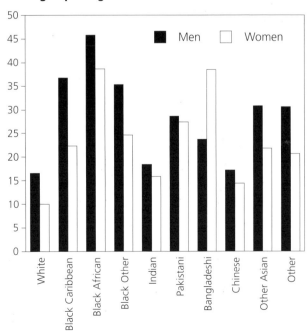

*Source: 1991 Census, LRC Commissioned Table LRCT15*

Bangladeshis aged 16 and over were in work, with the highest rate of two thirds among Bangladeshi men aged 40-44. Bangladeshi women had particularly low levels of employment, 13 per cent overall, rising to a high of only 23 per cent for those aged 18-19.

The pattern was different for the Black groups, however. Although Black Caribbean women were more likely to be economically active than women from other ethnic groups, unemployment rates among Black Caribbean women were higher than those of the White group and, for age groups up to 44, higher than those of the Indian and Chinese groups. Unemployment among residents included in the Black Other category followed a similar pattern to that among Black Caribbeans, although the younger age structure of the Black Other population meant that the overall rate was higher than for Black Caribbeans. The Black African population showed a somewhat different pattern. Unemployment among younger Black African men, up to the age of 29 was higher than for other groups, as was the proportion who were in the other economically inactive category. In contrast, the proportion of younger Black African women in this category was only a little above average, but the unemployment rate was still very high.

**Full-time and part-time working**

Some clear differences are found between the employment patterns of ethnic groups in London. Part-time employment (working 30 hours or less per week), as would be expected, is much more common among women of all ethnic groups than among men. It is particularly common among White women aged 35 and over and, to a slightly lesser extent, Bangladeshi women aged 25-39 although, as noted earlier, relatively few Bangladeshi women were in employment of any type. Around one in three White and Bangladeshi women aged 35-39 in work were part-time employees, rising to a high of more than half of White women aged 60 and over. In contrast, the lowest rate of part-time employment was among White women aged 20-24, with nearly 90 per cent of this group working full-time.

**Figure 7.10 Percentage of part-time employees among working women aged 35-39 by ethnic group**

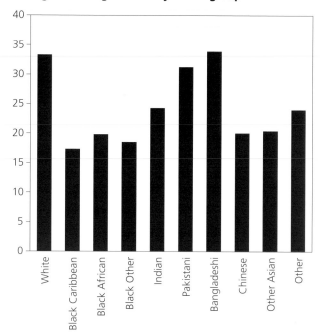

*Source: 1991 Census, LRC Commissioned Table LRCT15*

Full-time employment was customary among Black Caribbean working women, accounting for over three quarters of those in age groups 25-54.

For men, part-time employment was relatively uncommon, with the highest rates among Black Africans, peaking at nearly 30 per cent of working 18-19 year olds – probably a significant proportion of them also in full-time education. The same is also true for Black African men aged up to 44, for whom rates of part-time work were much higher than for men from other groups, as were the proportions in full-time education, as mentioned earlier.

The employment profile in age groups over retirement age was quite different to that of the main working ages. For men and women from all ethnic groups, the proportions working full-time were lower after retirement age, with relatively more working part-time and self-employed. The increase in part-time working is particularly noticeable among men, who may be taking part-time jobs having retired from their career job.

## Qualifications

Many factors can affect educational achievements. Family background, in particular, is known to have an important influence on young people's progress. In general, children whose fathers are in the manual social classes tend to have lower achievements at school, which may account for the low proportions of Black and Pakistani/Bangladeshi people continuing into higher education. For some children from ethnic minority groups, lack of fluency in English may also be a factor that hinders performance in exams and so again progress into further and higher education is not an option. However, this should be less of a problem for younger age groups who are more likely to have been born in the United Kingdom.

In the 1991 Census, residents aged 18 and over were asked for details of degrees and professional and vocational qualifications obtained. Because this information was difficult and time consuming to code, qualifications, along with various other data was only processed for a ten per cent sample of returned Census forms. The highest level of qualifications were classified and then grouped into three educational levels in the 1991 Census:

> level a – higher degrees of UK standard
> level b – first degrees and all other qualifications of UK first degree standard
> level c – qualifications that are generally obtained at 18 and over, above GCE A level standard and below first degree standard. This level also includes most nursing and many teaching qualifications, although degrees in education are classified as level b.

Levels a and b are grouped together in this analysis.

Table 7.1 and Figure 7.11 show those in ethnic groups aged 18-29 by their qualification level. This age group largely represents those who were educated in Britain, while the numbers of qualified ethnic minority residents in older age groups tend to be much lower.

**Figure 7.11 Qualified residents by ethnic group and gender for ages 18-29**

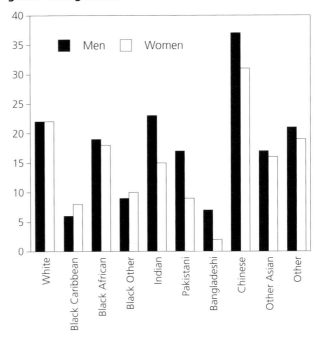

Source: 1991 Census, LRC Commissioned Table LRCT39

The Chinese, in this age range, are the most qualified group by far, (28 per cent with a first or higher degree) which is not surprising given the high proportion of younger Chinese people who were full-time students (see earlier section on economically inactive). This is true for both Chinese men and women, although the percentage is higher for men – 31 per cent compared to 25 per cent. Particularly noteworthy is that more than 40 per cent of Chinese residents aged 23-26 were qualified, which is double the proportion among Whites and Indians of the same ages.

The reasons behind the larger proportions of Chinese and Indian residents staying on and doing well in higher education are complex but may include strong family encouragement to continue in full-time education and the difficulties which some young ethnic minority people face in finding employment. Many Indian and Chinese people, if recently arrived in the UK, already have a degree obtained in their home country which they themselves consider to be of equal status to a degree obtained in the UK. Almost half of all ethnic minority group members with a degree had obtained that qualification outside the UK and over half of those with higher education qualifications below degree level had obtained their qualification outside the UK (Owen, Mortimore, Phoenix 1997). Moreover, the proportion arriving with qualifications varies between ethnic group.

The White group had the second highest percentage qualified for 18 to 29 year olds – over 16 per cent were qualified with a first degree or higher. Again there is a difference between males and females – 16 per cent of White women compared to 18 per cent of White men were qualified to at least degree level. More White women, however, had a level c qualification.

Around one in six Indian men aged 18-29 had a qualification above A-level standard, which was close to the proportion among White men but Indian women were much less likely to have a higher qualification than White women – just 11 per cent had a first degree, although this is still much higher than among Pakistani

and Bangladeshi women. The Bangladeshis, having only relatively recently arrived in the UK, are less established. It usually takes a generation or so (as with Indians) for improved participation in higher education to take place. Of all Bangladeshi women aged 18-29, 98 per cent were 'unqualified' – the highest proportion of any ethnic group.

Black Caribbean and Black Other groups also had a small percentage of 18-29 year olds with a higher qualification. Only four per cent of all 18-29 year old Black Caribbeans had a degree or equivalent – the same as Bangladeshis and only 6 per cent of Black Others. Indeed, Black Caribbean men had the lowest percentage qualified of all men in ethnic minority groups with only three per cent. Black Caribbean women also had a low percentage who were qualified at levels a or b (four per cent) but this is higher than their male equivalents – the only ethnic group where this is the case.

**Table 7.1 Qualification levels by gender and ethnic group** (percentage)

| Males | Total 18-29 | White | Black Caribbean | Black African | Black other | Indian | Paki-stani | Bangla-deshi | Chinese | Other Asian | Other |
|---|---|---|---|---|---|---|---|---|---|---|---|
| A or B | 16.3 | 17.6 | 3.3 | 11.2 | 5.9 | 17.0 | 12.4 | 6.2 | 31.0 | 11.0 | 15.7 |
| C | 4.4 | 4.3 | 2.9 | 7.3 | 3.3 | 5.7 | 4.5 | 0.6 | 6.0 | 6.1 | 5.5 |
| Non-qual | 79.2 | 78.1 | 93.8 | 81.5 | 90.8 | 77.3 | 83.2 | 93.2 | 63.0 | 82.9 | 78.9 |
| Female | | | | | | | | | | | |
| A or B | 14.0 | 15.6 | 3.8 | 9.6 | 5.5 | 11.2 | 7.3 | 1.8 | 25.4 | 9.4 | 12.9 |
| C | 6.0 | 6.3 | 4.1 | 8.0 | 4.9 | 4.1 | 2.0 | 0.4 | 5.2 | 6.9 | 6.1 |
| Non-qual | 80.0 | 78.2 | 92.1 | 82.4 | 89.6 | 84.7 | 90.7 | 97.8 | 69.4 | 83.6 | 81.0 |
| All | | | | | | | | | | | |
| A or B | 15.1 | 16.5 | 3.6 | 10.3 | 5.6 | 13.9 | 9.9 | 3.8 | 28.2 | 10.2 | 14.3 |
| C | 5.2 | 5.3 | 3.5 | 7.7 | 4.3 | 4.9 | 3.3 | 0.5 | 5.6 | 6.5 | 5.8 |
| Non-qual | 79.6 | 78.1 | 92.9 | 82.0 | 90.1 | 81.2 | 86.9 | 95.7 | 66.3 | 83.3 | 79.9 |

*Source: 1991 Census, LRC Commissioned Table LRCT39*

**Figure 7.12 Percentage of qualified residents who were unemployed by ethnic group**

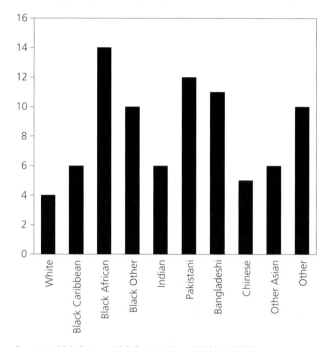

*Source: 1991 Census, LRC Commissioned Table LRCT39*

Black Africans are more qualified than the other Black groups which again follows on from the high proportion of students discussed earlier in this chapter. One in ten 18-29 year olds were qualified to degree level. There was little difference between Black African men and women – 11 per cent of men had a first degree or above compared to 10 per cent of women. Half of all qualified Black Africans were aged 30 to 44 – this is the highest amongst all ethnic groups with the exception of Other Asian. This may indicate the preference amongst this group to study in the UK as mature students or show that younger Black Africans are finding it harder to obtain a qualification in the UK compared to the generation before who may have got their qualifications before they arrived in the UK.

Women from ethnic minorities, and especially those from Pakistani and Bangladeshi groups, are further disadvantaged because some are restricted to choosing from educational institutions which are located in their home region – they may need to be near support mechanisms which are both emotional and financial and they may be responding to family and community pressures (Bhavnani 1994). Family pressures may also restrict the range of subjects available to them. Males from all ethnic groups were more likely than their female counterparts to be studying sciences (Modood and Shiner 1994). Another reason could be that Pakistani and Bangladeshi women are mostly Muslims, a stricter culture which limits the choices available for some women.

Figure 7.12 shows the percentage of all qualified people aged 18 and over in each ethnic group who were unemployed. Whites had the lowest percentage unemployed at just 4 per cent, compared with 14 per cent for Black Africans – the highest percentage unemployed. Pakistani, Bangladeshi and Black Other all had rates of 10 per cent or higher. Many people in ethnic minority groups live in areas with high social deprivation, which are often also areas with limited local employment opportunities. In order to increase their chances of finding suitable employment, these same people have a desire to go into further education. However, Figure 7.12 seems to show that even after overcoming the difficulties of getting into a higher education establishment and then obtaining a higher qualification, people from ethnic minorities still face discrimination when applying for jobs.

**Occupation**

The 1991 Census data shows that the most significant differences in occupational distribution were between men and women, although there were also considerable differences by ethnic group. The nine major occupation groups used here are as shown in Table 7.2, which summarises the occupational distribution for men and women.

*Managers and administrators*

The largest occupation category for men overall and the second largest for women, this group includes nearly 500,000 of London's working residents. It is clear from Table 7.2 that Black Caribbeans, particularly men and to a lesser degree other Black residents, were much less likely to be working in these types of occupations than

**Table 7.2 Occupation distribution by ethnic group and gender** (percentage)

| | All ethnic groups | White | Black C'bean | Black A'can | Black other | Indian | Paki- stani | Bangla- deshi | Chinese | Other Asian | Other |
|---|---|---|---|---|---|---|---|---|---|---|---|
| Total Males | 100 | 100 | 100 | 100 | 100 | 100 | 100 | 100 | 100 | 100 | 100 |
| 1 Managers and administrators | 21 | 21 | 8 | 11 | 13 | 23 | 22 | 17 | 22 | 25 | 22 |
| 2 Professional occupations | 11 | 11 | 4 | 12 | 6 | 13 | 9 | 6 | 19 | 11 | 15 |
| 3 Associate professional and | | | | | | | | | | | |
| technical occupations | 11 | 11 | 8 | 9 | 12 | 7 | 6 | 3 | 10 | 10 | 12 |
| 4 Clerical and secretarial occups. | 9 | 9 | 10 | 15 | 14 | 13 | 13 | 6 | 8 | 13 | 13 |
| 5 Craft and related occupations | 18 | 18 | 27 | 8 | 19 | 15 | 13 | 17 | 4 | 9 | 10 |
| 6 Personal and protective | | | | | | | | | | | |
| service occupations | 7 | 7 | 9 | 11 | 9 | 3 | 5 | 34 | 23 | 9 | 8 |
| 7 Sales occupations | 5 | 4 | 3 | 5 | 5 | 7 | 8 | 4 | 4 | 7 | 5 |
| 8 Plant and machine operatives | 10 | 9 | 17 | 10 | 11 | 11 | 15 | 3 | 3 | 5 | 7 |
| 9 Other occupations | 7 | 7 | 12 | 13 | 9 | 5 | 5 | 6 | 4 | 7 | 6 |
| Occupation not stated or inad. desc. | 2 | 1 | 3 | 5 | 2 | 2 | 3 | 4 | 2 | 2 | 3 |
| | | | | | | | | | | | |
| Total Females | 100 | 100 | 100 | 100 | 100 | 100 | 100 | 100 | 100 | 100 | 100 |
| 1 Managers and administrators | 14 | 15 | 7 | 8 | 12 | 13 | 12 | 7 | 15 | 9 | 13 |
| 2 Professional occupations | 9 | 10 | 5 | 6 | 7 | 7 | 10 | 15 | 13 | 8 | 11 |
| 3 Associate professional and | | | | | | | | | | | |
| technical occupations | 13 | 13 | 16 | 17 | 12 | 8 | 8 | 9 | 23 | 14 | 14 |
| 4 Clerical and secretarial occups. | 33 | 34 | 33 | 22 | 39 | 32 | 30 | 20 | 20 | 28 | 33 |
| 5 Craft and related occupations | 2 | 2 | 2 | 4 | 3 | 4 | 4 | 8 | 3 | 2 | 2 |
| 6 Personal and protective | | | | | | | | | | | |
| service occupations | 10 | 10 | 14 | 12 | 12 | 5 | 7 | 15 | 13 | 16 | 9 |
| 7 Sales occupations | 8 | 8 | 4 | 7 | 7 | 10 | 12 | 11 | 6 | 9 | 8 |
| 8 Plant and machine operatives | 2 | 2 | 4 | 3 | 2 | 13 | 10 | 4 | 0 | 3 | 2 |
| 9 Other occupations | 7 | 7 | 11 | 20 | 5 | 6 | 3 | 5 | 5 | 11 | 6 |
| Occ'n not stated or inadequate descr'n. | 1 | 1 | 2 | 4 | 2 | 2 | 3 | 5 | 2 | 1 | 2 |

Source: 1991 Census, LRC Commissioned Table LRCT27

men from other ethnic groups. What the figures in the table do not show is that White men and women were most likely to be managers or administrators in large establishments, including both the private and public sectors, whereas the high proportions in this occupation category among Indian, Pakistani and Chinese workers are mainly due to large numbers running smaller businesses. This relates closely to high proportions of residents from these ethnic groups in self-employment, and is particularly a feature of older age groups, aged 45 and over.

*Professional occupations*
Accounting for around one in ten of all London's residents in work, this occupation category shows some of the biggest contrasts between ethnic groups for both men and women. The high proportion of Chinese men in professional occupations (almost one in five) clearly relates to the large proportion qualified to degree level or above (see the previous section on qualifications). The comparatively small proportion of Black Caribbean men in this category (just one in 20) is similarly related to the low levels of qualifications among this group. Chinese women and Indian and Black African men – groups which also show higher academic levels – also had above average proportions in professional occupations.

The high proportion of Bangladeshi women in this category shown in Table 7.2 is particularly noteworthy, although since relatively few Bangladeshi women were in employment, as discussed in earlier sections, this was a small number in absolute terms. This, too, demonstrates the importance of looking at the figures in more detail when exploring differences, as most of the Bangladeshi women in professional occupations, and many of the White women were teachers, whereas Chinese and Black African professionals were more likely to be in all the non-teaching professional occupations. These range from natural scientists, through civil and software engineers to health professionals, such as doctors, dentists, pharmacists, ophthalmic opticians and veterinarians, to lawyers,

librarians, business and financial professionals, architects and surveyors, psychologists, social workers and clergy.

*Associate professional and technical occupations*
This group of occupations covers a wide range of jobs, and again reveals differences between ethnic groups and between men and women. While 16 per cent of Chinese women, 12 per cent of Black African and 11 per cent of Black Caribbean women worked as associate professionals in health – a category including, for example, physiotherapists, chiropodists and environmental health officers, as well as nurses and midwives – only two per cent of Pakistani and three per cent of Bangladeshi women did so. Another, possibly significant point, is that the proportions of Chinese, Black African and Black Caribbean women working in these jobs were much lower in the under 30 age groups than among older ages.

Men from all ethnic groups were more likely than women to work in science and engineering associate professional jobs, such as scientific technicians, computer programmers and quantity surveyors or other associate professional occupations, including ship and aircraft officers, legal, business and financial and social welfare associate professionals and literary, artistic and sports professionals. The low proportion among the South Asian ethnic groups was a feature of all these categories with the exception of above average proportions of Indian men in science and engineering associate professional occupations.

*Clerical and secretarial occupations*
Among the most striking features from Table 7.2 are the high proportions of women from all ethnic groups in clerical/secretarial occupations (around one in three overall), but particularly among the Black Other category. Almost 40 per cent of working Black Other women were included in this category, with those in clerical occupations outnumbering those in secretarial jobs by almost two to one. In contrast, nearly half of the White women in this occupation group were doing

secretarial work. Women in the Black Other category were almost twice as likely as Bangladeshi or Chinese women to be employed in these occupations, but even so, this was the largest occupation group for Bangladeshi women. This type of work was particularly common among younger women, with the highest proportions for all ethnic groups among those aged under 30.

Men were much less likely than women overall to be in either clerical or secretarial occupations, but particularly in secretarial jobs, which accounted for one in every seven working women, but fewer than one in a hundred working men. The highest proportion of men in this category was among Black Africans, at 15 per cent. This was the only ethnic group with a higher proportion of men than of women in clerical occupations.

*Craft and related occupations*
The two outstanding features of this occupation group are the high proportion of men compared to women (18 per cent and two per cent respectively) and the very high proportion of Black Caribbean men (27 per cent), contrasting with a well below average proportion of Black African men (eight per cent) and even fewer Chinese men (four per cent).

Above average proportions of Black Caribbean men were in each of the three groups making up this major occupation category – skilled construction trades, skilled engineering trades and other skilled trades, but were most likely to be working in other skilled trades. This last category includes occupations as diverse as plumbers, motor mechanics, knitters, printers, carpenters, bakers, piano tuners and gardeners, among a wide range of others. The proportions working in craft and related occupations tended to be higher for all ethnic groups among older people.

*Personal and protective occupations*
This occupation category also displays the massive contrasts between ethnic groups and between men and women. More than one in three working Bangladeshi

men were in jobs in this category, along with nearly one in four (mainly older) Chinese men, compared with just three per cent of Indian men. Nearly all of these men were in personal service occupations, a category which covers a range of occupations as diverse as chefs, waiters, travel attendants, dental nurses, ambulance staff, care assistants, playgroup leaders, hairdressers, caretakers and bookmakers. Almost all of the relatively high proportions of Black Caribbean, Bangladeshi and Other Asian women were also in personal service occupations.

It is worth noting that although the proportion of Bangladeshi men working in personal services was very high compared to the White group (four per cent), in terms of actual numbers, there were far more White men working in this occupation group (nearly 50,000, compared with just over 3,000 Bangladeshi men).

Perhaps one of the more surprising findings is that Black African men were more likely to be in protective service occupations than men from any other ethnic group. This occupation category, which covers three per cent of London's working men and one per cent of working women, includes, for example, NCOs and other ranks in armed forces, police, fire, prison, customs and immigration officers other than those in management, traffic wardens and security guards.

*Sales occupations*
There was relatively little difference between groups in respect of the proportion working in sales. However, men were more likely to be buyers or brokers, whereas women were more likely to be shop assistants, window dressers or telephone salespersons, and South Asians were much more likely than Black Caribbeans to be in sales occupations. Contrasts between age groups are also evident, with the highest proportions among the youngest age groups (over 30 per cent of working 16-17 year old women), tending to decrease with age for all ethnic groups.

*Plant and machine operatives*

Black Caribbean men were most likely to be working in both of the two occupational categories making up this group. One in ten of all working Black Caribbean men were drivers or mobile machine (such as fork lift trucks, earth moving equipment and cranes) operators, with a further eight per cent operating industrial plant or stationary machines. On the whole these are routine, manual occupations, mainly in a variety of manufacturing industries, such as food, textiles, chemicals and metal working.

The relatively large proportions of Indian and Pakistani women shown in this occupational group in Table 7.2 were nearly all working in this latter category and were particularly concentrated in older age groups. The contrast with the extremely small number of Chinese women in this occupational group is particularly strong. Pakistani men, too, had above average proportions of both drivers and stationary machine operators.

*Other occupations*

This wide ranging group of occupations covers largely unskilled, manual jobs, such as labourers in manufacturing or construction, road and rail construction workers, refuse collectors, postal workers, porters, shelf fillers, window cleaners and car park attendants. As Table 7.2 shows, this occupation category was largest for Black Africans (particularly women, at one in five) and Black Caribbeans, whereas Black Others were less likely to be in this type of job. The highest percentages for most ethnic groups were among the youngest and oldest age groups (age 16-17 and 60 and over).

## Industry

The industry in which a person is employed is determined by the main business or activity of the organisation for which he or she works. This means that several people with the same occupation could be employed in different industrial sectors. For example, a secretary doing similar tasks could work in any of the industrial sectors below – if the employer was a water company, then the secretary would work in the energy and water supply industries, but if the employer was a taxi firm, the secretary would be employed in the transport sector. Table 7.3 gives the industrial distribution for men and Table 7.4 for women. Each of the industrial sectors in London employing more than two per cent of residents is discussed below.

*Manufacturing metal, etc*

This industrial sector, sometimes referred to as 'heavy manufacturing', incorporates the manufacture of metal goods (rather than the manufacture of the metals and alloys themselves), such as a wide range of machinery, electrical and electronic equipment, motor vehicles (and parts) and other transport equipment and instrument engineering. As might be expected, this industrial sector employed a far higher proportion of men than of women. Nearly six per cent of working men living in London worked in this sector, compared to just two per cent of working women.

The ethnic distributions of residents working in this sector differ for men and women. The ethnic group with the highest proportion of men working in this industrial sector was Black Caribbean (nine per cent), with the smallest proportion among Bangladeshis (one per cent). Indian women were most likely to be employed in this sector (seven per cent), which was almost as high as the proportion among Indian men (eight per cent), and the same as among Pakistani men. The proportions of Black African and Black Other women working in this sector were very small (one per cent). Chinese residents were among those least likely to be working in this sector (two per cent of Chinese men and one per cent of Chinese women).

Generally, the highest proportions were among the 45-59 age group, with 12 per cent of Black Caribbean men in this age group being employed in heavy manufacturing. Similarly, ten per cent of working Indian, Pakistani and Bangladeshi women in this age group were employed in this sector. Among Indian men, however, the highest proportion was from the

**Table 7.3 Industrial distribution by ethnic group and gender** (percentage)

| | All ethnic groups | White | Black C'bean | Black A'can | Black other | Indian | Paki- stani | Bangla- deshi | Chinese | Other Asian | Other |
|---|---|---|---|---|---|---|---|---|---|---|---|
| Total Males | 100 | 100 | 100 | 100 | 100 | 100 | 100 | 100 | 100 | 100 | 100 |
| 0 Agriculture, forestry and fishing | 0 | 0 | 0 | 0 | 0 | 0 | 0 | 0 | 0 | 0 | 0 |
| 1 Energy and water supply | 1 | 2 | 1 | 0 | 1 | 1 | 0 | 0 | 1 | 1 | 1 |
| 2 Extraction of minerals and ores | | | | | | | | | | | |
| other than fuels, manufacture of | | | | | | | | | | | |
| metals, mineral products,chemicals | 1 | 1 | 1 | 1 | 1 | 1 | 1 | 0 | 1 | 1 | 1 |
| 3 Metal goods, engineering and | | | | | | | | | | | |
| vehicles industries | 6 | 6 | 9 | 4 | 6 | 8 | 7 | 1 | 2 | 5 | 5 |
| 4 Other manufacturing industries | 7 | 7 | 7 | 6 | 7 | 8 | 11 | 19 | 3 | 4 | 5 |
| 5 Construction | 11 | 12 | 11 | 3 | 7 | 6 | 2 | 1 | 2 | 3 | 4 |
| 6 Distribution, hotels and catering, | | | | | | | | | | | |
| repairs | 19 | 17 | 16 | 18 | 21 | 31 | 28 | 52 | 46 | 29 | 25 |
| 7 Transport and Communication | 12 | 12 | 23 | 14 | 17 | 15 | 17 | 4 | 5 | 12 | 11 |
| 8 Banking, finance, insurance, | | | | | | | | | | | |
| business services and leasing | 20 | 20 | 10 | 17 | 15 | 15 | 16 | 8 | 22 | 22 | 20 |
| 9 Other services | 22 | 22 | 19 | 30 | 23 | 13 | 14 | 11 | 15 | 21 | 25 |
| Ind. not stated or inadequately. desc'd. | 1 | 1 | 3 | 5 | 2 | 2 | 3 | 4 | 2 | 2 | 3 |
| Workplace outside United Kingdom | 0 | 0 | 0 | 1 | 0 | 0 | 0 | 0 | 0 | 0 | 1 |

*Source: 1991 Census, LRC Commissioned Table LRCT28*

30-44 age group, with ten per cent of this group working in this sector. Overall, the age group with the highest proportion working in this sector was 60-64 year old men, with nine per cent of all working men from this age range employed in heavy manufacturing. This may be partially related to earlier retirement ages in some other industrial sectors.

*Other manufacturing*
The 'light manufacturing' sector, as this is sometimes called, encompasses manufacturing of food, drink and tobacco, textiles, clothing, furniture and paper, processing of timber, plastics and rubber, printing and

publishing and other manufacturing industries such as jewellery, toys and sports goods. Overall, this sector employed seven per cent of men and six per cent of women living in London.

Whereas Bangladeshi men were the least likely to be employed in heavy manufacturing, the proportion in light manufacturing was higher than from any other ethnic group. At 19 per cent, this was nearly three times the overall proportion of men employed in this sector. The next highest proportion was of Pakistani men, with 11 per cent working in this sector. The proportion of Bangladeshi women working in light manufacturing

**Table 7.4 Industrial distribution by ethnic group and gender** (percentage)

| | All ethnic groups | White | Black C'bean | Black A'can | Black other | Indian | Paki- stani | Bangla- deshi | Chinese | Other Asian | Other |
|---|---|---|---|---|---|---|---|---|---|---|---|
| Total Females | 100 | 100 | 100 | 100 | 100 | 100 | 100 | 100 | 100 | 100 | 100 |
| 0 Agriculture, forestry and fishing | 0 | 0 | 0 | 0 | 0 | 0 | 0 | 0 | 0 | 0 | 0 |
| 1 Energy and water supply | 1 | 1 | 1 | 1 | 1 | 1 | 1 | 0 | 0 | 0 | 1 |
| 2 Extraction of minerals and ores | | | | | | | | | | | |
| other than fuels, manufacture of | | | | | | | | | | | |
| metals, mineral products,chemicals | 1 | 1 | 0 | 0 | 0 | 1 | 1 | 0 | 0 | 0 | 1 |
| 3 Metal goods, engineering and | | | | | | | | | | | |
| vehicles industries | 2 | 2 | 2 | 1 | 1 | 7 | 5 | 3 | 1 | 2 | 2 |
| 4 Other manufacturing industries | 6 | 5 | 4 | 5 | 6 | 10 | 10 | 11 | 4 | 3 | 5 |
| 5 Construction | 1 | 1 | 1 | 1 | 1 | 1 | 0 | 0 | 1 | 1 | 1 |
| 6 Distribution, hotels and catering, | | | | | | | | | | | |
| repairs | 20 | 20 | 13 | 18 | 17 | 29 | 24 | 27 | 31 | 26 | 20 |
| 7 Transport and Communication | 5 | 4 | 7 | 7 | 5 | 7 | 9 | 2 | 3 | 6 | 5 |
| 8 Banking, finance, insurance, | | | | | | | | | | | |
| business services and leasing | 21 | 22 | 16 | 12 | 20 | 15 | 17 | 9 | 23 | 15 | 21 |
| 9 Other services | 42 | 42 | 54 | 51 | 47 | 28 | 31 | 42 | 33 | 44 | 42 |
| Ind. not stated or inadequately. desc'd. | 1 | 1 | 3 | 4 | 2 | 2 | 3 | 5 | 2 | 1 | 2 |
| Workplace outside United Kingdom | 0 | 0 | 0 | 0 | 0 | 0 | 0 | 0 | 0 | 1 | 0 |

*Source: 1991 Census, LRC Commissioned Table LRCT28*

was also higher than for any other ethnic group, at 11 per cent, although the proportions of Pakistani and Indian women were only a little lower, at ten per cent. Chinese and Other Asian men and women were among those least likely to be employed in this sector.

The overall proportions of men employed in this sector increased slightly with age, although the highest proportion of all was among Bangladeshi men in the 30-44 age range, of whom 23 per cent were employed in this sector, along with 20 per cent of the 45-59 age group. In contrast, the proportions of women in this sector were similar across the age groups, but were

highest among Indian (14 per cent) and Pakistani (15 per cent) women in the 45-59 age group.

*Construction*
The construction industry employed 11 per cent of working men, but just one per cent of working women. The highest proportion was of White men (12 per cent), although the proportion of Black Caribbeans working in this sector was only just below (11 per cent). At the other end of the spectrum, less than one per cent of Bangladeshis and just ten per cent of Chinese and Pakistani men were employed in construction. The proportion of White men working in the

construction industry was similar for each age group, whereas the proportions of Black Caribbeans were higher among the middle and older age groups – just 6 per cent of the 16-17 age group, compared to over 12 per cent in the 30-44, 45-59 and 60-64 age groups.

*Distribution and catering*
This industrial sector includes both wholesale and retail distribution, hotels and catering and repairs of consumer goods and vehicles. Altogether, this sector employed 20 per cent of working women and 19 per cent of working men.

The differences in the proportions of men from the different ethnic groups working in this sector were greater than for any other industrial sector, ranging from just over half of Bangladeshi men and 46 per cent of Chinese men to 16 per cent of Black Caribbean and 17 per cent of White men. The differences, although a little less conspicuous, were also apparent for women, with nearly a third of Chinese women working in this sector, compared with just 13 per cent of Black Caribbean women. For both men and women, all the Asian ethnic groups had higher proportions working in this sector than the Black and White groups.

For both men and women, the proportions working in distribution and catering were highest for the youngest age group (16-17 year olds), with 45 per cent of this age group employed in this sector. For men from the Black and White ethnic groups, this proportion decreased with age, but there was no clear decrease with age among men from any of the Asian groups. A similar decrease with age in the proportion working in this sector was apparent for Black and Bangladeshi women, but not among White women or women from any of the other Asian groups.

*Transport and communications*
This sector covers all forms of transport (road, rail, sea and air) as well as communication – both postal and telecommunications. The transport and communications sector employed 12 per cent of men

and five per cent of women living in London.

Nearly a quarter of Black Caribbean men worked in this sector, along with 17 per cent of Pakistani men and men from the Black Other group. Among women, Pakistanis were most likely to be working in this sector (nine per cent), along with seven per cent of Black Caribbeans, Black Africans and Indians. For both men and women, Bangladeshis were least likely to be employed in this sector.

For all ethnic groups, the highest proportions of men employed in the transport sector were among the 45-59 age group, including 30 per cent of Black Caribbean men aged 45-59. In contrast, women were most likely to be employed in this sector in the 16-17 and 18-29 age groups.

*Banking and finance*
The banking and finance sector is wider than the term implies. In addition to banking and finance, this sector covers insurance, renting of movables, owning and dealing and real estate and business services, which includes estate agents, legal services, accountants, advertising and computer services, among others. In all 20 per cent of working men and 21 per cent of working women were employed in this sector.

For both men and women, Chinese were the most likely to be employed in this sector (22 per cent of Chinese men and 23 per cent of Chinese women), while Bangladeshis were least likely (eight and nine per cent of men and women respectively). There were some differences between men and women, however, as 22 per cent of men from the Other Asian category worked in this sector – among the highest proportions – whereas just 15 per cent of Other Asian women worked in this sector – among the lowest. Conversely, quite a high proportion of Black Other women (20 per cent) worked in this sector, compared with 15 per cent of men from the same ethnic category.

The proportion of Black Caribbean women working in

banking and finance was also higher than of Black Caribbean men (16 and 10 per cent), whereas the proportion of Black African men was higher than the proportion of Black African women (17 and 12 per cent). All these proportions were below average, however.

The proportions working in this sector were highest among the 18-29 age group for both men and women and for most ethnic groups. Over a third of Chinese and 24 per cent of White men in this age group worked in banking and finance, while the proportions were even higher for women, at 38 per cent of Chinese and 29 per cent of White women aged 18-29. The proportions decreased with age generally, but nearly a quarter of working White men aged 65 and over were employed in this sector.

*Other services*
This sector was the largest in London, as in the rest of Great Britain, employing 22 per cent of men and 42 per cent of women living in the capital. The vast majority of people in this industrial sector are employed in the public sector in one of the three major spheres of public administration (in both national and local government), education and health. Private companies within these spheres, including driving schools and veterinary practices also fall within this industrial sector, as do a wide range of other services in both the public and private sectors. These include national defence, research and development, television, libraries, sport, trade unions, religious organisations, hair dressing, refuse disposal, domestic services, diplomatic representation and international organisations.

The proportions working in this sector varied considerably between ethnic groups, ranging from over half of Black Caribbean and Black African working women to under a third of Indian and Pakistani women and from 30 per cent of Black African men down to just 11 per cent of Bangladeshi men. These figures reflect the generally higher proportions from Black groups working in this sector, and the relatively low

proportions of Asians, although there were exceptions, with just 19 per cent of Black Caribbean men employed in other services, along with 42 per cent of working Bangladeshi women. For both men and women, the proportions from the Other Asian categories working in this sector were close to average.

There were also clear differences with age, which applied across all ethnic groups. The proportions working in this sector increased with age, so that the proportions of both working men and women employed in this sector were highest from the 60-64 age group, up to over 80 per cent of Black African and over 70 per cent of Black Caribbean working women in this age group. The only exceptions to this were for Chinese men and Bangladeshi and Other women, each of which had the highest proportions from the 44-59 age group. The proportions from the oldest age group (age 65 and over) employed in this sector were also high, remaining close to the overall proportions. These high proportions translate to substantial numbers, with over 20,000 women aged 60-64 working in this industrial sector.

**Social class**
The social class of a person is determined by his or her occupation, with occupations grouped in such a way as to bring together, as far as possible, people with similar levels of occupational skill. This is done at the individual occupation level, rather than occupation groups, as described earlier in this chapter. A person's employment status may also be taken into account so that foremen and managers are generally assigned to a higher social class than those they are supervising. Table 7.5 gives the social class distribution for London residents.

Social class I covers professional occupations, although this is not the same definition as the professional occupations category under the Standard Occupational Classification used to form the occupational breakdown. Social class II includes managerial and technical occupations, social class III covers skilled occupations, further subdivided into III(N), non-

**Table 7.5 Social class distribution by ethnic group and gender** (percentage)

| | All ethnic groups | White | Black C'bean | Black A'can | Black other | Indian | Paki-stani | Bangla-deshi | Chinese | Other Asian | Other |
|---|---|---|---|---|---|---|---|---|---|---|---|
| Total Males | 100 | 100 | 100 | 100 | 100 | 100 | 100 | 100 | 100 | 100 | 100 |
| I Professional etc. occupations | 9 | 9 | 2 | 11 | 4 | 12 | 8 | 5 | 19 | 10 | 12 |
| II Managerial and technical occups. | 33 | 34 | 16 | 22 | 26 | 32 | 29 | 15 | 27 | 37 | 35 |
| IIIN Skilled occupations - non manual | 14 | 14 | 12 | 19 | 19 | 18 | 21 | 15 | 17 | 19 | 18 |
| IIIM Skilled occupations - manual | 26 | 26 | 39 | 18 | 28 | 21 | 21 | 24 | 24 | 16 | 18 |
| IV Partly skilled occupations | 12 | 11 | 19 | 18 | 15 | 13 | 15 | 32 | 8 | 13 | 10 |
| V Unskilled occupations | 4 | 4 | 7 | 8 | 5 | 3 | 3 | 5 | 2 | 3 | 3 |
| Armed forces | 0 | 1 | 0 | 0 | 0 | 0 | 0 | 0 | 0 | 0 | 0 |
| Occupation not stated or inad. desc. | 2 | 1 | 3 | 5 | 2 | 2 | 3 | 4 | 2 | 2 | 3 |
| | | | | | | | | | | | |
| Total Females | 100 | 100 | 100 | 100 | 100 | 100 | 100 | 100 | 100 | 100 | 100 |
| I Professional etc. occupations | 3 | 3 | 1 | 3 | 2 | 5 | 6 | 3 | 11 | 4 | 5 |
| II Managerial and technical occups. | 33 | 34 | 31 | 29 | 30 | 24 | 24 | 27 | 37 | 28 | 34 |
| IIIN Skilled occupations - non manual | 41 | 41 | 37 | 29 | 46 | 41 | 43 | 32 | 30 | 38 | 41 |
| IIIM Skilled occupations - manual | 5 | 5 | 6 | 7 | 6 | 4 | 6 | 10 | 6 | 8 | 5 |
| IV Partly skilled occupations | 11 | 10 | 15 | 16 | 10 | 20 | 17 | 20 | 11 | 15 | 10 |
| V Unskilled occupations | 5 | 5 | 8 | 13 | 4 | 4 | 2 | 3 | 3 | 7 | 4 |
| Armed forces | 0 | 0 | 0 | 0 | 0 | 0 | 0 | 0 | 0 | 0 | 0 |
| Occupation not stated or inad. desc. | 1 | 1 | 2 | 4 | 2 | 2 | 3 | 5 | 2 | 1 | 2 |

*Source: 1991 Census, LRC Commissioned Table LRCT29*

manual and III(M), manual. Social classes IV and V cover semi-skilled and unskilled manual occupations respectively.

*I Professional etc occupations*
This social class included nine per cent of working men and just three per cent of working women living in London. This is somewhat less than the proportion categorised in professional occupations earlier, particularly for women. This is because some professional occupations, such as teachers, librarians and social workers (occupations more often followed by

women) are included in social class II. Conversely, senior civil servants, who are categorised as corporate managers and administrators in the occupational classification are allocated to social class I.

Nearly one in five working Chinese men was in social class I, the highest proportion of any ethnic group. Similarly, Chinese women were also more likely than other women to be in this class, although at 11 per cent, the proportion was still considerably lower than for men. Indian and Black African men were also more likely than average to be in social class I, along with men classified in the Other ethnic groups category. In contrast, a very small proportion of Black Caribbean men, and well below average proportions of Black Others and Bangladeshis were in this class.

There were some similarities in the pattern for women, as well as differences. As already noted, Chinese women were most likely to be in social class I, but unlike their male counterparts, the proportion of Pakistani women in this class was also well above average (six per cent). This higher proportion was not apparent from the figures on occupation, suggesting that working Pakistani women in professional occupations, like the Chinese, are more likely to be in the higher prestige professions. The proportions of Indian and Other ethnic group women in social class I were also above average. As for the men, the proportions of Black Caribbean and Black Other women in social class I were lower than for other groups.

The highest proportions of men in social class I were generally among the 30-44 age group, but for Chinese men, the proportion was highest for the 18-29 age band (26 per cent) then decreased with age, but remaining above average for all age groups up to 59. Overall, 11 per cent of the 30-44 age group were in social class I, but the proportion was just four per cent of Black Caribbeans in this age group and one per cent of Black Caribbeans in the 45-59 age band. The pattern for women was slightly different, with several ethnic groups having the highest proportions among the 18-29 age group, such as Chinese (20 per cent) and Indian (seven per cent).

## II Managerial and technical occupations

This is by far the largest social class for London residents, accounting for a third of all working men and women. Social class II groups together people in the managerial occupations, professionals not included in social class I, most associate professionals and managers in occupations which would otherwise be included in social classes III(N) or III(M).

The differences between ethnic groups were more pronounced for men than for women. Just 15 per cent of Bangladeshi men and 16 per cent of Black Caribbean men were in social class II, ranging up to 37 per cent of men from the Other Asian ethnic groups. For women, the proportions ranged from 24 per cent of working Indians and Pakistanis and 27 per cent of Bangladeshis up to 37 per cent of Chinese women. Whereas the proportion of Black Caribbean men in social class II was very low the proportion of Black Caribbean women was only just below average (31 per cent).

For both men and women, the highest proportions were among the 30-44 age group overall (39 per cent), but there were exceptions for some ethnic groups. For example, 30 per cent of Pakistani men in the 30-44 and 45-59 age groups were in social class II, compared with over 40 per cent of the 60-64 age group, and 30 per cent of Black African women aged 30-44 were in this class, compared with 39 per cent of the 45-59 age group.

## III (N) Skilled occupations: non-manual

Social class III(N) was the largest social class of all for working women, including just over 40 per cent of all those in work. However, the proportion of working men in this class was much smaller, at just 14 per cent. This social class includes most secretarial and clerical occupations, along with assorted other occupations, such as draughtspersons, professional athletes, driving instructors, police and fire officers, playgroup leaders and sales assistants.

There were substantial differences between ethnic groups, following different patterns for men and women. The proportions ranged from 46 per cent from the Black Other group and 43 per cent of Pakistanis down to 29 per cent of Black Africans and 30 per cent of Chinese for women and from 21 per cent of Pakistanis and 19 per cent of Black Africans, Black Others and Other Asians down to 12 per cent of Black Caribbeans and 14 per cent of Whites for men.

For both men and women, the proportions were

generally highest among the youngest age group (16-17 year olds) and decreased with age. Over 70 per cent of working women in the 16-17 age group were in social class III(N), but ranging from over 80 per cent of the Black Other group down to just 20 per cent of Chinese women. The proportion of Chinese women in this social class was lowest in the youngest age group, but was around 30 per cent of most other age groups.

*III (M) Skilled occupations: manual*
In contrast to the skilled non-manual occupations, skilled manual occupations, represented by social class III(M) had far higher proportions of men than of women. Just over a quarter of all working men were in this social class, compared to just 5 per cent of women. Social class III(M) incorporates a range of occupations from the groups given above, but not the whole of any group. For example, a bricklayer (who is not a manager) is in social class III(M), whereas tilers are generally included in social class IV unless they are managers or foremen, in which case, they too are included in social class III(M). All of these are included in the skilled construction trades occupation group.

The proportions of Black Caribbean men in social class III(M) was by far the highest at almost 40 per cent with the second highest proportion among Black Other men (28 per cent). At the other end of the spectrum, just 16 per cent of working men from the Other Asian ethnic groups were in this class. The picture was very different for women. Bangladeshis were most likely to be in social class III(M), (ten per cent) followed by Other Asians (eight per cent), while the lowest proportion was among Indians (four per cent).

For most ethnic groups, there was relatively little difference between the proportions in social class III(M) at different ages. However, the proportion of younger Black Caribbean men (aged 16-29) in this class was clearly lower than of older age groups, with well over 40 per cent of Black Caribbean men from the 30-59 age range in skilled manual occupations.

*IV Partly skilled occupations*
Overall, the proportions of men and women in social class IV were similar, at 12 and 11 per cent respectively. Partly skilled occupations cover a range of occupations from waiters to care assistants to many factory workers, among others. The differences between ethnic groups were substantial for women, with the proportion of Indians and Bangladeshis, at 20 per cent, twice the proportion of White women in this social class. The disparity was even greater for men, with the proportion of Bangladeshis (32 per cent) four times the proportion of Chinese. The proportions of Black Caribbean and Black African men in social class IV were also well above average, as were the proportions of Pakistani and Black African women.

For most ethnic groups, the proportions of men in social class IV were higher for the youngest age group (16-17) and the older age groups (age 45 and over) and lower for the middle age groups (18-44), but the proportion of Bangladeshi men in this class was highest for the 16-17 age group and then decreased with age. Overall, a similar pattern was apparent for women, with higher proportions in the youngest and older age groups, but the differences were less marked than for men.

*V Unskilled occupations*
Overall, this was the smallest social class, encompassing just four per cent of men and five per cent of women. Examples of occupations in this class are railway station staff, road construction workers, kitchen porters and window cleaners.

The highest proportions of both men and women in social class V were among Black Africans and Black Caribbeans – up to 13 per cent of Black African women were in social class V. In contrast just two per cent of working Chinese men and Pakistani women were in unskilled occupations. Generally, the age patterns were similar to those for social class IV – higher in the youngest and older age groups. For Black Africans, the pattern was different, with higher proportions of residents in the age groups up to 44 and lower proportions of the older age groups in social class V. The pattern for Black Caribbeans was the opposite of this – lower for the younger age groups, and increasing for the older age groups. These patterns were apparent for both men and women.

## References

Owen C, Mortimore P, Phoenix A, Chapter 1– *Ethnicity in the 1991 Census*, ONS 1997

Modood T and Shiner M, *Ethnic Minorities and Higher Education*, Policy Studies Institute 1994

Bhavnani R, *Black Women in the Labour Market*, Equal Opportunities Commission 1994

# Chapter 8
# Means of travel to work

# Means of travel to work

## Introduction

The transport people use to get to work is affected by where they live, where they work and what transport services are available, and is not necessarily a matter of choice. Nevertheless, it is important information for provision of services, studies of the labour market and for estimating travel flows. There are differences between how people living in an area travel and how people who work in the area travel, as well as differences between means of travel used by different ethnic groups. This chapter concentrates on London's residents and how they travel. An initial analysis of means of travel to work by ethnic group was included in the report *London's Workers* published by the London Research Centre in July 1997. This chapter takes that analysis a stage further.

The Census includes only travel to work, and not travel for any other purpose, so it does not include journeys to school or college, shopping trips or journeys for any other purposes. Travel to work, though, is a major part of the overall picture of travel patterns in the London boroughs. Means of travel to work is very much affected by where people live and work, for example people working in Inner and Central London are more likely to travel by public transport than people working in Outer London. There are other differences too, for example in the levels of car ownership, which may have some effect on decisions about how to travel to work but the effect of differences in things like levels of car ownership is likely to be far less important than the effect of the areas in which people live and work.

This chapter includes sections on how people who live in London travel to work and how this has changed since 1981 for both men and women; where London's ethnic minorities live and work in London; the differences between ethnic minority groups in London and how they travel; and distance travelled by ethnic minority groups by each means of travel.

The Census question on travel to work asked respondents to specify the main means of transport used and not about the various means which may be used regularly. The decision on how to define the main means of travel when more than one was used was left to the individual, but with the advice that the main means of travel should be the one which covered the longest part of the journey by distance. A large number of people use more than one means of travel to work, including, for example, a bus to the station, a British Rail train and the underground, so how people interpreted 'main means of travel' might vary. The assumption here is that this did not result in significant bias in the data. The term 'underground' in this chapter includes the Docklands Light Railway.

## Means of travel to work used by London's residents

Travel is vital to London's economy when considered in the context of 2.7 million people living and working in London; more than 672,000 people commuting into London from outside; almost 150,000 residents travelling outside London to work. This results in almost 3.5 million people travelling to work into, around or out of London each day.

**Figure 8.1 Means of travel to work by gender, all residents 1991**

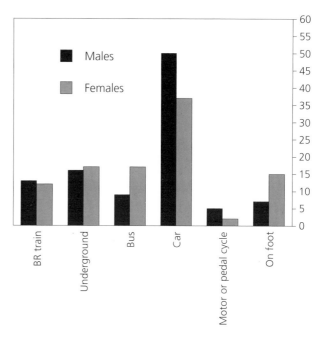

*Source: 1991 Census, Commissioned Table LRCT86*

**Table 8.1 Means of travel to work used by London's residents by gender, 1991**

| | Persons | Males | Females |
|---|---|---|---|
| British Rail train | 12 | 12 | 12 |
| Underground | 16 | 16 | 17 |
| Bus | 12 | 8 | 17 |
| Car | 45 | 52 | 37 |
| Motor cycle | 1 | 2 | 0 |
| Pedal cycle | 2 | 3 | 2 |
| On foot | 11 | 7 | 15 |
| Total | 100 | 100 | 100 |

*Source: 1991 Census, Workplace and Transport to Work Report, Table 6*

**Table 8.2 Means of travel to work used by London's residents by gender, 1981**

| | Persons | Males | Females |
|---|---|---|---|
| British Rail train | 11 | 11 | 11 |
| Underground | 13 | 13 | 14 |
| Bus | 18 | 12 | 25 |
| Car | 39 | 48 | 26 |
| Motor cycle | 2 | 3 | 1 |
| Pedal cycle | 3 | 3 | 2 |
| On foot | 14 | 9 | 21 |
| Total | 100 | 100 | 100 |

*Source: 1981 Census, Workplace and Transport to Work Report, Table 6*

The most widely used means of travel for London residents was car, although there was a considerable amount of variation across London in the proportion of residents travelling to work by car. Car use was far higher in Outer than Inner London, where residents were far more likely to travel by public transport than to drive a car to work. Residents in Outer London did not necessarily drive into London to work but were more likely to travel around the M25 or drive out of London. Even so, there were considerable numbers of cars travelling into Central and Inner London and far more than is desirable.

Figure 8.1 shows the means of travel to work for London residents by gender. It shows that a much larger proportion of men than women travelled to work by car, while a much larger proportion of women than men travelled by bus or walked to work.

Car use had increased from 39 per cent in 1981 to 45 per cent overall in 1991, reflecting a national pattern of increasing car use. The increase was far more evident for women than for men, as shown in Tables 8.1 and 8.2. Looking at the changing proportions between 1981 and 1991 does not give the complete story in this case.

There was a fall of around 300,000 residents in work (and who stated a means of travel) between 1981 and 1991, which consisted of a very large fall in the number of male and very small fall in the number of female residents in work. There were falls in the numbers of residents travelling by all means except underground and driving a car, which had increases of approximately 38,000 and 80,000 respectively. The largest falls were in residents travelling by bus (-193,000) and walking to work (-130,000).

Many of these changes applied to both men and women, but the change in car driving affected men and women in different ways, as illustrated in Figures 8.2 and 8.3. The overall increase of 80,000 residents driving cars to work resulted from a fall of around 64,000 male drivers and an increase of more than 144,000 female drivers. There were corresponding falls of around 102,000 women travelling by bus and 84,000 women walking to work. The final result was an increase of 60 per cent in the number of female residents driving to work. This reflects a considerable change in the position of women in London's labour force, and major changes in how they travel.

**Figure 8.2  Change in means of travel to work for women, 1981 to 1991**

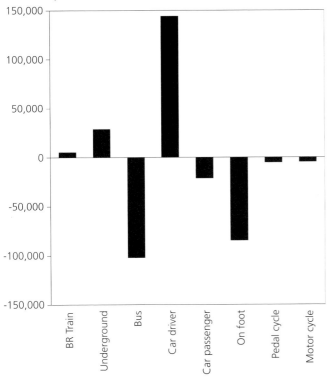

*Source:1991 Census, Commissioned Table LRCT86*

**Figure 8.3  Change in means of travel to work for men, 1981 to 1991**

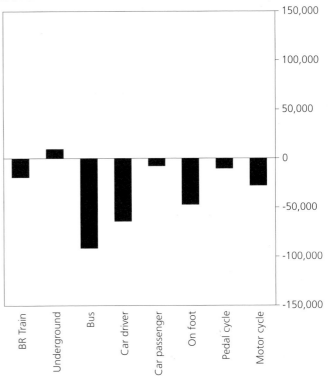

*Source:1991 Census, Commissioned Table LRCT86*

### Ethnic groups living in London and where they worked

Where people live and work has a crucial effect on how they travel, so this section looks at differences between where ethnic groups in London live and work. The following section then looks at differences in how they travel. There are also differences in levels of car ownership between ethnic groups, but the main effect is likely to be based on the areas of residence and workplace and therefore the areas that people are travelling from and to. The following sections include consideration of how many work in London or outside, what proportions live and work in the same borough, and the proportions working in Central London as defined by the City of London, Westminster, Kensington and Chelsea and Camden.

Around 95 per cent of all London residents worked in London and only 5 per cent worked elsewhere. The proportion of White residents working in London was 94 per cent, with the remaining 6 per cent working in Surrey, Hertfordshire, Essex, Kent and other areas outside London. Over 131,000 White residents travelled outside London to work. The proportions, and numbers, of residents of Black ethnic groups working outside London were much smaller. More than 98 per cent of Black Caribbean residents worked in London, with just over 2,600 working outside London out of a total of around 120,510. Similar proportions of Black African and Black Other residents worked in London, with around 1,220 and 480 respectively travelling outside London to work out of totals of 42,550 and 20,030.

The proportions of residents of all the other ethnic groups working within London were much closer to the proportion for White residents – 95 per cent of Indian, Other Asian and Other groups, 96 per cent of Pakistani, and 94 per cent of Bangladeshi and Chinese residents working within London.

Looking in a little more detail at those working within London, less than half of White residents, 45 per cent, worked in the borough in which they lived, compared with 41 per cent of Black residents, 43 per cent of Indian and 40 per cent or less of most other ethnic groups. The only ethnic group with a higher proportion than the White group living and working in the same borough was the combined Pakistani and Bangladeshi group (combined because of small numbers). These figures are also likely to be affected by the types of jobs done by different ethnic groups (see Chapter 7).

The proportions of residents working in the four central London boroughs varied considerably between ethnic groups and between London boroughs. A quarter of White residents of London worked in central London compared with only 17 per cent of Indian and 18 per cent of Pakistani and Bangladeshi residents. The corresponding proportion of Black residents was 24 per cent – but this overall figure masks the difference between Black Caribbean residents and residents in the Black African and Black Other groups, who were both more likely than Black Caribbeans to work in central London. The figures were 22 per cent of Black Caribbean and 28 per cent of both Black African and Black Other residents working in central London. The proportions of Chinese and Other groups working in Central London were much higher than the proportions of White residents – 36 to 38 per cent of Other groups worked in Central London compared with 25 per cent of White residents.

Where the numbers were large enough, they show the proportion of White residents working in the City of London to be higher than the proportions of Black, Indian, Pakistani and Bangladeshi residents. The proportions of Other groups working in the City of London were higher than that for White residents. The ethnic group with the largest proportion of residents working in the City of London was Other Asian.

The pattern for residents working in Westminster showed the same sort of differences between ethnic

**Figure 8.4  Means of travel to work by gender, White residents**

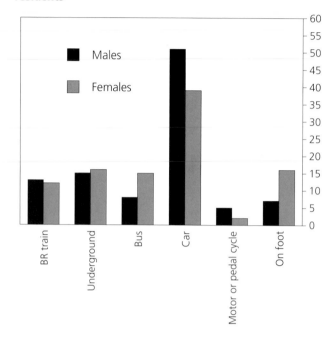

*Source: 1991 Census, Commissioned Table LRCT86*

**Figure 8.5  Means of travel to work by gender, Black Caribbean residents**

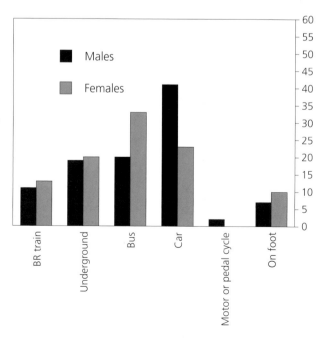

*Source: 1991 Census, Commissioned Table LRCT86*

**Figure 8.6 Means of travel to work by gender, Black African residents**

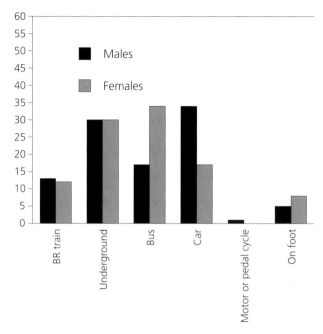

Source: 1991 Census, Commissioned Table LRCT86

**Figure 8.7 Means of travel to work by gender, Black Other residents**

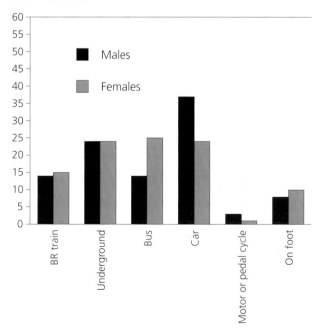

Source: 1991 Census, Commissioned Table LRCT86

groups – with Black Caribbean residents having lower proportions than Black African and Black Other residents; very low proportions of Indian, Pakistani and Bangladeshi residents; and relatively high proportions of Other ethnic groups working in Westminster. Chinese residents had the highest proportion working in Westminster.

### Means of travel to work used by residents by ethnic group, 1991

There were some interesting differences between the means of travel used by different ethnic groups, some of which result from where different ethnic groups live in London.

The figures for the White group, illustrated in Figure 8.4, were very similar to those for all residents because they formed the largest individual group. The only small difference was that a slightly higher proportion than average of White residents travelled by car and a slightly lower proportion than average travelled by bus. White men were more likely than White women to travel by car, whereas White women were more likely than White men to walk or travel to work by bus.

Black Caribbean residents were less likely than average to travel by car or walk to work, and more likely than average to travel by bus or underground. This pattern of travel is likely to be linked to the areas in which Black Caribbean residents of London lived and worked. The differences between Black Caribbean men and women were pronounced, with Black Caribbean and Black African women being the least likely of any ethnic group to travel to work by car and the most likely to travel to work by bus. Black Caribbean women were much less likely than White women to walk to work. Figure 8.5 illustrates the distribution for Black Caribbean residents.

Figure 8.6 shows that Black Africans were more likely to travel by underground and bus than by any other means, as they commonly worked in Westminster, Camden and Hackney. They were the only ethnic

**Figure 8.8 Means of travel to work by gender, Indian residents**

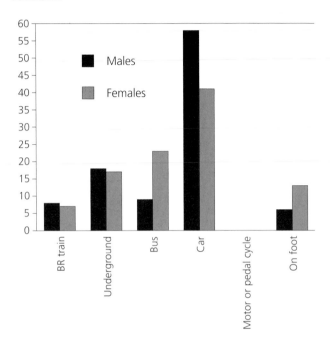

*Source: 1991 Census, Commissioned Table LRCT86*

**Figure 8.9 Means of travel to work by gender, Pakistani residents**

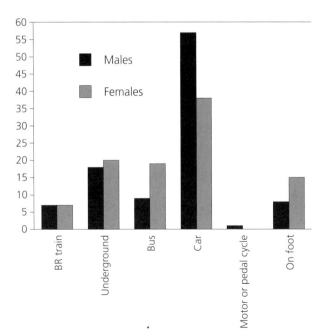

*Source: 1991 Census, Commissioned Table LRCT86*

group for which a car was not the most commonly used means of travel to work. There were almost equal proportions of Black African men and women travelling by underground, but large differences between the proportions of men and women travelling by bus and car. A very large proportion of Black African women travelled by bus, roughly equal to the proportion of Black African men travelling by car. The proportions of Black African men travelling by bus and Black African women travelling by car were also very similar.

Figure 8.7 shows that Black Others were more likely than average to travel by bus and underground, but car was still the most common means of travel. The distribution of means of travel was similar to that of Black Caribbean residents with slightly lower proportions of men and women travelling by car and bus and higher proportions travelling by underground. All Black groups had lower than average proportions travelling to work by car.

More than half of Indian residents travelled to work by car and a slightly higher than average proportion travelled by bus. A slightly lower proportion travelled by underground. Both Indian men and women had the largest proportions of any ethnic group travelling to work by car. Far more Indian women than men travelled by bus or on foot. Figure 8.8 shows this.

More than half of Pakistani residents travelled to work by car, and the overall distribution was similar to that of Indian residents as shown in Figure 8.9. Pakistani men and women, as with Indian men and women, were among the most likely to travel to work by car.

Higher than average proportions of Bangladeshi residents travelled by underground and bus, while a lower than average proportion travelled by car, shown in Figure 8.10. The most striking feature of the travel patterns of Bangladeshi residents was the very high proportion who walked to work, 22 per cent of residents. The proportions of both male and female Bangladeshis walking to work were very large.

**Figure 8.10  Means of travel to work by gender, Bangladeshi residents**

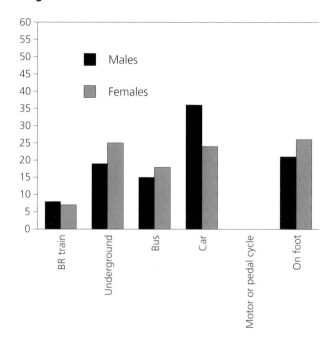

*Source: 1991 Census, Commissioned Table LRCT86*

**Figure 8.11  Means of travel to work by gender, Chinese residents**

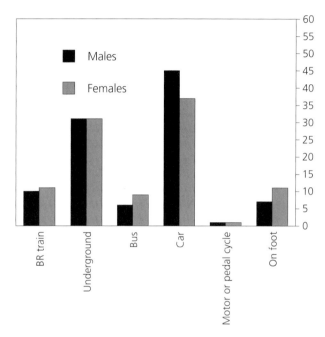

*Source: 1991 Census, Commissioned Table LRCT86*

**Figure 8.12  Means of travel to work by gender, Other Asian residents**

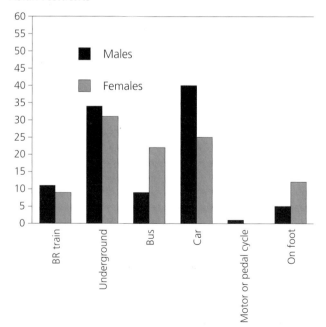

*Source: 1991 Census, Commissioned Table LRCT86*

**Figure 8.13  Means of travel to work by gender, Other residents**

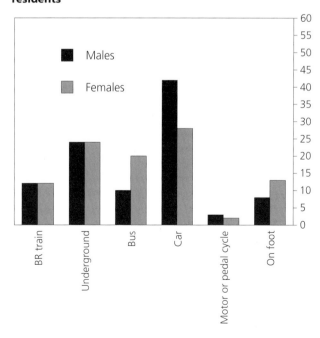

*Source: 1991 Census, Commissioned Table LRCT86*

**Figure 8.14  Distance travelled to work by White residents by gender, 1991**

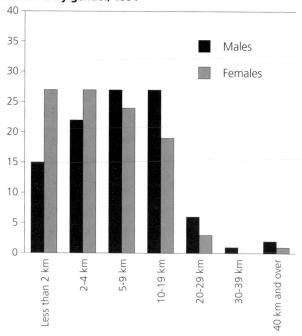

*Source: 1991 Census, Commissioned Table LRCT86*

**Figure 8.15  Distance travelled to work by Bangladeshi residents by gender, 1991**

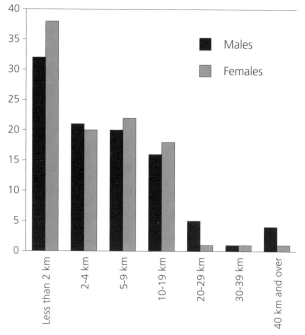

*Source: 1991 Census, Commissioned Table LRCT86*

Chinese residents had a different distribution of means of travel, shown in Figure 8.11, with 31 per cent of residents travelling by underground and 42 per cent travelling by car. This is probably explained by the fact that almost a third of Chinese residents worked in Westminster. A lower proportion of Chinese women than men travelled to work by car, but the difference was relatively small, and was smaller than for any other ethnic group.

Larger than average proportions of Other Asian and Other residents travelled to work by underground, and lower than average proportions travelled by car, see Figures 8.12 and 8.13. The differences between men and women were similar to those for most other ethnic groups, with larger proportions of men than women travelling by car and larger proportions of women than men travelling by bus and on foot.

**Distance travelled to work**

Another measure from the 1991 Census allows a comparison of distance travelled to work for different ethnic groups. This also shows some interesting, and different patterns. The vast majority of residents of London travelled less than 20 kilometres to work. Men tended to travel further than women in all ethnic groups, more than half of all women travelled less than 5 kilometres compared with only 37 per cent of men. Figure 8.14 shows the distance travelled for White men and women, reflecting the overall pattern.

Distance travelled is a factor of where people live and work, and we said earlier that most Black Caribbean, Black African and Black Other residents worked in London with very few travelling outside the capital. This explains why all Black groups had considerably lower proportions travelling more than 20 kilometres to work than the White group. The proportions travelling less than 2 km were slightly lower than for White residents and the proportions travelling between 2 and 9 km were larger than those for White residents. The same patterns applied to the differences between Black and White women and men. The main contrast between men and women was that the proportions of Black Caribbean and African women travelling less than 2km were only three quarters of the corresponding proportions for White women.

The proportions of Indian and Pakistani residents travelling the various distances to work were similar to those of White residents, with slightly fewer travelling 20 km or more.

The largest differences between ethnic minority groups and the White group were for Bangladeshis in London. One in three Bangladeshis travelled less than 2 km to work, rising to 38 per cent of Bangladeshi women who worked, as shown in Figure 8.15. At the other end of the scale Bangladeshis were more than twice as likely as White residents to travel 40 km or more to work. This is a result of Bangladeshi men being more likely than White men to travel 40 km or more, while Bangladeshi women were less likely than White women to travel long distances to work.

Chinese, Other Asian and Other women were all less likely than White women to travel less than 5 km to work, while only Chinese women were more likely than White women to travel 30 km or more. Figure 8.16 shows that Other Asian men travelled longer distances than White men up to 20 km and had a very different distribution to Other Asian women.

**Figure 8.16  Distance travelled to work by Other Asian residents by gender, 1991**

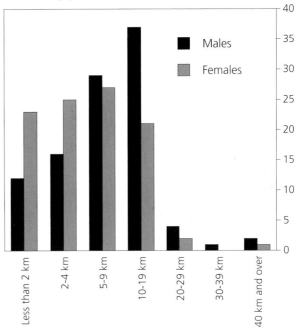

*Source: 1991 Census, Commissioned Table LRCT86*

# Chapter 9
# Looking ahead

# Looking ahead

## Change in London's population

Since the mid 1980s the population of London has increased slowly to over seven million after decades of decline, and the city has gradually become more cosmopolitan. Since 1991, 92 per cent of the growth in London's population has occurred through natural change – more births than deaths. London is a young city, with young people tending to move in, and people moving out as they become older. Less than four per cent of London's growth since 1991 has been through migration. London has high levels of in-migration, but it also has high levels of out-migration, and throughout the 1990s in and out migration have been almost identical.

Since 1991 the population of ethnic minority groups has grown, whilst those who record themselves as White are declining as people in this group leaving the city (as they have done since the Second World War) exceed those moving to the city (which they are doing in large numbers too). Ethnic minority populations have young age structures, and much of the growth in these populations is natural growth. International in and out migration has been high. A large component of international in-migration (31 per cent at present) is of asylum seekers and visitor switchers.

An understanding of the overall changes in London's demography, and the composition of those changes is important for the future success of the city. This section presents a detailed analysis of the latest estimates and future expected trends in London.

## Current estimates of London's ethnic minority communities

More than one in three Londoners is now from an ethnic minority group (including White minority groups such as some Irish, Cypriots and Turks), and around 300 languages are spoken. The latest estimates show that 1.8 million Londoners now belong to ethnic minority groups. Of people of ethnic minority origin recorded in London in the 1997-98 Labour Force Survey, 39 per cent were Black and 35 per cent of

Indian, Pakistani or Bangladeshi origin. A further 26 per cent were of mixed ethnic origin or from other ethnic minority groups (see Table 9.1).

**Table 9.1  London's Ethnic Minority Population, percentage by group**

| | |
|---|---|
| Black | 39 |
| Indian | 23 |
| Pakistani/Bangladeshi | 12 |
| Mixed/Other | 26 |
| | |
| Total ethnic minorities | 100 |
| Total number | 1,794,000 |

*Source: 1997/98 Labour Force Survey, Regional Trends 34*

Changes within the ethnic minority population in each borough in London are shown by the Local Authorities Database of the Labour Force Survey. The figures for the four years for which the annual database has been constructed are shown in Table 9.2.

Table 9.2 shows figures for those boroughs with an ethnic minority population of ten per cent or more. The borough with the largest ethnic minority population is Newham, where the majority (56 per cent) of the population were recorded as ethnic minorities in 1997-98. There are several boroughs in London with ethnic minority populations of less than ten per cent, as can be seen by the empty cells in the table. The boroughs with the smaller ethnic minority populations tend to be the Outer London boroughs to the east and south. The confidence intervals attached to these data are high. Actual figures could vary by as much as five per cent.

The Labour Force Survey uses the same ethnic group categories as the 1991 Census. It is important to recognise that this classification places some ethnic minority groups within the White group. This includes a number of Cypriots, Turks and Arabs who would record themselves as White. In London it is estimated

**Table 9.2 Ethnic Minority Population (percentage) in London boroughs 1994-95 to 1997-98**

| | 1997-98 | 1996-97 | 1995-96 | 1994-95 |
|---|---|---|---|---|
| Barking & Dagenham | | 15.59 | | |
| Barnet | 27.73 | 22.03 | 19.99 | 19.61 |
| Bexley | | | | |
| Brent | 48.97 | 48.07 | 52.65 | 50.08 |
| Bromley | | | | |
| Camden | 24.13 | 16.08 | 18.08 | 18.77 |
| Croydon | 21.31 | 18.36 | 19.06 | 18.82 |
| Ealing | 35.37 | 34.81 | 35.01 | 35.14 |
| Enfield | 20.06 | 19.23 | 16.06 | 16.43 |
| Greenwich | 18.13 | 17.65 | 14.58 | 16.35 |
| Hackney | 41.88 | 42.57 | 38.34 | 35.05 |
| Hammersmith & Fulham | 19.19 | 16.96 | 21.00 | 19.15 |
| Haringey | 35.49 | 31.03 | 34.77 | 31.68 |
| Harrow | 35.22 | 31.11 | 27.85 | 28.52 |
| Havering | | | | |
| Hillingdon | 12.97 | 11.31 | 12.58 | 13.56 |
| Hounslow | 30.82 | 32.60 | 26.64 | 25.63 |
| Islington | 17.88 | 25.07 | 21.08 | 21.54 |
| Kensington & Chelsea | 18.21 | 17.28 | 12.48 | 15.93 |
| Kingston upon Thames | | | | |
| Lambeth | 39.15 | 36.82 | 31.65 | 32.51 |
| Lewisham | 26.51 | 25.10 | 22.04 | 21.98 |
| Merton | 24.08 | 20.17 | 16.12 | 17.00 |
| Newham | 55.94 | 52.60 | 54.87 | 53.06 |
| Redbridge | 23.88 | 25.67 | 25.72 | 25.26 |
| Richmond upon Thames | | | | |
| Southwark | 37.10 | 34.73 | 30.90 | 27.65 |
| Sutton | | | | |
| Tower Hamlets | 47.14 | 37.77 | 43.72 | 40.60 |
| Waltham Forest | 31.58 | 30.34 | 25.34 | 23.87 |
| Wandsworth | 21.22 | 20.78 | 18.39 | 19.81 |
| Westminster | 22.82 | 24.68 | 24.43 | 28.23 |
| | | | | |
| Greater London | 29.58 | 27.77 | 26.63 | 26.31 |

*Source: Labour Force Survey Local Authorities Database*

**Table 9.3  Ethnic group populations 1991 to 2011, London**

| | 1991 | 1996 | 2001 | 2006 | 2011 | % change 1991 to 2011 |
|---|---|---|---|---|---|---|
| White | 5,492,927 | 5,380,973 | 5,359,376 | 5,351,329 | 5,329,830 | -3 |
| Black Caribbean | 301,561 | 328,076 | 340,193 | 332,252 | 318,184 | 6 |
| Black African | 172,187 | 249,136 | 276,522 | 308,655 | 332,339 | 93 |
| Black Other | 84,516 | 108,839 | 117,014 | 116,121 | 113,810 | 35 |
| Indian | 356,776 | 401,552 | 425,449 | 428,489 | 422,350 | 18 |
| Pakistani | 90,736 | 116,625 | 130,568 | 139,069 | 143,931 | 59 |
| Bangladeshi | 89,248 | 112,139 | 120,126 | 124,855 | 128,030 | 43 |
| Chinese | 59,100 | 69,700 | 75,202 | 81,539 | 86,299 | 46 |
| Other Asian | 116,935 | 149,334 | 163,180 | 180,880 | 194,284 | 66 |
| Other | 125,966 | 162,745 | 173,048 | 180,696 | 187,009 | 48 |
| Total (non-White) ethnic minorities | 1,397,021 | 1,698,147 | 1,821,302 | 1,892,556 | 1,926,236 | 38 |
| Total | 6,889,948 | 7,079,120 | 7,180,678 | 7,243,885 | 7,256,066 | 5 |

*Source: 1998 LRC Ethnic group projections (1/M96)*

that at the time of the 1991 Census around ten per cent of London's ethnic minority population were White, including around five per cent Irish and another five per cent Cypriots, Turks, Arabs and others.

## The growth in London's ethnic minority communities

The LRC has developed a computer model projecting the populations of different ethnic groups. Figures show the (non-White) ethnic minority population growing from 20.3 per cent in 1991, to 25.4 per cent in 2001 and 26.5 per cent in 2011. Earlier in this report it was estimated that ten per cent of London's population are from White ethnic minority groups such as white Irish, Cypriot and Turkish people. If this percentage is maintained, the total ethnic minority population in London is estimated to be up to 35 per cent in 2001.

London's population is set to grow very gradually over the next decade. The White ethnic group shows a decline from 1991 to 2011 of three per cent, whilst all the other ethnic groups increase by an average of 38 per cent. Ethnic minority groups vary in the rates at which they are growing. The two largest minority groups, the Indian and Black Caribbean groups are growing by the smallest amounts (18 and six per cent respectively). The next in terms of growth is the Black Other group which is growing by around a third over the 20 years. Five of the nine groups are growing by around half over the two decades including the Pakistani and Bangladeshi groups, the two Other groups and the Chinese group. The Black African group is set to grow the fastest, with a growth of over 90 per cent, almost doubling in this time.

Overall the number of children in London is expected to grow by 11 per cent over the period although this masks an increase up to 2006 and a small decrease to 2011. The ethnic minority groups combined show a larger increase of 22 per cent. The ethnic minority

**Table 9.4  Ethnic group populations aged 0-17 1991 to 2011, London**

| Population aged 0-17 | 1991 | 1996 | 2001 | 2006 | 2011 | % change 1991 to 2011 |
|---|---|---|---|---|---|---|
| White | 1,033,206 | 1,073,432 | 1,104,091 | 1,111,063 | 1,095,973 | 6 |
| Black Caribbean | 73,633 | 82,841 | 87,224 | 85,296 | 78,409 | 6 |
| Black African | 53,894 | 84,044 | 93,104 | 101,067 | 103,005 | 91 |
| Black Other | 42,887 | 54,035 | 54,899 | 50,189 | 43,997 | 3 |
| Indian | 108,173 | 110,866 | 110,535 | 109,090 | 107,134 | -1 |
| Pakistani | 34,886 | 42,547 | 45,105 | 47,019 | 48,836 | 40 |
| Bangladeshi | 46,148 | 48,938 | 49,389 | 49,530 | 49,933 | 8 |
| Chinese | 14,419 | 15,370 | 16,495 | 17,417 | 18,009 | 25 |
| Other Asian | 30,146 | 36,970 | 39,673 | 42,977 | 45,175 | 50 |
| Other | 50,133 | 64,257 | 64,903 | 63,419 | 61,163 | 22 |
| Total (non-White) ethnic minorities | 454,318 | 539,867 | 561,327 | 566,005 | 555,663 | 22 |
| Total | 1,487,524 | 1,613,298 | 1,665,418 | 1,677,068 | 1,651,636 | 11 |

*Source:  1998 LRC Ethnic group projections (1/M96)*

groups show more of an increase mostly because these groups have a large proportion of women of childbearing age, so even if fertility levels are low, a large number of children have recently been born and this will continue for a short time. Overall fertility rates are slightly higher for these groups, which contributes to the increase in children.

Again the extent by which each ethnic group changes differs.  The Indian group shows a small decline over this time period, although this masks an increase up to 1996. All other ethnic groups show an increase between 1991 and 2011. For the Black Other, White, Black Caribbean and Bangladeshi groups the increase in numbers of children is small – less than 10 per cent. In the White ethnic group the population of those aged 0 - 17 contains the children of the baby boom people born in the early 60s. Although the average number of children these people are having is low compared with other ethnic groups, there are, as with the minority

groups, proportionately a large number of women in their peak childbearing years. For most ethnic groups there is more growth in the period 1991 to 2001 than between 2001 and 2011. This is partly a reflection of the way the model works in that the future population of London is not able to grow much above seven million unless there are radical changes in household densities. Therefore this constraint limits future growth in London's population.

The Black Other group is expected to increase the most over this period, as a result of the increasing number of children likely to be Black British, or Black of mixed parentage, who would be included within this group.

The population of working aged people is set to grow more than the population of children over this time. The differential rates of change will have important implications for the labour market. Overall the number of people aged 18 - 64 is set to rise by eight per cent.

**Table 9.5  Ethnic group populations aged 18-64 1991 to 2011, London**

| Population aged 18-64 | 1991 | 1996 | 2001 | 2006 | 2011 | % change 1991 to 2011 |
|---|---|---|---|---|---|---|
| White | 3,536,285 | 3,449,602 | 3,472,356 | 3,517,264 | 3,533,812 | 0 |
| Black Caribbean | 212,561 | 219,942 | 217,125 | 203,446 | 195,178 | -8 |
| Black African | 116,452 | 161,498 | 178,273 | 199,895 | 219,305 | 88 |
| Black Other | 40,505 | 53,267 | 60,149 | 63,524 | 66,971 | 65 |
| Indian | 232,819 | 267,628 | 284,689 | 282,830 | 274,855 | 18 |
| Pakistani | 54,200 | 70,989 | 80,499 | 84,852 | 86,457 | 60 |
| Bangladeshi | 42,023 | 60,329 | 66,268 | 69,105 | 71,308 | 70 |
| Chinese | 42,675 | 51,584 | 55266 | 59,893 | 63,325 | 48 |
| Other Asian | 83,890 | 107,811 | 117,328 | 129,556 | 138,278 | 65 |
| Other | 71,320 | 92,617 | 101,212 | 109,102 | 116,392 | 63 |
| Total (non-White) ethnic minorities | 896,445 | 1,085,664 | 1,160,810 | 1,202,203 | 1,232,069 | 37 |
| Total | 4,432,730 | 4,535,266 | 4,633,166 | 4,719,467 | 4,765,881 | 8 |

*Source: 1998 LRC Ethnic group projections (1/M96)*

Contained within this is a slight (less than one per cent) decline in the numbers of White people in this age group, and a growth of ethnic minorities of 37 per cent.

The largest community (Indian) has a lower rate of growth at 18 per cent, whilst others such as Black African and Black Other groups are set to grow by around two thirds. The Black Caribbean group shows a small decline over this 20 year period.

London is set to have declining numbers of older people in this period, a trend which has been evident for many years as people choose to spend their later years outside London. This is particularly so of the White group which is expected to lose 24 per cent of its population over this time. However this loss is offset by the increase in ethnic minority older people of 200 per cent, increasing almost three fold. In fact a number of ethnic groups do triple in number over this time, including the Black African, Pakistani and Bangladeshi communities.

The ethnic minority communities with the largest populations of older people, Indians and Black Caribbeans, are set to grow significantly in size, more than doubling over these two decades. In this age group in particular, the change in numbers is not a new trend, but the change in composition of the older population in London is considerable.

**Asylum seekers and other international migrants**
Refugees have become an important feature of London's demography in the 1990s – a trend which looks set to continue into the next millennium. Between mid 1991 and mid-1998 it is estimated that 212,500 asylum seekers and visitor switchers became residents of London, an average of just over 30,000 per year. (The number of refugees who leave is not recorded). The yearly figures are shown in Table 9.7. Asylum seekers include all those applying for asylum, whilst visitor switchers are people who have entered the country with a short-term visa, such as a tourist, and

### Table 9.6 Ethnic group populations aged 65 and over 1991 to 2011, London

| Population aged 65+ | 1991 | 1996 | 2001 | 2006 | 2011 | % change 1991 to 2011 |
|---|---|---|---|---|---|---|
| White | 923,436 | 857,940 | 782,929 | 723,002 | 700,045 | -24 |
| Black Caribbean | 15,367 | 25,293 | 35,843 | 43,510 | 44,597 | 190 |
| Black African | 1,841 | 3,594 | 5,144 | 7,693 | 10,029 | 445 |
| Black Other | 1,124 | 1,537 | 1,967 | 2,407 | 2,841 | 153 |
| Indian | 15,783 | 23,059 | 30,225 | 36,568 | 40,361 | 156 |
| Pakistani | 1,651 | 3,089 | 4,964 | 7,198 | 8,637 | 423 |
| Bangladeshi | 1,078 | 2,872 | 4,469 | 6,220 | 6,789 | 530 |
| Chinese | 2006 | 2,747 | 3,441 | 4,230 | 4,964 | 147 |
| Other Asian | 2,896 | 4,553 | 6,179 | 8,348 | 10,831 | 274 |
| Other | 4,513 | 5,872 | 6,933 | 8,175 | 9,454 | 110 |
| | | | | | | |
| Total (non-White) ethnic minorities | 46,258 | 72,616 | 99,165 | 124,348 | 138,504 | 199 |
| Total | 969,694 | 930,556 | 882,094 | 847,350 | 838,549 | -14 |

*Source: 1998 LRC Ethnic group projections (1/M96)*

have then had a more permanent status granted, such as a student or spouse, allowing them to remain in the UK for a year or more. The main countries in 1997 from which the highest numbers of refugees came were

### Table 9.7 Asylum seekers and visitor switchers assigned to London

| | |
|---|---|
| 1991-92 | 32,900 |
| 1992-93 | 29,200 |
| 1993-94 | 22,200 |
| 1994-95 | 28,800 |
| 1995-96 | 36,300 |
| 1996-97 | 29,100 |
| 1997-98 | 34,000 |
| | |
| 1991-98 | 212,500 |

*Source: ONS mid-year estimates change analysis, published in LRC DSS Technical Paper 99/3*

Somalia, former Yugoslavia, former Soviet Union, China and Sri Lanka. Asylum seekers in the 1990s have often come from countries where there were only very small communities beforehand in London, such as Somalia, Zaire, Bosnia and Kosova. This has added to London's diversity. It is very difficult to identify where the next refugee movements might come from, but the Foreign and Commonwealth Office currently currently identifies nearly 30 areas or countries experiencing political unrest.

International migration has been high and has increased during the 1990s, averaging a net inflow of around 50,000 international migrants a year. This pattern looks set to continue. The out-migration of persons who had sought asylum in the UK is included in the overall outflow of migrants from London measured by the International Passenger Survey (IPS). The IPS samples both international inflows and outflows. The estimated total in, out and net flows since mid 1991 are recorded

**Table 9.8 London's International Migration, 1991-1998 (excludes asylum seekers and visitor switchers)**

|  | Inflow | Outflow | Net |
|---|---|---|---|
| 1991-92 | 60,200 | 65,600 | -5,400 |
| 1992-93 | 57,700 | 52,700 | 5,000 |
| 1993-94 | 76,100 | 56,600 | 19,500 |
| 1994-95 | 71,800 | 62,100 | 9,800 |
| 1995-96 | 84,800 | 53,000 | 31,800 |
| 1996-97 | 84,900 | 60,000 | 24,900 |
| 1997-98 | 111,200 | 73,700 | 37,500 |

*Source: ONS MIG2 forms published in LRC DSS Technical Paper 99/3*

in Table 9.8. The table shows the considerable rise in the inflows coupled with more stable outflows. This has led to a small net loss in 1991-92 changing to gains of over 24,000 in each year since mid-1995.

Detailed IPS results for 1997 show that 24 per cent of migrants into the UK are British. Of those who are not British, over a third are European Union citizens, just under a quarter (23 per cent) are Old Commonwealth citizens, 17 per cent New Commonwealth citizens and the remaining 24 per cent are from other countries.

Whether international migration will increase, remain constant or decrease will depend on all kinds of factors such as the UK economy, the ability of London to attract employers including perhaps the type of employers attracted, the cost of housing and staff, and government and EC policies influencing the right of European and other workers to employment. An interesting fact is that 37 per cent of homes in central London are now purchased by overseas buyers (Source: Savills 1999). Perhaps in the future today's Londoners will not be able to afford to live in the centre at all. London might have a corporate city centre by then!

A large and growing ethnic minority population, and an inflow of international migrants and refugees will add to London's ethnic diversity and will lead to many opportunities and issues which Londoners must address

in the future. This diversity offers London opportunities such as the business strength from a workforce which has good networks in countries around the world, and which speaks 300 different languages. There is also an extensive artistic diversity borne from communities celebrating their heritages. This report shows how different communities fare within the labour and housing markets. There is undoubtedly race discrimination occurring both directly and indirectly across the city. How different identities and communities are shaping the city and how the London is dealing with ethnic diversity issues, will have a big impact on social cohesion and the success of London in the future.

**Future data**

There has been considerable debate over the last few years about how the next census should present a question on ethnic group. There is a lot of interest in developing the question further, in the light of knowledge gained and social change since the 1991 Census. There is also interest in maintaining a degree of comparability between the 1991 and 2001 ethnic group categories, so that change over the decade may be studied. The final result looks like being a compromise between these two interests.

The 2001 Census Order has confirmed that the ethnic group question used in the Census Rehearsal in April 1999 is the one which will be used in the 2001 Census. It is shown on the following page.

It is also hoped that a question on religion, similar to that on the next page, will be included. These are in addition to a question on country of birth, which will hopefully give more detail than in 1991. The ability to cross-tabulate ethnic group, religion and country of birth should lead to a far better understanding of ethnicity in London in the coming decade.

## What is your ethnic group?

Choose one section from a to e, then tick the appropriate box to indicate your cultural background.

a       White

- [ ] British
- [ ] Irish
- [ ] Any other White background, please write in

......................................................

b       Mixed

- [ ] White and Black Caribbean
- [ ] White and Black African
- [ ] White and Asian
- [ ] Any other Mixed background, please write in

......................................................

c       Asian or Asian British

- [ ] Indian
- [ ] Pakistani
- [ ] Bangladeshi
- [ ] Any other Asian background, please write in

......................................................

d       Black or Black British

- [ ] Caribbean
- [ ] African
- [ ] Any other Black background, please write in

......................................................

e       Chinese or other ethnic group

- [ ] Chinese
- [ ] Any other, please write in

......................................................

## What is your religion?

Tick one box only.

- [ ] None
- [ ] Christian (including Church of England, Catholic, Protestant and all other Christian denominations)
- [ ] Buddhist
- [ ] Hindu
- [ ] Muslim
- [ ] Sikh
- [ ] Jewish
- [ ] Any other religion, please write in

......................................................

**References**

Yolande Barnes of FPD Savills in a talk 'Population change – the market impacts' given at a Joseph Rowntree Foundation conference *The People – where are they coming from? The housing consequences of migration* in September 1999

# Chapter 10
## Notes and definitions

# Notes and definitions

The 1991 Census was organised in the traditional way by OPCS (now the Office for National Statistics, ONS) and was the nineteenth decennial census. This report includes special tables from the 1991 Census commissioned by the London Research Centre, data from the National Topic Report on Housing and Availability of Cars and data from the standard datasets, that is the local base and small area statistics.

## Size of standard datasets

The statistics made available from the 1991 Census are more extensive than those produced for any previous census of Great Britain. Census users generally had been requesting more output than had been produced previously, particularly arising from the inclusion of the new questions on ethnicity, long-term illness, term-time address of students, possession of central heating and hours worked weekly in main job. With developments in technology over the previous decade, ONS was able to produce a larger number of tables without substantially increasing the cost to users. ONS decided that, to protect confidentiality of individuals, it would produce a more detailed standard dataset at ward level than it would at enumeration district level. Hence the Small Area Statistics were produced, as in 1981, for enumeration districts and above, but additionally the Local Base Statistics were produced at ward level and above.

## Imputation

OPCS encountered some unique problems in taking the 1991 Census, and new efforts had to be made to account for the level of non-contact which was apparent as the Census was being taken.

Imputation was a new method of accounting for wholly absent households, who did not return a form voluntarily in the 1991 Census. It was a procedure whereby missing households were added back on and various household characteristics imputed for those absent households. Overall in London 292,000 absent (or not contacted) people were imputed in the 1991 Census statistics. The number varied considerably across

London, from 24,000 imputed in Lambeth to less than 2,000 in Bexley and just over 500 in the City of London. Far more people were imputed in Inner London than in Outer London, illustrating how difficult enumerators experienced in contacting everyone in some parts of Inner London. The difficulties were many and varied. They included entry phones and security systems which made it difficult to get into some buildings, and the increase in single person households making it more difficult to find anyone at home.

## Undercounting

After the imputation process, there is still thought to have been some residual undercounting in the 1991 Census. The overall amount is small, less than two per cent of the population nationally, but the effects of it are very important for London.

Undercounting is thought to have been particularly concentrated among specific age groups, those aged 20 to 49 (and particularly men aged 20 to 29) and those aged 85 and over. ONS has published two reports based on the Census Validation Survey, the Coverage Report and the Quality Report. Both of these may help inform Census users about the data they are using, and the potential pitfalls.

## Definitions

*Usually resident population* – is a count of all persons recorded as resident in households in an area, even if they were present elsewhere on census night, plus residents in communal establishments who were present in the establishment on census night. This population is 'topped up' with persons from enumerated wholly absent households and imputed wholly absent households.

*Household*

A household is either one person living alone or a group of people living at the same address who share at least one meal a day or a common living room.

## Ethnic group

People were asked to tick a box showing ethnic group. The main output categories were:

White
Black Caribbean
Black African
Black Other
Indian
Pakistani
Bangladeshi
Chinese
Other Asian
Other

The notes to the question stated that 'If the person is descended from more than one ethnic or racial group, please tick the group to which the person considers he/she belongs, or tick the Any other ethnic group box and describe the person's ancestry in the space provided'.

For some of the tables commissioned by the LRC a more detailed breakdown was used – this was the full 35 code classification used for coding responses to the question and includes more detail on the written-in answers. These categories were then recoded to the ten main output categories. For example, 'Greek (including Greek Cypriot)' was a category in the full coding system (before recoding), which was recoded to the White category for the main output (after recoding). People ticking Black Other and writing in a Caribbean Island, West Indies or Guyana were given a separate code in the detailed breakdown and were recoded to Black Caribbean in the main output classification.

## Pensioner

In this report the term pensioner refers to anyone who has reached state retirement age, that is 65 for men and 60 for women.

## Pensionable age/retirement age

Age at least 65 for men and age at least 60 for women.

## Central London

Central London is the City of London and boroughs of Camden, Westminster and Kensington and Chelsea.

## Inner London

The definition used in this report and in 1991 Census output generally includes the City of London and the London boroughs of Camden, Hackney, Hammersmith and Fulham, Haringey, Islington, Kensington and Chelsea, Lambeth, Lewisham, Newham, Southwark, Tower Hamlets, Wandsworth and Westminster.

## Outer London

The definition used in this report and in 1991 Census output generally includes the London boroughs of Barking and Dagenham, Barnet, Bexley, Brent, Bromley, Croydon, Ealing, Enfield, Greenwich, Harrow, Havering, Hillingdon, Hounslow, Kingston upon Thames, Merton, Redbridge, Richmond upon Thames, Sutton and Waltham Forest.

## Migrant

A migrant in the Census data is anyone with a different usual address one year before the Census.

## Head of household

The head of household is defined as the person entered in the first column of the census form, provided that the person was aged 16 or over and usually resident at the address. Form fillers were asked to enter the 'head of joint head of household' in the first column but neither term was defined.

## Family

A family is one of the following:
• a married couple with or without their never married children, including a childless married couple
• a co-habiting couple (one male and one female stating that they 'live together as a couple' with or without their never married children, including a childless couple
• a lone parent together with her or his never married child(ren)

A family contains a maximum of two generations. Grandparents with grandchildren are classified as a family if there are no apparent parents of the children resident in the household. Childless in this context means that no child of the couple is apparent and resident in the household. Dependent children are in the second generation of a family and are aged 0-15, or 16-18 and never married, in full-time education and economically inactive.

## Household space
A household space is generally defined as the accommodation available for a household. Household spaces in permanent accommodation are unshared dwellings purpose built, converted or not self-contained, shared dwellings not self-contained, and unattached household spaces not self-contained. There is also non permanent accommodation which is included in the full household space type classification.

## Rooms
The number of rooms is defined as the number of rooms a household has for its own use, excluding small kitchens under two metres wide, bathrooms and toilets.

## Overcrowding
For the purposes of this report, overcrowding refers to households having more than one person per room. Severe overcrowding refers to households with more than 1.5 persons per room.

## Amenities
The amenities about which information is collected in the census are inside WC, bath and/or shower and central heating. The basic amenities referred to in this report are inside WC and bath/shower.

## Central heating
Includes night storage heaters, warm air and underfloor heating systems, whether actually used or not. The form asked whether central heating was available in all bedrooms and living rooms, some or none.

## Limiting long-term illness
The statistics on long-term illness are based on responses to the question 'Does the person have any long-term illness, health problem or handicap which limits his/her daily activities or the work he/she can do?

## Economically active
A person is economically active if, in the week before the Census, the person had a paid job, was unemployed but looking for a job, or was unemployed and sick but would be looking for a job after recovering from illness.

## Economic activity rates
Economic activity rates are defined as the number of people economically active as a percentage of those aged 16 and over.

## Full-time working
Full-time working is defined as working 31 hours or more per week in a person's main job in 1991. In the 1981 Census, full-time working was part of the question on economic activity, as a question on hours worked was not included.

## Part-time working
Part-time working is defined as working 30 hours or less in a person's main job. In the 1981 Census, part-time working was part of the question on economic activity, as a question on hours worked was not included.

## Occupation
The occupation of a person depends on the type of work they do. Occupation codes are allocated from the write-in answers to the Census question on the main things done in the person's job and their full job title. These codes are based on the Standard Occupational Classification (SOC), 1992 published by HMSO. There are nine major and 22 sub-major groups.

## Industry
The industry in which a person works is determined by the business or activity in which his or her occupation is followed. The industrial classification has regard only to

the nature of the service or product to which the labour contributes. Industry codes are assigned, as far as possible, by reference to the Standard Industrial Classification (SIC) 1980. This classification was revised in 1992, too late for use with the 1991 Census.

*Social class based on occupation*
Social class is based on occupation for people who had a job in the ten years before the Census. Occupations are grouped in such a way as to bring together, as far as possible, people with similar levels of occupational skill. A person's employment status may also be taken into account so that foremen and managers may be assigned to a higher social class than those they are supervising.

Members of the armed forces and those with inadequately described occupations are not allocated to a social class.

*Means of travel to work*
Means of travel to work relates to how the longest part, by distance, of the person's normal daily journey to work is made.

*Asylum seekers*
Anyone who has applied to the Home Office for asylum and is awaiting a decision.

*Visitor switchers*
Visitor switchers are those who have entered the country with a short term visa, such as a tourist, and have then had a more permanent status granted, such as a student or spouse, allowing them to remain in the country for a year or more.

**100 per cent and ten per cent sample data**
Some census questions, for example that on occupation, are so difficult to code that they have been processed for only a ten per cent sample of census forms. It is for these difficult to code topics that data is only published in the ten per cent sample statistics. Other topics included in this are social class, socio-economic group, industry, qualifications and family composition. The sample was drawn by randomly selecting one complete (but not imputed) household form from each stratum of ten sequentially numbered forms, together with one person randomly selected from each stratum of ten sequentially numbered individual forms from communal establishments.

**Copyright**
All Census data is Crown Copyright and this must be acknowledged whenever the statistics are quoted.

# Appendices

# Appendix 1

**Table A.1  New country of birth figures from commissioned data unavailable from the standard Census output**

| | Brazil | Colombia | Iraq | Jordan | Lebanon | Saudi Arabia | Syria | Taiwan | Thailand |
|---|---|---|---|---|---|---|---|---|---|
| City of London | 2 | 0 | 12 | 2 | 4 | 1 | 0 | 1 | 8 |
| Camden | 379 | 251 | 262 | 27 | 235 | 50 | 48 | 40 | 136 |
| Hackney | 84 | 213 | 65 | 32 | 81 | 9 | 16 | 7 | 33 |
| Hammersmith and Fulham | 290 | 189 | 413 | 43 | 301 | 45 | 63 | 17 | 169 |
| Haringey | 172 | 147 | 188 | 19 | 489 | 25 | 42 | 22 | 60 |
| Islington | 141 | 255 | 89 | 10 | 75 | 37 | 34 | 26 | 104 |
| Kensington and Chelsea | 588 | 454 | 554 | 129 | 1,206 | 112 | 169 | 29 | 370 |
| Lambeth | 251 | 444 | 205 | 20 | 100 | 26 | 21 | 2 | 85 |
| Lewisham | 88 | 76 | 109 | 16 | 50 | 17 | 48 | 22 | 74 |
| Newham | 38 | 55 | 67 | 13 | 86 | 31 | 15 | 5 | 124 |
| Southwark | 139 | 268 | 161 | 15 | 74 | 18 | 12 | 21 | 91 |
| Tower Hamlets | 36 | 62 | 44 | 6 | 54 | 32 | 2 | 6 | 61 |
| Wandsworth | 339 | 178 | 300 | 39 | 165 | 35 | 32 | 25 | 189 |
| Westminster | 635 | 353 | 831 | 158 | 1,230 | 212 | 247 | 74 | 249 |
| Barking and Dagenham | 9 | 6 | 22 | 8 | 7 | 5 | 7 | 3 | 19 |
| Barnet | 258 | 193 | 671 | 45 | 150 | 40 | 73 | 93 | 116 |
| Bexley | 18 | 6 | 64 | 5 | 10 | 6 | 13 | 0 | 22 |
| Brent | 184 | 164 | 596 | 28 | 321 | 58 | 106 | 48 | 179 |
| Bromley | 66 | 36 | 120 | 9 | 63 | 23 | 10 | 17 | 56 |
| Croydon | 82 | 40 | 177 | 27 | 105 | 36 | 22 | 21 | 70 |
| Ealing | 165 | 63 | 1,339 | 70 | 461 | 142 | 186 | 54 | 115 |
| Enfield | 21 | 63 | 106 | 16 | 84 | 27 | 22 | 6 | 34 |
| Greenwich | 39 | 46 | 127 | 9 | 28 | 21 | 2 | 3 | 45 |
| Harrow | 49 | 64 | 213 | 4 | 96 | 21 | 32 | 73 | 32 |
| Havering | 10 | 12 | 39 | 4 | 14 | 6 | 8 | 22 | 14 |
| Hillingdon | 74 | 26 | 174 | 12 | 77 | 12 | 24 | 14 | 80 |
| Hounslow | 92 | 54 | 340 | 25 | 302 | 33 | 68 | 18 | 100 |
| Kingston upon Thames | 54 | 54 | 293 | 17 | 93 | 20 | 31 | 16 | 76 |
| Merton | 64 | 54 | 217 | 41 | 172 | 26 | 54 | 26 | 158 |
| Redbridge | 39 | 44 | 156 | 9 | 54 | 21 | 33 | 9 | 33 |
| Richmond upon Thames | 146 | 41 | 178 | 27 | 163 | 24 | 43 | 11 | 101 |
| Sutton | 42 | 25 | 162 | 13 | 28 | 11 | 12 | 2 | 43 |
| Waltham Forest | 36 | 55 | 59 | 11 | 66 | 18 | 10 | 10 | 71 |
| Inner London | 3,182 | 2,945 | 3,300 | 529 | 4,150 | 650 | 749 | 297 | 1,753 |
| Outer London | 1,448 | 1,046 | 5,053 | 380 | 2,294 | 550 | 756 | 446 | 1,364 |
| Greater London | 4,630 | 3,991 | 8,353 | 909 | 6,444 | 1,200 | 1,505 | 743 | 3,117 |

*Source: 1991 Census, LRC Commissioned Table LRCT14*

# Appendix 2

**Data sources**

## 1991 Census

There are limitations to both the ethnic group and the migration data from the Census which have been discussed at length elsewhere. Difficulties occur with the migration data because the Census only marks two points in time and does not pick up intermediary moves. For example, a respondent may have moved from the address one year ago (A) to another (B) before moving again before the Census date (C). In this situation the intermediary move (B) will not be recorded and the Census will show the migration flow as being from A to C. In addition, respondents who moved back to their original address (from A to B to A) will not be recorded as migrants at all. Although people who moved from outside Britain to each borough are recorded, the opposite flow of international emigrants cannot be measured by the Census.

Other data sources which include information about migration and ethnic group are the Labour Force Survey (LFS) and the ONS Longitudinal Study (LS). The LFS enables detailed analysis of migrants'

economic position to be undertaken, although the addition of ethnic group as a variable often means the sample becomes very small. The LS enables migrants to be tracked over time as three censuses have been linked to vital registration and other health data . Useful though these two surveys are, the small numbers mean that analysis is restricted to London. Despite the drawbacks of the census data, it is still the most comprehensive source of information on migration by ethnic group, and the only source for robust local analysis of migration patterns.

In order to obtain the data which best suited the LRC's requirements (primarily for input to population projection models), a table was commissioned from ONS which was based initially on Table 11 in the national migration report. The data were a 100 per cent sample of migrants for broad age groups, for males and females separately, at borough level, for the ten main ethnic groups classified in the Census, for four main types of move and a count of the total resident migrants. The details of the data can be seen in Table B1.

**Table B1**
**Details of the commissioned migration data - LRCT49**

| Ethnic groups | Age groups | Gender | Type of move |
|---|---|---|---|
| White | 1-4 | female | moves within a borough |
| Black Caribbean | 5-15 | male | moves between boroughs |
| Black African | 16-19 | | move between the Rest of |
| Black Other | 20-29 | | GB and each borough |
| Indian | 30-44 | | moves from outside GB to each borough |
| Pakistani | 45-pensionable age | | total migrants |
| Bangladeshi | pensionable age and over | | |
| Chinese | | | |
| Other Asian | | | |
| Other | | | |

*Source: 1991 Census, LRC Commissioned Table 49*

## Adjustments to the data

The data were provided as unsupressed flows for each type of move by age, sex and ethnic group. ONS was asked not to include migrants who did not state a previous address in within area moves, as had been done for the published tables. This enabled a count of these people to be made. They could then be assigned origins to their moves in proportion to the known flows into each area.

An important point to note is that in- and out-migration flows include the sum of all people moving in and out of London boroughs, and not just all people moving in and out of London as a whole. Because of this movers between London boroughs will be included as in-migrants to one area and out-migrants of another. Migration matrices were constructed to facilitate this process.

Finally an estimate of international out-migration was made using the International Passenger Survey. As stated previously, the census is unable to include migrants who moved overseas during the year before the census. International immigration is a very important component of population dynamics of the capital, but no estimates of net migration can be produced without information about the extent to which international immigration is compensated for by international emigration. The IPS also has its limitations as a data source, and does not include ethnic group within its survey. Taking an average of three year's data (1990-1992), factors were calculated which related inflows to outflows for selected countries representing each ethnic group. For example flows to and from the Caribbean were chosen to represent the Black Caribbean group. The factors were then applied to the census international in-migration for each ethnic group in order to estimate international out-migration for that group.